POLICING LAS VEGAS

How I Was Hired, Trained, and Policed in Las Vegas for Twenty Years

JOSEPH SOBRIO

authorHOUSE®

AuthorHouse™
1663 Liberty Drive
Bloomington, IN 47403
www.authorhouse.com
Phone: 833-262-8899

Published by AuthorHouse 04/20/2022

ISBN: 978-1-6655-5790-0 (sc)
ISBN: 978-1-6655-5788-7 (hc)
ISBN: 978-1-6655-5789-4 (e)

Library of Congress Control Number: 2022907562

Print information available on the last page.

This book is printed on acid-free paper.

This is my first book; although, I intend it to be the first of many works. Because it is my first book, I struggled, fought, and learned as I went. I received a tremendous amount of support from my wife, who has stood by me through life's adventures. Cheryl, thank you for all your support, I truly love you.

CONTENTS

INTRODUCTION

This book covers quite a bit of information that is applicable to most of the police agencies in the United States. It will cover how to get hired by a police department from a unique perspective: that is, the perspective of the person who was responsible for hiring for all positions within the Las Vegas Metropolitan Police Department. I will go into detail on how to get hired, and to complete both the academy and field training. Because of the uniformity of hiring within governmental agencies, this book will give you a serious advantage over other candidates.

As you learn from my insider perspective, I will also give you a glimpse of what policing is like. All the stories in this book are true and representative of any police officer in a major metropolitan area. I have changed names to protect the privacy of those still doing the job. I also changed names so I could remain as honest as possible. I will be speaking very frankly about the inner workings of a police department in the twenty-first century, giving praise where it is deserved and being very critical when that is called for.

I hope you enjoy the book and take something from it. Whether your goal is to become a traditional police officer, detective, corrections officer, or any position within a law enforcement agency, this book will help you. Even those seeking positions that are not necessarily thought of as law enforcement, such as probation and parole officers, will benefit from this book. Further, if you are attempting to become any part of an agency, including a dispatcher or crime-scene analyst, this book will help.

Finally, I will tell you the story of my career and show you what being a cop is really like not an opinion or a theory, but a real account of police work from someone who lived it. Because this is a real story, some of the content may be upsetting to some readers. This is certainly not intentional, but an unfortunate thing about the truth is that not everyone likes it. I say this because the contents of this book are not *my* truth or *a* truth, but *the* truth.

I chose to write this book for many reasons, more than I could list. As I gave this some thought, however, I managed to narrow it down to a top few. First and most important is to document my career. I spent twenty-one years in law enforcement and two years in private corporate security. My experience in law enforcement was extensive. I spent just about a year working at a state prison in Nevada, then twenty years in policing. I was a cop through many infamous events, including 9/11; Hurricane Katrina; Mumbai, 2008; Islamabad, 2008; Ferguson, 2014; Las Vegas, October 1, 2017; Minneapolis, 2020; and so much more.

Second, I came to discover very quickly that a small, very vocal subgroup in our United States has a very incorrect idea of policing. There is blame to be assigned. Primarily, this group seems unwilling to educate themselves, which is very puzzling. A more informed citizen is usually a safer citizen. There is also a significant amount of blame to go around between politicians, the media in general, and Hollywood. Each group has its own reasons for portraying the police in a particular light.

Politicians, I came to learn, blame policing for their failed policies. Hollywood tends to use policing as a source of material but then blames the material when they decide to become politically motivated. Within the category of Hollywood, I have to include the news media, who also use policing as a means of revenue generation and also turn their backs on policing when it follows an undesirable narrative. It is easy to have two sides to a position; however, it is difficult to stand a line and represent only one side. When you can have two sides to a position, you never really have to take a stand. You can simply stir up each side and watch the battle. When you have to stand for one side, and one side only, it forces character and courage upon you.

Sworn police officers do not have the ability to turn their backs on their trade. To be clear, police officers and police administrators are not blameless. There are bad police officers, bad police administrators, and bad police agencies. I will talk about the good and the bad. The reason

I had to wait to write this book until after I retired was because I plan on talking very pragmatically about the bad. Bad policing does exist, but not to the extent that you think.

I can honestly say that if it is police-related, I can almost guarantee I have done it during my career. This does not include taking a life. However, I have come very close many times. I say this not to glorify any activity, but to just give you a glimpse into my career.

Throughout this book, I plan on documenting my journey in policing. Everything I will talk about is truthful and did occur. Every story and example I've used happened. If I am offering my opinion, I will make that clear. But I will try to keep that to a minimum. Having said that, with pragmatism comes a great deal of hurt feelings. Thus, I will be changing the names of everyone involved. I believe policing is an incredibly noble profession, and those who are still doing it or who are retired deserve their privacy.

When it comes to names of well-known political figures, actors, police chiefs, or elected sheriffs, however, I *have* used their real names. I do this because nothing I am writing is false, and quite frankly, some of them deserve credit for the things they have done. I also think that when you enter the public spotlight, you lose some of your anonymity.

It is difficult to condense an entire career into a book, regardless of its length. In addition to that, I have an obligation to keep it somewhat entertaining. Further, I think I have an obligation to be honest. The last thing we need is another book glorifying a political cause or giving a one-sided view of an issue. I plan on being fair, transparent, and critical where needed.

From 2000 forward, I began to pay attention to the political climate in the United States. Prior to that, I think I was willfully ignorant. Books have been written and careers have been built on drawing correlations political correlations among reasons for poverty, crime, entitlements, war, and justice. While I do not have a PhD, I do have a large amount of real-world, on-the-ground, face-to-face experience. My experience has allowed me to have a unique perspective on life.

During my twenty-one years in law enforcement, the diversity of my experience has shown me life at its a basic level. I began working in corporate security for a large entertainment company. I was doing basic property protection, which evolved into security consultation, internal investigations, large event planning, executive protection, and property management. I left this and spent about a year working at a state prison, where I supervised inmates and spent some time doing case-management work.

After this, I started as a police officer for the Las Vegas Metropolitan Police Department. LVMPD employs six thousand people, four thousand of whom are sworn officers. I spent nine years as a police officer. During that time, I worked in traditional patrol, which is the absolute backbone of policing. I conducted undercover work, business licensing, and chronic nuisance investigations. I was assigned to a problem-solving unit whose responsibility really was multifaceted: it involved violent crime investigations, undercover narcotics operations, high-profile investigations, search-warrant preparation and service, various surveillance activities, and a very generalized direct-action team. I spent quite a bit of time as a field training officer, training new academy graduates.

After nine years as a police officer, I was promoted to sergeant and supervised various squads of police officers. Really, I supervised all aspects of police activity. I was a sergeant in patrol, on a utility team, and in field training. I spent some time as a sergeant in the agency's advanced officer-skills training program and the reality-based training section also.

After five years as a sergeant, I was promoted to police lieutenant. I supervised patrol and detective sections, community-oriented policing, and specialized patrol operations groups, as well as leading various squads and police activities on the Las Vegas Strip, including counterterrorism activities. While I was a lieutenant, I supervised response to large-scale demonstrations and dignitary protection. I was selected to represent the agency as the patrol administrative lieutenant.

During this time, I was one of the agency's representatives to the collective-bargaining associations, and I was primarily responsible for staffing allocation. I was involved in development of deployment plans for traditional patrol and investigative functions, as well as large-scale major events. I was involved in the creation of the agency's first homeless outreach team. This was a massive undertaking that involved identifying homeless crime trends for both victims and defendants a task that had never been done before.

After three years as a police lieutenant, I was promoted to the rank of director. Before I give you a brief idea of what I did as a director, I almost always have to explain what a director is in policing. It's not a common rank that people are used to hearing.

A director is an appointed captain. In order to be a police officer, you have to pass a civil-service test (I will go in-depth into this later). In order to maintain a fair promotional structure, police officers are usually promoted using their results on testing instruments and time in their department, kind of like the military. After lieutenant, the next logical civil-service promotion is captain. But this requires another test. You take the captain test, which I did, and are selected off of a list based on your performance. As a captain, you are placed in charge of a bureau, and you tend to rotate positions about every two or three years.

Some agencies forgo a test for captains and appoint them directly. The director position that I held in my agency is a position equivalent to a captain. However, it is much more specialized. It is used in cases where special skills or knowledge is required to supervise that bureau. For example, the Southern Nevada Counter Terrorism Center is a bureau. The agency may require the director who runs that bureau to have a security clearance. It would not be fiscally or operationally responsible to rotate new captains in and out of that bureau every two years. By the time they received the needed clearances, they would be on to another assignment.

Another example could be a digital investigation bureau. The leader of that bureau would need to be a sworn officer, but years of extensive cybersecurity training would be required to run that bureau. This is a case where a director would be more desirable. A captain, in comparison, could run a police station and be transferred to another police station, and the agency would not really feel any pain. Further, a captain who is supervises a traffic bureau could be moved to a specialized detective bureau, no problem. It would take a minimum amount of acclimation for that individual to assimilate.

A director is a hyper-specialized bureau commander who is selected for a position rather than testing for it. To be selected for these highly specialized positions is flattering, as you are personally picked by the head of the agency. There is no test, and you can be selected based on some specialized training, education, or experience you may have. But it comes with some risk. You did not test for that position, so if you mess up, it can be taken from you.

I had been selected based on my experience with staffing allocation and collective bargaining. I had also been injured at one point in my career, so this was a good selection for me. I was promoted to director and placed in charge of the Human Resources Bureau.

Why would a police agency require a sworn, commissioned police employee to run a Human Resources Bureau? As I will explain quite a bit, the LVMPD is not a typical police department, and our Human Resources Bureau was not the typical Human Resources Bureau. As bureau commander, I supervised all hiring, including all testing of both new hires and promoted personnel. Background investigations, polygraph investigations, psychological testing, recruiting, staffing allocation, compensation and classification reviews and studies, and really anything else that did not fit anywhere else in the agency fell to us. The bureau was a mix of civilian personnel, managers, detectives, sergeants, lieutenants, and polygraphers. You would likely be surprised by the amount of actual police work that took place in what seems on the surface to be a purely administrative bureau.

During my time as the director of human resources, I learned quite a bit about entry-level and promotional law enforcement positions, from test creation and getting hired or promoted, to retiring. Which is why I suspect some of you picked up this book. Do not worry; by the end, you will understand everything there is to know about getting hired into a law enforcement agency.

Policing in the United States is not as broken as you are being told. There are areas that can be improved; however, the improvement falls on other entities also. Some main concepts I will talk about are uneducated decision-makers; the real effects of poor political decisions; the unreliability of the media; police misunderstandings; the damage that filmmakers do to the profession; and blame. Blame is to be found on all sides.

When it comes to problems, real or perceived, we as humans wish to assign blame; it provides balance. If we can point to who is at fault, we can first separate ourselves from them and second feel a relief that the world has order. There is comfort in placing ourselves outside of the blame group, and there is a great deal of comfort in trying to provide explanations for tragic events. If we cannot separate ourselves from the party to blame, that implies we could be to blame for a similar circumstance. Also, if no one is wrong, then we must realize that our world is one that we have no control over. It is uncomfortable to realize that terrible things occur and we cannot stop them.

When it comes to blame, there are two categories of blame that, in this context, let us move on quickly and with the least amount of effort. First, in a working environment, it is very comforting to blame the person at the very bottom of the ladder. We can say, "This was a rogue employee", or "the employee's actions do not represent us." Further, the lowest person on the ladder has no way to defend themselves.

The second category is to blame the police. This is very common, the police are blamed for making the arrest, for pursuing the vehicle, for failing to prevent a crime, or not showing up in time. If we can blame the police, we can shift blame away from a poor political decision, poor legislation, schools, family dynamics, culture, or our failures. The police make a great scapegoat. Come at the subject with an open mind and admit that you may not know everything.

We will talk about the ups and downs of my career, policing in general, police leadership, reform, and how politics affects policing in the United States.

PART ONE
About Policing

Part one of this book will cover the process you will undergo to apply, get hired and trained by a police agency. This process will remain relatively consistent as you go from state to state. The Department of Justice does place some conditions on how agencies undergo these processes. Because of this, federal law, and the United States Constitution the road man to becoming a cop is very similar across the country. As we take this journey, I will give you both facts and my observations. You will be uniquely instructed by a person who successfully navigated the process as a candidate, and a person who wrote the testing processes for the Las Vegas Metropolitan Police Department.

I also have given you my personal life experiences that assisted me along the way. I truly learned what not to do, several times. The reader here is given the benefit of learning from my many life mistakes, without suffering the consequences. I wish the reader good luck, and I hope you accomplish your goals.

1

Overview

When I spent two years working in corporate security, I was very surprised how well I was paid in relation to what I did each day. It was a very high-liability job, but it was not rewarding, and to be frank, my goal was to be a police officer. After working corporate security, I took a job working for the State of Nevada as a corrections officer. After graduating from the Corrections Academy, I was a member of the opening staff of High Desert State Prison in Southern Nevada. After working at the prison for about a year, I was hired by the Las Vegas Metropolitan Police Department (LVMPD).

When I talk about agency structure, I will usually refer to the structure of the LVMPD. However, when I was researching this book, I found that almost all police agencies are structured the same, just with some dissimilar terminology. Mostly, agencies are structured very similarly to other employers. You have line-level employees, first-line supervisors, second-line supervisors, and so on. Each step up the ladder has more responsibility and thus carries more liability.

For those of you with limited knowledge in this area:

- Sergeants are first-line supervisors who are responsible for a squad of officers, usually numbering from seven to fourteen. For example, a sergeant could supervise a team of narcotics detectives.
- A lieutenant (section commander), being a second-line supervisor, is responsible for a section. In our example, the lieutenant would be responsible for either all the narcotics squads or potentially a specific group of them, like day watch

or night watch. Sections are made up of numerous squads with the same mission.

- A captain or director (bureau commander) supervises a bureau. A bureau consists of numerous sections that are not identical but have a similar mission. For example, a captain or director could be responsible for the narcotics section, repeat-offenders section, and the robbery section.

I must give you a general overview of police agencies in order to discuss the functions therein. Police agencies usually are built based upon the Incident Command System Model (ICS), which is a Federal Emergency Management Agency (FEMA) standard. It helps during mass agency incidents. The federal government usually has significant influence on the structure of a police agency; usually this is due to funding. The Department of Justice will usually establish rules, and these rules will be attached to federal funding to the police agency.

There are more myths and misunderstandings about policing than officers themselves, and I will try to work our way through these. I suppose we should start with structure. Staffing usually follows the model I have already explained. There are many different enforcement agencies throughout the United States. I could not possibly cover them all, so I have taken best practices and applied them as generally as I could.

Each county will have an elected sheriff, and in my opinion, this is the best policing model. County sheriffs have deputies; a deputy sheriff would be the equivalent to a police officer. County sheriffs and their deputies usually wear green or brown uniforms and are identified with a star. County deputy sheriffs will usually have a rank structure of deputy, corporal, sergeant, lieutenant, captain, chief deputy, assistant sheriff, and under sheriff, all led by an elected sheriff.

Within the United States, county sheriffs are responsible for both unincorporated areas of the county as well as urban areas. Sheriff's departments are usually funded by a county revenue source, such as property or sales tax funds.

Police departments are usually the result of an area incorporating itself into a city. City police departments are usually led by a police chief. Some have civilian oversight in the way of a police commission or a mayor. Police commissioners are usually only seen in very large agencies, such as New York and Los Angeles. Most police agencies in the United States are small agencies.

City police departments are traditionally led by a police chief who is appointed by either the mayor or the city manager. Police departments usually have a rank structure of officer, corporal, sergeant, lieutenant, captain, commander, deputy chief, assistant chief, and then the police chief. City police officers usually wear blue uniforms and are identified with a badge or shield. City police departments are usually funded through city-generated revenue and taxes, such as income tax or a combination of other city revenue sources.

In some jurisdictions, policing entities have combined. You see this in some counties in the United States. The most common combination is when a county sheriff and a city police department combine. This will usually result in a "metropolitan" police department. For example, in 1973, the Las Vegas Police Department and the Clark County Sheriff's Office combined to create the Las Vegas Metropolitan Police Department. The main reason for this consolidation was revenue savings. Policing is very expensive, and combining two entities into one creates a significant opportunity for financial savings, including fewer jails, fewer crime labs, less bureaucracy, and lower payroll.

There is not a huge push for this to occur nationally, mostly due to mayors wanting to have a police department at their disposal. A combined county and city department would likely be led by an elected sheriff who only answers to the people of his or her county. This is not an idea embraced by mayors, who feel they should control the police in their city.

Although mayors may want to retain control of their various city police departments, there is a benefit to having the department led by an elected official, as seen in the civil unrest and riots following the killing of George Floyd on May 25, 2020. Remember that while the city of Portland burned for months, riots in Las Vegas lasted just over one week. In Portland, the city police were controlled by a partisan mayor. This failed, as the city and its residents suffered. The mayor made enforcement decisions with no experience or understanding of policing. Meanwhile, in Las Vegas, the elected sheriff, Joseph Lombardo, suppressed the demonstrations when they became unlawful, deploying officers and gas to control the crowds. While there is no perfect policing model, the benefit of an elected nonpartisan sheriff who is a career law enforcement officer versus a partisan mayor who is driven by partisan party agendas is obvious.

Each state also has a designated state police force. The state police may be the elite organization in the state or the least-funded and poorest trained. State police officers are known as *troopers*. A typical state police agency rank structure is trooper, sergeant, lieutenant, captain, commander, major, colonel, or chief. State police usually wear the same color as their state flag. The head of the agency is generally appointed by the governor.

Depending on the state in question, state police can have unique responsibilities. These include parole and probation; state regulatory enforcement; and dignitary protection. In Nevada, the Gaming Control Board and the Taxicab Authority are state entities.

Federal departments tend to cover the gaps and are really the source of the greatest myths when it comes to policing. The Bureau of Indian Affairs supervises police activities on tribal lands and reservations. Federal law enforcement agencies tend to be the most terrifying to deal with, as they are usually led by political appointees whose motivations seem questionable at times. We saw an example of the turmoil this caused when in 2021, President Joe Biden reversed President Donald Trump's immigration policies, and the Customs and Border Patrols were forced to completely change their policies based on executive action.

I am not taking a position on this matter; I am just explaining the turmoil that can be caused when politics enters policing. Regardless of your political position, it is scary to see a single person, not duly elected for the position of running an agency, with sole control of a law enforcement agency. The takeaway here is that if we enforced the laws that are already established, with no political interference, things would be so much better.

2

Criminal Law

Generally speaking, in the United States, crimes are broken up into two major categories: misdemeanors and felonies. Misdemeanors are generally minor crimes that could result in a fine up to about $1,500 and no more than a year in a county jail, whereas a felony would generally start at a fine of about $1,500 and more than a year in a state prison. These two crime categories are present in the federal justice system as well as the local.

Generally, federal crimes are very intricate and, by nature, require movement beyond state lines or a violation of a federal statute. Federal statutes are very complicate they are the result of two hundred years of legislative action. Federal laws are rarely repealed and tend to stack on top of each other. Federal criminal statutes are very hard to enforce and are sometimes based on what is called *administrative law*.

Federal agencies that enforce these federal statutes have a very difficult job. Some laws that could be hundreds of years old are just not relevant now. Administrative law is a process that federal agencies and, quite frankly, politicians use to completely circumvent the lawmaking process of the federal government. Federal law begins as a bill that is voted upon and then sent to the president for signature or veto. That process takes time and effort, so how do administrative laws get around this?

Imagine you are the president, and due to political pressure, you decide that the Drug Enforcement Agency (DEA) should no longer enforce marijuana trafficking or possession laws. The attorney general reports to you, as does the DEA, so you tell them to not enforce these statutes. Now for all intents and purposes, marijuana is now federally legal, and you completely bypassed Congress.

Or perhaps you direct the Bureau of Alcohol Tobacco and Firearms (ATF) to rewrite the definition of a machine gun. The definition should now include any firearm with a caliber larger than 9mm. The ATF reports to you, so it changes the definition, and now anyone who owns a firearm that has a larger caliber than 9mm is in possession of a machine gun.

Here is one more: you direct the US Border Patrol to no longer search vehicles entering the country under any circumstances. Now trafficking narcotics across the border is essentially legal.

These administrative laws are sometimes called *executive actions*, and both political parties use these tools, depending on who is in the White House, to get something done. Executive orders written by both governors and the president were flying around the country during the pandemic of 2020–2021. Mask mandates were one example of this power. Regardless of your position on these issues, you can understand that circumventing the law-creation process can be very dangerous.

One thing I will explain later is that in any organization, as you go higher up, authority will almost always come down to one person. The President of the United States oversees all of the military, and all federal agencies, including federal law enforcement. If the president decides that the federal tax code should be changed, the IRS will change it, and you will be jailed for violating it. Now, it is likely that if the decision is unconstitutional, eventually it will make its way to the US Supreme Court, and you may win. But by that time, the president who made the decision will have long since retired. The founders of our country never meant for the courts to make laws; however, they are.

Because federal law is incredibly complicated, very specialized people are needed to enforce it. Therefore, you have law enforcement officers who work for the IRS, or the treasury department. The mystique of federal law enforcement being an elite group of enforcers who are above reproach is just false. They are the subject of such insane fictional movies and television shows that it is laughable to those who are actually in law enforcement.

Pick any movie or television show that glorifies any federal law enforcement agency. Watch it and wait for the scene when they assert themselves. It will go one of two ways: Either you will see some inept, stupid, or rogue local police officer who can only be corrected by the elite standards of some federal agency, or the federal agency will show up at some crime scene and assert some fictional, ridiculous jurisdictional argument over some local police agency.

Please understand that police officers are the ones who are outside daily enforcing the laws. There is no elite federal agency that investigates everything from mass homicides to bomb disposal in the middle of a city. I don't want to get in trouble here, but just watch any television show that is titled with an acronym and that represents a federal law enforcement agency, or any movie whose main character is employed by a federal law enforcement agency. It is insulting to the true heroes who run into schools to stop the active shooter who is killing children, or the cop who shows up to help you at the most traumatic moment of your life and saves you. Federal entities have their place, but unfortunately, their role has become so politically driven that their potency has been reduced to a joke in the law enforcement world.

Because of these issues, federal law enforcement, in my experience, is very hampered in its efforts. It is not all the officers' fault—there are some very great federal law enforcement officers. Federal statutes and administrative agency policies are hundreds of years old and are so overly complicated that enforcement of them creates legal issues in itself. Ruby Ridge; Waco, Texas; Bunkerville, Nevada … I could just keep listing events. Because federal law is so overly complicated, in order to get around it, federal agencies will partner with local police on task forces in order to get things done. Political opinions should not but do influence the federal enforcement of statutes.

Laws in the United States are naturally layered. State laws can be more restrictive than federal laws, but not usually less restrictive. For example, a federal law may regulate safety features in your car, but a state law could further regulate your vehicle by requiring it to be registered, or for the emissions to be checked annually. County and city statutes can be more restrictive than state law. An example of this would be a federal regulation for a state to establish traffic laws; however, the state would establish the actual speed limit.

The United States of America is not perfect; however, I feel that we do have the finest justice model on the face of the earth. The

US Constitution granted us rights, and these rights are inalienable. However, as time has gone on, with more and more laws passed and more and more federal agencies created, laws have literally become unenforceable. It is easy to pass a law and point to the police for help. However, is your passed law constitutional? Is it ethical to jail persons for the matter?

In Las Vegas, at one point, there was a push by the city to make it unlawful to feed the homeless. I was a lieutenant and had to explain to the city government that passing a law to stop people from feeding the poor is unenforceable. The good news is, you do not have to be a legal expert to live in the United States, and the laws of our land are intended to apply to all equally.

Before I get into specifics on laws, there are a few more points I must make, just to keep the reader informed. Most laws that you are responsible for require two things. The first is intent, and the second is an act or omission. With one exception (strict liability), some type of intent is required for you to be found guilty of a crime. I learned the best way to explain this concept from a college professor. He said that intent comes in many gradients, such as neglect. If you are so neglectful of your duties as a parent that your child dies, that could be foundational to establish intent.

My college professor further explained it this way: Imagine you went to a very fancy, expensive restaurant. When you entered, the hostess took your jacket. You enjoyed and paid for your meal. When you left, you retrieved your jacket. But unbeknownst to you, you were given someone else's jacket. So far, you have not committed a crime. You certainly have taken someone else's property, but you do not know it yet. You may go the rest of your life having taken someone's jacket and never knowing it. You never established intent.

The problem is introduced when intent and act meet. For our example, you arrive home, and you take off the jacket and realize it is not yours. Intent is getting very close to the act. You have now identified that this jacket is not yours, and you are in possession of it. However, still no crime. But this is much nicer than your jacket, and you decide that you will keep this jacket. The second you decide to keep it, you have now committed a crime.

There is a notable exception to the intent and act rule. This exception is "strict liability" crimes. People seem to confuse strict liability crimes with status offences. Status offences are crimes based on your age, where an adult who committed the act would not be committing a crime. Possession of alcohol is a status offence: if you are under twenty-one, this is a crime, but if you are twenty-one, there is no crime. Curfew and smoking are also examples of status offences.

Strict liability crimes are those you can commit and be found guilty of regardless of your intent to commit the crime. Serving alcohol to a minor if you are a bartender is a good example. Your intent is irrelevant; if you sell alcohol to a minor, you are guilty. Another great example is speeding. If you are stopped for speeding, try pleading that you had no intent to speed—you will still get a ticket.

One final point in this crash course on criminal law: There are so many laws—local, state, and federal—that there are far too many to explain. I don't say this from a political viewpoint but from experience. Layers of laws, passed with political motivations, often become unenforceable. This leads to the problem they were trying to solve being exacerbated, and yet more laws being passed. I am not a constitutional scholar; I was just the tool the government used to enforce its laws.

Misdemeanor offences that occur in the city will be processed by the municipal court. That is, the offender will be arrested and taken to a city jail. However, felonies that occur in the city are handled differently. The defendant would be arrested and transported to a county jail, then the case would be disposed of in district court. All crimes occurring in the county would fall to the jurisdiction of the county jail. Whether misdemeanor or felony, all defendants end up at the county jail.

3

Becoming a Cop

I am going to walk you through how to get hired into the policing profession. We will go over a lot of inside information on the hiring process. I will walk you through the training police officers go through and point out some areas where I think things can be improved. I end the book with a brief insight into police supervision, leadership, and the big topic of police change. If you feel policing is very slow to change, you are right, but not for the reasons you may think. Some of the handicaps are built into the policing machine.

I am asked quite a bit why I chose the profession I did. I've found that people seem to be curious as to why people do this kind of work. There really is no one answer. Police officers come from all kinds of backgrounds, and people enter the profession for a lot of different reasons also. Cops are as different as the calls they respond to. I have, however, noticed some commonalities, some similar personality types, and some very similar political opinions.

To start, I will share a little about myself. I was a complete mess in high school—very rebellious, mostly out of boredom. High school was not an academic exercise for me; it was far more of a social experiment. My friend group seemed to be very similar to me. We had no long-term vision and could barely see to the end of the day. Rebellion, not getting assignments in on time, and mostly living for the social aspect of school was my reality.

When I look back, I realize I could have probably gone either way: bad or good. To be fair, most of my friends went the bad way. I have mostly lost touch with them. I made a decision halfway through my senior year that separated me from my friends, so it is really my fault. As I lost touch with them, I found out quickly that most of them went the wrong way. Some went to prison; some were in and out of jail.

I lacked any real vision up to the age of eighteen. Prior to that, I seemed to live for each day. I never looked further than a day into the future. It was relatively fatalistic, and naïve. I never really saw myself as having a future anywhere and just lived for what was right in front of me.

The one strange trait I had that separated me from my peers was sheer impatience. I wanted to grow up and move on. This may seem contradictory; however, it really is not. I was so bored and frustrated with my day-to-day, I just wanted it to be over. I had always looked older than I was, and this added to the issue. I found myself wanting to get away from school, to hurry and get it over with, even though I had no real plan. In middle school, I wanted to be in high school; in high school I wanted to be out on my own. I just did not want to be my age. I wanted my teenage years over so I could just move on.

This all came to a tipping point halfway through my senior year. I'd had enough of school and was just ready to live a life. So I dropped out with only one semester left and cut all contact with anyone I knew. It was incredibly impulsive, and I had no idea what I was doing, but I did know that I was done with the theater that I saw as high school.

Then, a grand total of two months after dropping out, something happened to me. Possibly I matured, and maybe some other force acted upon me. I came to the realization that I had no future. I had nowhere to go and nothing to do.

I could have pursued a GED, but like I said, my worldview had changed. I saw the world very differently. It was like some psychological switch had been flipped. I realized that to survive, I had to do something.

I was lucky enough to be able to reenroll in high school and graduate halfway through the following year. Going back to school even after such a short time, I found my life perception had significantly changed. I was still bored and rebellious, but I saw no need to make friends or pursue the typical lifestyle of a high school student. As I worked through this semester, I did look up my old friends but found them to be in prison, jail, or working toward that goal. Whatever had changed in me had not changed in them.

I was able to speak to an old friend named Jason. I had been put in contact with him by a girl I was dating. This was before social media, so this chance event was rare. I met with him, expecting to drop into the same routines as before. But my life perception had changed. Jason had graduated high school but had no goals; he was drifting. He had already been to jail and was bouncing from job to job. At the time we talked, he was working at a tire shop changing tires, and he explained that he was looking forward to learning how to work on brakes. This never happened. He left that job to deliver pizza.

This interaction really made me think in ways I never had before. Jason had graduated high school, but he had never changed. He was the same person. As unhappy as I was, I could not imagine remaining in that same mind frame. Although I expected us to drop into our old routines, I found them pointless and borderline ridiculous. It was repeating the same behavior and expecting a different result.

Halfway through my return to high school, I came to a very strong revelation: there had to be more people like me, people who saw no future, who only saw things day-to-day. I wasn't seeking them out to socialize with them; I was seeking them out to see if I could offer help, or maybe find a way out for myself. How could I stop people from entering this hopeless cycle of repetitive behavior? How could I get out of it?

As I pondered this idea, I realized that I had the power to do something about it, but I had no idea what to do. If you are reading this and you are a high school student, there is a concept I want to teach you that I learned the hard way. Regardless of your sex, race, religion, or background, there is only one person limiting you. That person is you.

The person who graduates high school and becomes a multimillionaire attorney and the high school dropout who goes to jail have only one difference. That difference is their own motivation. You are the only person in your way.

I thought about this for a few weeks. Then one morning, as I was walking through the courtyard of my high school to get to class, I noticed several school police officers in the courtyard. This was not necessarily an uncommon sight, as the high school I attended was known for crime. I turned to walk down a hallway, and a fight broke out between two students.

Without even giving it thought, I just kept walking to class. Meanwhile, the school police quickly broke up the fight. I sat in class thinking of what had just happened. Just one year prior, I would have been an active spectator in these schoolyard brawls. I began to ask myself, why not now? Why did I not care about the fight?

I spent weeks thinking about this situation, then I finally concluded that it just didn't matter. I found the fight pointless to watch or to get involved in. I also quickly realized the fight had likely started because the police were present and would quickly stop it. There was no courage involved, and it was likely an exercise in cowardice.

What conclusions could I draw from this? Over the next few weeks, as I grew closer to graduating, I gave this a lot of thought. If there were other people like me, people who had no direction, what did they do with their lives? It seemed that this idea was driving me toward an idea that I could find a solution and help people who were stuck in this pointless way of life. I realized that people might go their entire lives and have no direction, and this, to me, was a huge waste. I wanted to find direction and try to give people some guidance.

This went far beyond guidance counselors and therapy. I needed to find my own way and a way to stop people's cycle of endless nothingness. It did not seem to come from a place of compassion; it was more of a place of seeing the pointlessness of a goal-less life. I was just unaware of how I would find a goal.

Weeks later, I was sitting in class, still thinking about this. I don't remember what the class was. The teacher was going around the room asking students their plans after high school. She got to me, and I was lost in thought—so much so that she had to raise her voice.

"Joe, what are you going to do after school?" she asked.

I did not think, I just spoke. I said, "I'll be a cop."

I had never planned on being a cop, and the response seemed to come from some other person. The teacher's reaction will stay with me the rest of my life. She laughed and said, "Well, that fits."

I have no idea what she meant. Did I put off a vibe that I was unaware of? I thought about my answer, and the more I thought about it, the more it seemed to grow on me. I don't know how I reached policing as an occupation. However, I did, and my path was selected.

I graduated high school and started on my path. The problem is that you can't be a cop until you are twenty-one years old. I had three years to kill.

I bounced around and drifted from job to job, slipping right back into my previous idea of life. I met a girl in high school who I later married. She kept me grounded and really pushed me toward a goal, any goal.

I realized that I was only living for myself. As my girlfriend began to ground me, I decided I needed to serve a larger purpose. I was not getting anything accomplished, and I was not being productive. I needed a cause to serve; I needed to be a part of something that was bigger than myself. I needed purpose, so I enlisted in the army.

Although I had identified that I needed purpose, and that I needed to be part of a greater purpose, I was still incredibly impatient. I started to process into the army, and the physician who examined me told me I could not enlist until I finished a course of antibiotics I was taking for a respiratory infection. I had to finish the medicine and come back two weeks after that.

I mentioned I was impatient, right? I returned home, called my recruiter, and told him this was taking too long. Then I enrolled in college. In retrospect, not a great decision. College is not for everyone. Although I write this holding three college degrees, I encourage you to not see college as the only choice. Look toward the military, trade schools, apprenticeships, and college. Search, and do not allow anyone to tell you what you will do.

4

Corporate Security

Out of ignorance of how the world worked, I felt it necessary to develop a résumé at a young age based on protection services. My idea was that this would make me a better candidate for a law enforcement position. If you are reading this, are of high school age, and are planning on a career in law enforcement, do not get a job working security. It will do nothing for you and is an immense waste of your time. A tour in the military or steady uninterrupted employment in any field will help you more.

There are many levels of corporate security, and your duties will be as varied as your employer. I worked for a large private entertainment company. My duties over my two years in this field were not exciting and not worth writing about. However, I am two paragraphs into this chapter and you are still reading, so I will continue.

I began this career in a uniformed capacity, working nights so I could attend college during the day. If you think working security for a large entertainment and tourism-dependent company is exciting, well, it's not. You spend most of your time giving directions and reciting the same scripted lines a hundred times each shift.

The type of person who works a uniformed security job at an amusement park, casino, or tourist attraction can be categorized into several subcategories:

- There is a small population who choose this field as their primary career field, but I found that this is rarely by choice.
- Some are right out of military service, usually serving under one contract and choosing not to reenlist. These employees do not last long, usually working there for a very limited period until a better job comes up.

- What I call the *has-beens* are those who have completed a professional career in the protection services, as first responders or in the military, and are continuing their working life. As I will explain soon, these are the ideal candidates to attract to security work. They are already trained, they understand personal threat assessment and liability, and they usually have something to lose, so they are not wanting to take unnecessary risks.

- I also noticed a *wannabe* category. This category is the most prevalent, and the most dangerous. They are usually young (which is not the issue), short on life experience, and impulsive. Like me, they see the security field as a stepping stone into law enforcement. As I said before, do not do this. Employers, please, try to avoid these applicants. This category of applicants usually create far more liability than you realize as they reenact their idea of policing based on last night's episode of *COPS*. One of the issues of this candidate pool is that they tend not to see the line that separates them from the police. Which is strange, because they will draw a glaring line between them and civilians (everyone else).

Please know that I am being self-deprecating with that last category. I *was* that guy. I saw myself as the police for that small property I was being paid to protect ... well, paid to observe.

If you choose to go into the field of security, you can make a wonderful career out of it, but you must come to some realizations very quickly. First, you are not the police. Second, you are not the police. Third, understand that the police officers you interact with are the real police. They probably know what they are doing.

I remember running around that property, and every time I was able to interact with the police, I told them how I had career aspirations like theirs and I was going to be a police officer one day. Years later, I learned how annoying this is. I also learned how I contaminated countless crime scenes, involved the police either too late or too early, and saw myself as far more important than I was.

Tourism is a peculiar business for the security profession, as the security departments are seen as non-revenue-generating. Companies tow a line between the quiet professional security officer with a clandestine earpiece, suit jacket, and customer service motive versus the paramilitary armed-enforcement motive. I have found a need for both.

Within tourism, there is a need for a customer-service direction-giver who can help you find your car, as well as tell you when the next concert is playing. However, from a law enforcement perspective, if you have a need for security, you have a need for someone who can secure a property. Soft tourism attractions are common targets for criminals and terrorists. These properties are usually vast and require a familiarity in order to navigate them.

The issue is that when a terrorist event takes place, the police who are trained to handle these issues are minutes away, while your security guards are right there right now. This was a factor in Mumbai in 2008, Las Vegas in 2017, Islamabad in 2008, and so on. If you invite the public to your establishment, you have an obligation to provide some sort of protection. If you invite the public to your establishment and force them to disarm to enter, then you are obligated to protect them at the same level they could protect themselves.

A few ideas to talk about when it comes to private security: CEOs of these companies must move past their own perceived understanding of security and really evaluate their internal policies. As I have explained, when these attractions are on private property, the owners truly have all the advantages. However, most decision-makers fail to take advantage of this. Years later, when I was working as a cop, for a time I worked in a position of advising property owners and managers on security protocols. It was shocking to me how much they did not know.

There are a lot of issues to talk about. However, I noticed many concepts in life, I mean real life, that follow predictable patterns. One such principle that I will be talking about is that when a person or group pushes a specific issue without properly investigating it, the result tends to be the opposite of what their intent was. If you forbid your daughter from dating the tattooed guy with the earrings, she will date him. If you over-discipline your children to make them well-behaved, you will raise monsters. If you raise your children in an environment that protects them from any danger, the second you are not there, your child will get hurt. If you attempt to force a population to wear masks a great deal will rebel. If you are truly going to make a mandatory change you must do the proper research to ensure it will be accepted and yield the result you actually want.

The issue with policing is that people who are in very powerful private positions make uneducated decisions, and the repercussions end up backfiring much later or are blamed on police. Let's review some of these decisions.

Firearms are never a great talking point to bring up over a family dinner. However, for some reason, a necessity in a boardroom. There is a balance to be made here, and I will talk about both sides. If a property decides to prohibit all firearms, on the surface this seems wise. This is an example of an idea that is not thought through. It is purely security theater, and a CEO, general manager, or business owner who thinks otherwise has no experience in these matters.

For those of you unfamiliar, the term *security theater* is used to describe actions that have the appearance of being effective. The usual course of action is large signage declaring the property a gun-free zone. Metal detectors and security guards (usually unarmed) with wands are then added. The idea is that this stops all firearms from getting in.

The first, and probably most obvious, point is that terrorists and criminals will not abide by the gun-free zone rule. If it is terrorism, the unarmed guard with a wand manning the metal detector will be the first killed. Then the terrorist has hundreds of helpless trapped victims. Second, a general run-of-the-mill bad guy will get a gun in. One of the underpaid custodial employees or security guards will assist in this. Further, there are always gaps in fences, unlocked doors, and poorly searched bags.

The quality of staff matters. A large attraction or event will give a security contract to the lowest bidder. Remember, security is not revenue-generating. So, you hire a guard, or perhaps you contract it out. The underpaid guard working that gate has almost no incentive or training to prevent weapons from getting in.

Imagine yourself possibly working as a temp, or making under ten dollars per hour to check bags. Are you really willing to get into a confrontation with someone who insists the contents of the bag is medication, diapers, or filthy clothing? You could certainly prohibit entry; however, for ten dollars an hour, is the confrontation worth it?

Another thing to consider is if the metal-detecting wand activates and the patron explains it's because of a surgically implanted metal device, I am assuming the company is unwilling to make that individual submit to a strip search to enter. Additionally, over the years, I have found that the personnel using the wand must not receive any training in its proper use, because they are almost always held too close or at an incorrect angle.

As a cop, I got into the habit of carrying a firearm whenever I left the house. By the way, you should too. However, seek out good, well-established training prior to carrying a handgun. The concealed firearms class you may have taken is not enough. There are many organizations that provide these services, and if it saves your life, I am sure it is worth the cost.

I bring this up because I can tell you that I have carried firearms into "gun-free" zones, past metal detectors and security guards' wands. I am not going to tell the reader how to defeat security measures designed to keep firearms out, but I promise you, if people are determined to enter your establishment armed, they will. Many security consulting firms can help you understand these issues and show you where your security is weak. I have personal experience with this, and I know cops who took part in training with the Transportation Safety Administration (TSA) and were able to get past TSA at airports with firearms.

One more thing to consider before I get to the last issue: Let's assume you have discovered the magic procedure. You can 100 percent keep all firearms out of your private event, which please understand, you just cannot. The adage that law-abiding citizens will obey the gun-free zone is partially true. However, even the most law-abiding citizens must choose between being thrown out of an entertainment event and protecting their family's life, and the choice is obvious. They may not try to get their pistol in, but they will leave it in their car. Now your gun-free zone is a gun-loaded parking lot, and vehicle burglars know this.

When you draw this hard line against firearms at your event, you cripple the security of the event. Well-trained police, federal law enforcement, and military personnel do attend these events. If they obey the rules and do not enter with firearms, you have well-trained professionals who have taken oaths to protect this nation and you have rendered them useless. Maybe you have thought this through a little bit, and you have hired off-duty police officers to work your event. So you have an event or property with forty thousand attendees, and you have twenty police officers working it for you. If a shooting occurs, precisely how long do you think it will take those cops to navigate a stadium or property they are not familiar with, push their way through panicked citizens, locate the threat, and formulate a plan to stop the assailant without the cops' bullets hitting innocent people.

A moderately trained person can shoot several bullets a second; however, let's give you the benefit of the doubt and say the assailant can only shoot one bullet each second. (For context's sake, please realize that this is not reasonable. Some firearms can fire many rounds per second, even in an untrained hand.) When the shooting starts, how long will it take for the cops to stop the assailant after they locate him or her? One minute, maybe even five?

I did say I would remain balanced, so I will talk about the reason to attempt to prohibit firearms. The most common reason I am told for these hardline policies is the idea of a massive back-and-forth gun battle, with bullets flying all over the event. I suppose this is a risk; however, how do you weigh it? I am not implying that I have a solution. However, we can work through this logically.

In my experience, active assailants that is, people who are either killing or maiming numerous people with no justification, or to further a political cause, during a single event—are only ever stopped by one means: deadly force. I have been to many conferences, classes, and training events. These assailants either must have their body made incapable of continuing or must believe this is about to occur. A motivated suspect must be incapacitated. They are usually injured to a point of being unable to continue their activity; killed by themselves, citizens, or police; or this threat is made and they yield to it.

If an active assailant event occurs, whether armed with a pistol, sword, dagger, screwdriver, vehicle, or any other weapon, assailants either stop the event by killing themselves or are stopped by someone who can incapacitate them. The argument for disarming your invited guests is to prevent violence. However, the fact that you understand that violence is possible indicates your understanding that there must be a way to stop the violence.

The issue is balance. How do you invite the public to a large event that generates a lot of money and keep them safe? As I explained earlier, there are different categories of security for private property. Up until the 1990s, security was seen as a mini police force. Officers were armed, and their uniforms resembled police. A shift occurred around this time to customer-service representatives. The police-type uniforms were replaced by suits, and officers were meant to project calm customer-service ideas. It was a pendulum swing to a service-oriented employee. Since the events of 9/11, properties have taken steps to find a balance between customer service and protection.

There is a huge roadblock in this idea, however. The specific decision-makers, the CEOs and executive boards, speak of profit margin, as they should. Security being a non-revenue-generating department, there is a cost-benefit balance to be considered. The first is a militaristic type of security that presents a hard target, thus reducing the likelihood of a violent event. However, there is potential for overly sensitive guests not to patronize the business out of some sense of intimidation. The second is a security department that is not seen and observes. This makes the property a soft criminal target, but it is inviting to guests. There is quite literally a financial analysis and comparison between the cost of insuring an armed security department and not having armed personnel and paying individual lawsuits if guests are victimized.

The majority of tourist attractions are on private property and thus they enjoy the benefits of throwing people off their property, and making the rules on who can enter and under what circumstances. These companies, because they are on private property, can essentially create their own laws, enforceable by the company. If I own a tourism attraction and I don't like blue shirts, I will bar entry to all of those wearing blue shirts. Now there may be some civil issues I will be involved in, but my house follows my rules, in theory.

Based on this, larger tourist attractions should have a 100 percent pre-established protocol to follow when bad things happen, but surprisingly, they don't. Employees don't know where the nearest exit is and don't know who to contact for help. Something as simple as dialing 911 on a house phone may not work. If employees need to dial 9 for an outside line, there is no way they are going to remember to dial 9-911 in an emergency.

Companies have an obligation to properly train their people, especially when you consider the private property aspect. You have home-court advantage, and you set the rules. You will notice that many retired police officers find second careers as the directors of security departments at various properties. The property owner gets all the advantages and advanced training of career officers, and the officers can now apply their knowledge in an environment they control. It works well, usually.

Most employees at a tourist attractions are not even considered to be part of a property protection plan. In a real emergency be it a fire, natural disaster, or active assailant event most employees will have very limited direction as to how to proceed. The tragedy of this is that if, as a company, every employee was aware of what to do and was regularly trained on how to manage an emergency, the company liability would be reduced significantly. The severe disconnect occurs between middle management and executive staff, and the disconnect is usually labeled "general counsel."

After about a year, I was promoted to supervisor and was in charge of a shift. This was fun: I was twenty-two years old, making pretty good money, and working at a very popular attraction, with perks and discounts. Unfortunately, I was thrust into leadership ill-equipped. (I will go into leadership as an art much later in this book.) As a supervisor, I was privy to more information, had access to the surveillance rooms, and got to know some of the executives. Personal security was another perk. I was walking large amounts of money to different places in the property, conducting employee investigations, and seeing behind the curtain, as it is called.

I often wondered, as a line-level guard, why there were fewer cameras on the exterior of the property than the interior. I found out:

employees rob you. Employees steal from their employers often, quickly, and predictably. If you are a business owner, watch your employees; they are far more likely to steal from you than a patron is. I saw many of these theft events too many to put into words, too many to remember, quite frankly. I watched a video of an employee who very deliberately placed his shirt over a cash register drawer and then tried to walk off property with it under his arm; employees who pocketed tips that were to be pooled; waitresses and bartenders who would overcharge a patron by one or two dollars, such a low amount the patron doesn't notice, and the waitress or bartender pockets the balance. Do this about thirty times an hour, and it pays. Short-term, anyway, until you are caught.

After I hit the two-year mark, I realized I was bored. I began to speak with people around me who told me that they started in a similar situation to mine. They wanted a career in law enforcement, started in security, were promoted, and ended up making a good living working security. They gave up on law enforcement mostly due to not wanting to take a pay cut.

I even had a supervisor, Mike Schumer, tell me that if I stayed another year, I would no longer see the point in leaving or finishing college. Looking back, he was right. Had I stayed in the private sector, gaining the experience I was, doing the work I was, after twenty years, I would have been making double the amount I retired from the police department with. However, I found that most people do not go into law enforcement for the money. Some do; most do not. One theme you will see throughout this book is that I have learned not to place people into cookie-cutter categories, as they all have their own motivations.

I applied to every law enforcement agency I could: police, corrections, probation, parole. I applied everywhere. However, I was still far too impatient. I was hired very quickly to work for a state prison in Nevada, and I took the job thinking it would help me become a cop. I can tell you that working as a corrections officer at a prison was the worst job I ever had. There is nothing wrong with working at a prison; you can make a career out of it. However, I was there for all the wrong reasons, and I was not happy. Just be patient. If you want to be a cop, stay employed steadily in any field, and you'll be fine when you apply.

CHAPTER

5

Going to Prison

I worked for the Nevada Department of Prisons for about a year. My time working at a prison, I can honestly say, opened my eyes to a world that I had no idea existed. I am not a psychology major, nor did I study the sociological impact of incarceration. However, I did make some observations. I will share these observations as instruction to my law enforcement journey.

Working at a prison is a fascinating experience. It is very educational not in a formal way, but more of a sociological manner. I will share my unfiltered observations on the two prison facilities I worked in: High Desert State Prison and Southern Desert State Prison. The State of Nevada is, or at least was, very underfunded. I found myself very undertrained, under experienced, and unprepared. The application process for the prison consisted of a written application, a physical agility test, an interview, and a short background investigation.

I learned later that most of my classmates in the corrections academy had been hired before their background investigations were complete. It became commonplace for me to see my classmates not show up to work after being terminated due to an issue in their background that had been previously undiscovered. The fact that corrections officers who were working within the prison, who had inmate contact, had not been properly vetted was a little scary, but that turned out to be one of a great many major issues. We are going back twenty-one years at the time of this writing. I am sure things have improved since then.

Corrections Academy

I learned after I was hired that after my four weeks at the corrections academy, I would be part of the staff that would open the brand-new High Desert State Prison. I was excited, but as I indicated earlier, things became strange fast. The four-week course of instruction consisted of classroom time, some defensive tactics, and some firearms training. The defensive tactics were a four-hour block of instruction. Four hours to prepare me to supervise inmates at a ratio of about 185 to 1.

We received our firearms training in the classroom. Having very little training in this area, I was very open. Senior Corrections Officer Erick Paine was one of the academy instructors. He was like a corporal, between an officer and a sergeant. Quite frankly, he was the only one I remember. He discussed the policies and procedures when it came to firearms. He was our firearms instructor.

We received classroom instruction on a revolver, shotgun, and rifle. The revolver was a .38 caliber, the shotgun a 12 gauge, and the rifle a .223. We were taught in detail when to shoot an inmate. In fact, we received more training on *when* to shoot than *how* to shoot.

In the event of an escaping inmate outside of the prison, we were to aim center mass and fire our .38 revolver in the inmate's back to prevent his escape. This was a very troubling tactic; however, I later learned the legality of it. The irony was, I learned the legality of this type of shooting when I was training to be a police officer, not during the corrections academy.

We were taught how to break up inmate fights. More realistically, we were taught how to scare two fighting inmates. We were to give a verbal warning; we were then to work the action of our shotgun, chambering a blank shotgun round. Apparently, the sound of the action being worked was some kind of a deterrent. This is one of those policies that looks great on paper but in the real world makes no sense.

I realized later that the policies at the prison were really twenty years behind the rest of the world. Even working security, I was better trained than at the prison. The problem is if two people are alone in a small room, and one works the action of the shotgun, sure it is loud and intimidating. However, if you are in a prison housing module with two combatants and about 180 other inmates yelling and encouraging the fight, you can work that action five hundred times and no one will hear you.

After the useless bluff of chambering a round, if the fight did not stop, we were to fire a blank round in the air. This was very confusing to a new person. I knew that there were indoor posts that carried shotguns, so what about my eardrums? Moving on, after firing the blank, if the fighting continued, we were to work the shotgun action again, this time loading a birdshot cartridge. We were then instructed to fire the birdshot seven yards behind the inmate, "skipping" the birdshot into the inmate's shins. Every crazy thought you are thinking of right now, I was thinking then.

After the highlights I just wrote about, we were taught about fence-shooting procedures. We were taught to shoot to wound rather than to shoot center mass. For those of you who may not know, there is no shooting to wound. I have seen plenty of people die from being shot in arms, shoulders, and legs. I have also seen people live from being shot in the head. Shooting someone should only be for one reason: to stop them. The idea is that shooting them will destroy their body's ability to continue their actions.

I will go into further detail later, but police officers shoot to stop a threat. Someone who is goal-driven will continue to try to kill you after pepper spray, after being shot, after being hit with batons. Sometimes the only way to stop someone is to completely stop the body's ability to function. It's tragic, but true. However, I was young and in training, so I had an open mind.

At the time, I was a second-year criminal justice student at the University of Nevada, Las Vegas (UNLV), and these tactics were terrifying to me. Unfortunately, it got worse. The remaining training centered on a concept known as *con games*. When I say the remainder, 70 percent of the curriculum was dedicated to con games. The idea behind this extensive training was to prevent officers from passing information, goods, or drugs into or out of the prison on behalf of an inmate. This concept that seemed alien to me; I could not believe it happened.

I learned later why so much time and attention was devoted to this category. Inmates have time, nothing but time. They are skilled. They get to know each guard very well. It's scary how much information an inmate will remember about you.

The issue is, the inmates know how little money you make, and how uninvested most guards are. Based on this, they develop a very elaborate plan of manipulation to communicate with the outside via guards. Messages, drugs, and money are currency, and if a guard can be made a courier, it only has to happen once. Then the inmate owns that guard.

I can honestly say I never saw any of this. However, I did see inmates with items that had to have been smuggled in. I saw inmates with drugs and knives, and one with video cassettes. You must understand, there is only one way for these items to get into the prison, and that is a prison employee.

Before you become judgmental and think you would never be compromised, realize that you only know how you will react to any situation when you are in that situation. However, every time a news anchor, politician, or really anyone says, "If I were there, I would have …," realize those people have no idea what they are talking about. It's like a person with no children giving parenting advice, or a person who has never driven a car giving driving lessons. Even highly trained cops, SWAT members, or military special forces teams will only know how they will truly react in any given situation when they are in that situation.

The troubling, inadequate training followed by the fourteen-dollar-an-hour salary worried me. The salary was not a huge concern, but it is notable. I had taken about a 25 percent pay cut in order to serve my state. What very few knew at the prison was that my application for the LVMPD was being processed.

Graduating the corrections academy was an achievement. I still have the certificate and photos from the graduation. The graduation ceremony is supposed to be unforgettable; you have your badge pinned on ceremoniously, and it is supposed to be very impressive. However, the Nevada Department of Prisons did not order our badges. So, we graduated and never had uniform badges.

The interesting thing was that over the past four weeks, we had been told that we would be targeted by inmates for manipulation. We were to act experienced and not fall for manipulation. However, as soon as an inmate saw an officer with no badge, that officer was an instant laughingstock. We were set up for failure. What I learned very quickly is that prisons are out of sight and out of mind very intentionally.

I have a theory on this that I will share with you. Very few people see a prison daily. They are usually placed outside of urban areas, and this is intentional. As citizens of the United States, we have a sense of calm when we hear someone was brought to justice and went to prison. When we hear that, we subconsciously think that person is now out of society and the justice system worked. Really, when was the last time you thought about a prison, the guards, the inmates, or how many people work there? Because of this, we assume the staff are paid enough and that the incarceration of inmates is a foolproof way of keeping us safe.

That is a great idea, until you find out that guards are underpaid and undertrained. We saw the effect of underpaid and undertrained police during Hurricane Katrina, when New Orleans police officers walked off the job. Further, consider that most inmates serve about a third of their sentence, and "life in prison" does not mean life. Prisons are very strange places.

On the Job

My time at the prison was short; I was only there for about a year, and it went by quickly. I worked a variety of jobs, such as the front gate, towers, housing units, infirmary, and culinary. In the two prisons I worked, I saw many inmate fights. One inmate escaped on one of my days off. He hid in a trash compactor.

A few times every day, you count the inmates. It's monotonous. The count must be finished and correct before the prison can be let off of lockdown. The inmates want it over so they can get out of their cells, and the guards want it over so they can lock themselves in their offices.

We were opening a new prison; however, the inmates were real and the dangers were real. The training, staffing, and equipment used decades-old technology, and clearly the whole situation was just dangerous. Each post or position in the prison had "post orders" essentially, instructions for that assignment. If the assignment was an armed post (such as a tower) or a housing unit bubble, you had to check your weapons at the beginning and end of your shift. A bubble is a secured elevated room that gives you visual access to the entire housing unit. It is also where you control the cell doors.

The housing units each had a shotgun and a revolver. The revolver was a .38 caliber, and all six rounds were different types: some target ammunition, some hollow points, some obviously years old. The shotgun was loaded with a blank, a rubber bullet, and two birdshot rounds. If you recall prior, I never mentioned rubber bullets. I was never trained on them. When I was assigned to a housing unit, I read the post orders, and they also said nothing about rubber bullets. When I asked my supervisor, he referred me to the post orders. At this point, I began to realize I was not looking forward to twenty years in this position. I was undertrained, and it was a huge source of danger and liability.

Inmate-on-inmate sex was common and technically illegal. I wasn't aware of any rapes, but they may have occurred. I quickly became more concerned with my coworkers. As I said, they began to disappear after being hired due to failing their background investigations. Also, on several occasions, I saw officers and one nurse being walked out under arrest for various crimes. Prison crimes are investigated by the state attorney general usually. I would come to work and see an attorney general investigator walking out a prison employee in handcuffs. It was surreal. Although I was troubled by what I saw, I kept telling myself I could rise above the negativity and make a career out of this. Several events changed that idea.

I was standing outside of the culinary, supervising about three hundred inmates as they went from dinner to their cells. Yes, three hundred is a lot, but it was OK I had a partner. Officer Eric Cardiff was a twenty-year veteran. Standing next to him for about thirty minutes saying nothing, I was desperate to say something. I constantly heard guards complaining that the municipal corrections officers were paid more than the state. They said this was due to the municipalities having collective bargaining and the state not. Armed with that, I gave a shot at a conversation with Cardiff.

"So, I hear the legislature has set aside more money for our salary to make us competitive with the City of Las Vegas," I said in my most confident tone of voice.

Cardiff looked down at me, even though he was only about four inches taller. "Kid, I've been hearing that legislature line for twenty years. It's not going to happen. Get out now, while you can," he said.

He then broke eye contact and looked over the sea of blue-clad inmates we were watching. He and I became close after that interaction. It left an indelible impression on me. It wasn't the money, but everything costs money, so if salary was not going up, that meant training wasn't going to improve. Thus, my safety was not going to get any better. I wanted out quickly.

Search and Escort

Later that same week, I was assigned to a post named "search and escort." This was the best assignment to have. You didn't really have a post. You responded to housing units to search and escort inmates around. I was assigned to a segregation unit to do cell searches.

No one likes cell searches. The inmates don't like them for obvious reasons, but as a guard, you must search everywhere. It does not just involve opening the drawers and looking. We had to search in the toilet, in the trash, everywhere anything could be hidden, *everywhere*.

At the time, the prison was new and short on space. It had been opened while it was still under construction, another poor decision by the state. In the same housing unit were housed all the special inmates that is, the ones in protective custody, those who had discipline problems, and those being punished. All in the same unit, at the same time. Things were strange. Just to make sure you understand this: the inmates who needed protective custody were housed literally in the cell next to the type of people they needed protection from.

I was sitting at a table in the middle of the housing unit recording searches of cells. My job was to record which cells had been searched, by whom, and what was found. All the inmates were locked in their cells. I was at a table on the lower floor of the cell block, and my partner was searching cells. There was a third officer watching the inmate who was handcuffed behind his back, standing to the left of his cell door, and a fourth who was the officer assigned to the unit.

I was filling out the forms when I heard the argument. I looked up and saw the officer who was assigned to the housing unit arguing with the handcuffed inmate. The two were separated by about fifty feet of space, and my partner was next to the handcuffed inmate, so I returned to my forms.

Then the argument got louder. I didn't bother looking up, but I did hear footsteps. The argument soon calmed to conversation. I then heard the inmate ask the housing unit officer, Randolph Foster, for water. I looked up to see Officer Foster walking the inmate to the water fountain, leaving my partner in the cell.

As you can probably guess, the argument started again. It grew in volume and became impossible to ignore. However, there were two other officers in the unit to address it. I frankly was the only one in a position *not* to address it, as I was seated and writing a report. At this point the argument was so loud, other inmates were looking out of a small plexiglass window in each of their doors to see what was happening.

Then I heard a very peculiar sound. As I would learn in the police academy, your brain works much faster when it senses danger. This is why people say that life-threatening events seem to take hours when they were only seconds. Your brain will process stimuli much faster than you are perceiving it. Thus, you process a large amount of information very quickly. What would normally take you a few seconds to process, you are able to process in a fraction of a second. I heard what sounded like the footsteps of a horse, and the horse sounded like it was running toward me.

What seemed like thirty minutes went by, but was probably only a few seconds. When I looked up, I saw that Officer Foster was running. He was running away from the water fountain. In front of him was the handcuffed inmate, who was also running. It almost looked like the inmate was running from Officer Foster, but the two were neither gaining nor losing ground. Puzzled, my mind tried to understand what I was seeing.

I then realized that Officer Foster's right hand was firmly gripping the back of the inmate's neck. His arm was straight, and he was forcing the inmate forward at a runner's pace. I looked back in my ignorance to see what they were running from, but they were running from nothing, I then looked to their ultimate destination, which appeared to be the open cell for the inmate. I glanced back at the two just in time to see the inmate's face slam into the wall just next to his cell. I don't remember the inmate or what he did, but he had just been forced at a runner's pace into a block wall with his hands behind him. The bleeding was immense.

The two were separated by my partner, and I called our supervisor, a lieutenant named Carrington. Lieutenant Carrington did not immediately respond. I say that because the nurse who treated the inmate arrived before he did. I later brought up the incident, and Carrington chuckled and made a comment I don't remember. I had heard of inmate abuse, but I had never seen it.

I requested to work in the towers for a while after this incident, mostly in protest, but no one knew this. Carrington allowed it, and I worked in a few towers for a few weeks. Working in a prison tower is very boring. Except for the random coyote walking by, there is not much to see.

New Assignments

After a few weeks of working in the towers, I got the opportunity to work a more desirable shift with better days off, but this was an eight-hour shift instead of the traditional twelves. Days off mattered, so I took the shift change. I spent two shifts in the towers on my new shift. When I showed up for my third, I checked in with my sergeant for my post. Sergeant Patterson told me I was a waste in the towers and asked if I would like to work somewhere else. My care level was at a huge low, so I really didn't care.

Patterson then assigned my tower shift to Officer Fetner, a fifteen-year veteran of the state prison system and the local labor union steward. I was not aware of this; all I knew was I was not going to the tower.

Apparently, having a new guy with less than a year take your assignment was taboo. I watched Officer Fetner throw a fit like a child. The first thing he threw was his lunch box across the room; he then began throwing every item he passed as he walked to collect his lunch box. He was screaming so loud I could not understand him.

As he got closer to me, I heard him say, "Fucking new guy and I get the tower." It all made sense now. That was the last time I ever saw Fetner, but the impact of his behavior will be with me forever. I was now convinced I would not spend a career in the prison system of Nevada. Perhaps things have changed, and the prison is a desirable place to work now. At the time, I felt that it was not a comfortable place for me. I felt there was no integrity and no accountability.

I was assigned to the infirmary for a while after that. That was easy duty, as most of the inmates were sedated. After a few weeks, a new inmate arrived from death row. He had suffered a stroke and was being treated at our prison, which did not normally house death row inmates. Death row inmates are very easy to supervise. People with no experience in the area assume that death row is full of hard-to-manage inmates, and that short-time inmates are easy to manage. An unusual thing I noticed is that when assumptions are made by people who have no experience in an area, their assumptions are often quite the opposite of the realistic nature of the experience.

In fact, new, short-time inmates are very difficult to manage. They are usually attempting to gain status and are traditionally young and immature. Death row inmates are normally very easy to manage. They are usually acclimated to the prison culture and are almost always waiting for an appeal process. Based on this, they do not want to create even a small wave. They are like supervising statues.

This death row inmate was very ill. I was briefed that two officers would have to be present to open the door to the cell with the death row inmate. I did not care, as he was sedated and rarely moved. There was some sort of supervisory switch, as Lieutenant Carrington was now again in my chain of command, just above Sergeant Patterson.

It was count time, and I was counting the inmates in the small infirmary. I walked up to the door of the cell housing the death row inmate, and I saw him standing. This was new. He was standing and attempting to walk to the end of his bed. He was noticeably having difficulty, as the stroke he has suffered had rendered his left side useless. I told him to sit down, but he ignored me and continued to try to walk. A small step later, he fell to the ground.

For the benefit of the reader, if you are a little squeamish, maybe skip this paragraph. At that point, I remembered that the inmate was sedated, had a stroke, and had a catheter inserted into his penis for urine. I am not a doctor or a medic; I know very little of these things. However, apparently, when a man has a catheter inserted, some sort of balloon is inflated in his bladder. When this inmate fell, the catheter was forcibly pulled from his penis. It was quite graphic. It is amazing how much blood a human has.

I ran to the phone and called my supervisor. Lieutenant Carrington answered the phone. I told him what had happened. I will never forget his response: "You will not crack that door until another officer or a nurse shows up."

In retrospect, even if I had opened the door, I'm not sure what I would have done. Even today, I don't know how to treat, well, *that*. About fifteen minutes went by, and a nurse showed up. I never learned what happened to the inmate; I can't imagine he survived.

Moving On

As life goes by, you are introduced to moments you quickly forget and ones you will remember forever. I saw many inmate fights and beatings so many that I have forgotten most of them. However, that event in all its graphic reality will be with me forever.

From the day I graduated high school, I had been going to college one class here, two there, mostly to have a goal to work toward. Right around the catheter incident, I had earned enough credits to graduate from community college with an associate's degree. I then began taking college a little more seriously, transferring my associate's degree to the UNLV.

My bachelor's classes were harder. I was charging tuition to a credit card and paying it off during the semester. I would get off work at the prison at around eight in the morning, drive to UNLV, sleep in the parking lot for about an hour, and attend class. College requires commitment more than intelligence. I was just stubborn, not smart.

One morning, I was asleep in the UNLV parking lot and my cellular phone rang. It was the LVMPD offering me a job as a police officer. I accepted the job and gave the State of Nevada my resignation notice, enthusiastically.

Sergeant Patterson was the supervisor who received my resignation notice. As I said, as life goes by, you are introduced to moments you quickly forget and ones you will remember forever. He found it very strange that I was going the police route and not going to work at the county jail. He asked me about seven times, "Police, not Corrections?"

I affirmed each time, "Police."

He then asked me to sit down. He did not give me an assignment that day. Everyone else received their assignment and went to their posts. The room emptied, and it was just the two of us. For a very awkward minute or two, he just stared at me.

The supervisor's office at the prison at that time was always a hub of activity. The only time it was quiet was just after assignments were given. At that time, officers went to their posts and relieved the officers who were there. For about a fifteen-minute window, the office was empty. As soon as the officers were relieved, they came to check out with the sergeant and the office was jumping with people again. During the shift, there was always something going on in the sergeant's office, except for shift change.

During this fifteen-minute window of quiet time, Patterson began the conversation. "You don't have to say anything in fact, don't. I am not going to give you an assignment the rest of the time you are here. You will have an easy two weeks."

Then he added, "I drive drunk a lot. I can't be arrested. If you stop me, just let me go."

As my mind fought for the words to say, someone walked in and broke the tension. True to his word, Sergeant Patterson let me sit my last two weeks in his office and do nothing. I promise you, if I had ever stopped him, and he was drunk, he would have gone to jail the same as everyone else.

6

Getting Hired

Urban myths abound in this arena, propagated by television. Everyone knows someone, who knows someone, who applied to be a cop and was not selected because of not passing a background investigation for some trivial reason like getting into a fight in high school. When I researched this book, I found that almost all police agencies utilize the same basic steps to get in the door. They have different names, but the steps are essentially the same.

I take the time in this book to explain the police application process more than I did for corporate security or the prison. To be fair, security required a job interview, and the prison was in such need of people that they held my hand throughout the process. However, if you want to know more about that, I am sure some of this information will help you.

There is one glaring truth that is unknown to the general public: police departments have a recruiting problem. The problems with recruiting are getting worse with societal changes. Police agencies struggle to keep cops on the streets. When there are fewer cops on the streets, crime increases. With the anti-police messaging that occurred in 2020 and 2021, this recruiting issue will only get worse. Recruiting is a problem, and there are a lot of reasons for this. Some I understand and some I do not; regardless, I will explain as best I can.

The main problem with policing is sheer numbers. Most police agencies are small in size; in fact, some are tiny, with twenty employees. Then you have the New York Police Department, which tops out at around 40,000 sworn officers. Attrition is a problem at any agency; as officers retire, resign, or are terminated, they must be replaced. From application to police officer on the street, the timeline can be eighteen months to two years.

Recruiting has many challenges, and in 2020 and 2021, these challenges multiplied. With the events surrounding the killing of George Floyd in 2020, the riots, COVID-19 and the Defund the Police movement, recruiting became almost impossible. Policing is dangerous, both physically and civilly. You may be attacked, and you may be killed. As a human being, you may make an error and be sued. Since police officers are human beings, errors happen. The issue is the high stakes. If a mechanic makes a mistake, it can be fixed. If a police officer makes a mistake, people lose their freedom or their life.

Police officers must be very well trained. They will be called upon to respond to you on quite literally the worst day of your life. They must arrive quickly, make a sound decision, and resolve an issue in minutes, that likely took years to create. While they solve the problem, they may be attacked or killed, or you may need to be protected by them. If they make a reckless mistake, they will be imprisoned; if they make an administrative error, they may be terminated from their agency. If they are on the wrong side of a political issue, their entire life will be destroyed. They will be tried by the press and vilified by their political officials.

Officers are human beings with spouses and children, car payments and mortgages. Some protections must be put in place. That is, officers must have some level of protection due to the nature of the job they hold. If police officers make a mistake that they were improperly trained for or that is politically unpopular, what should occur? If you do not provide the police with some protections, no reasonable ethical person will do the job. The only people who would sign up for that would be unreasonable and unethical.

Police officers are often blamed for any governmental wrong that is committed. It is easy to blame the police. If you have a governmental grievance, what portion of the government can you call at any time of the day or night, and they will show up? The police. Therefore, the police require some level of protection from issues that are beyond their control.

If recruiting police becomes harder than it already is, who will be negatively affected by this? Less police means more crime, so groups who purport to represent the poor and the residents of high crime areas but support naïve ideas like defunding police have no idea what they are creating. High-crime neighborhoods become unlivable.

As of this writing, violent crime has escalated to levels not seen since the early 1980s. This is the product of the Defund the Police political movement. Everyone wants law enforcement until they are enforced. Everyone wants speeders to get tickets, just not them. The issue is complicated, and police do hold some responsibility. The Ferguson Effect was a term coined to describe when police stop doing any proactive police work out of fear of political or civil ramifications.

When police are threatened with defunding, fear for their career, and are scared to take any risk, they will only act when they are statutorily obligated to. When police do not enforce crime and only respond when they must, you see crime go up. Both sides have some culpability in the crime rates of 2020 and 2021.

As politicians force the issue of less police, the results are predictable. The issue is, there is tremendous imbalance. Police budgets are paid via tax revenue. The citizens who pay the higher percentage of this tax use police services very rarely. Those who live in high-crime areas are traditionally low-income and pay a very small percentage of this tax revenue but disproportionately use police services. If police services are reduced, the citizens in high-crime areas will require more police services that will not be available. As this continues, the citizens in low-crime areas, when they do require police services, will be subject to severe, extended wait times, as police calls for service are prioritized by severity, not the time of the call.

Further, as policing becomes a less desired profession, there will be fewer applicants. I discovered a more than 25 percent decrease in police and corrections officer applications when I compared average LVMPD application numbers prior to May of 2020 to those after the nationwide anti-police, Defund the Police movement. You must understand the gravity of the problem. Only about 7 percent of applicants who apply to be police officers finish the hiring process. That means seven applicants out of every hundred finish the hiring process; at least this was the case at LVMPD.

These numbers are relatively reflective of other agencies also. If applications drop by 25 percent, this affects your safety. The police and corrections academies that I was responsible for filling in mid-2020 to mid-2021 were not full. That is, the budgeted number of positions allotted was far higher than the number of applicants that I could get hired, based directly on reduced applications.

As fewer people apply to be police and corrections officers, there are serious ramifications. Police departments have an obligation to keep the community safe, but no applicants means there is no one to train, so no one to come to your house when you call 911. Police agencies will be forced to lower hiring standards, putting a lower-quality product on the street. These low-quality officers will abuse their authority at far greater rates and will create further crime.

With less money comes less training, less salary, less quality, and less ethics. Police officers usually don't become police officers for the money; they can far exceed their salary in the private sector. However, there is a significant number of officers who remain in their agencies once they are vested in the agency.

Some barriers must be set up when hiring officers. I will talk about them in detail; however, the barriers to employment for the position of police officer are designed to protect the public from potential police abuse. Background investigations, psychological tests, polygraph investigations, and so on must be part of the process. Police officers have a tremendous amount of power and discretion. In order to have an ethical, transparent department that values integrity, barriers must be put in place.

When it comes to policing, you are reliant on someone to get you through the absolute worst moment of your life. Do you want the name brand product, or will a generic, lower-quality product do for you? Force politicians to properly fund police agencies, and force police agencies to hire the very highest quality candidates who will enforce the law with ethics and integrity candidates who will not run from danger but stand between you and the danger, candidates who have something to lose and will be held accountable for errors. If not for you, do it for the weakest populations in our communities. Poorly trained, unethical police officers are bullies who have the potential to kill you or take your freedom.

Applying for the Job

Back to recruiting. The ideal police-officer-to-citizen ratio changes with trends. When I was in college, it was 1.7 to 1,000. Now there are jurisdictions with more than three per thousand. If you want a career in law enforcement, pay attention. This is good news for you as an applicant.

I have already explained the typical police department makeup, so I won't go over that again. However, what do you have to do to get hired? Well, first, apply. You have to understand that police departments have to hire and hire a lot. Even a small agency with a thousand sworn officers will hire a lot. People retire. Assuming a normal distribution by age, I found that most agencies lose about 10 to 20 percent per year. There are a lot of factors that play into this, but let's start at the lower end and say 10 percent.

If an agency of 1,000 officers loses 100 officers annually, and applicant hiring is, as I have stated, about 7 percent of applicant total, it takes just over 1,400 applications to get to 100 officers. On top of that, agencies lose about 10 percent in the academy and another 10 percent in field training. So, our target is actually to hire 120.

Now we need more than 1,700 applications for those 100 positions. Also, this is a moving figure. Remember, from application to cop on the street can take almost two years. So, after a year goes by, now you need 1,700 more applicants. Once you hire the second group, the first group is just finishing the police academy, and you are now looking at the third recruitment of 1,700.

Based on this, police departments are hiring. Pay attention to how many agencies advertise. Police agencies cannot keep up with their attrition. I say this because we couldn't. At LVMPD, we only hired about 7 percent of those who applied. This worked out to about twenty applicants per hired employee mostly because not everyone finishes the hiring process, or they are hired by another agency, or they decline employment when it is offered.

This is significant, especially when you consider that a police department's background investigation costs between $2,000 and

$2,500. Larger agencies will conduct their own, where smaller agencies may use the state police or county sheriffs to do their backgrounds.

Research the issue. I often hear candidates say that they want to hire onto a smaller agency so they have less competition throughout their career. This is competition for promotions, specialized assignments, and perks. However, the percentages do not change. A very small agency will still lose 10 to 20 percent annually. A tiny agency may have one promotional opportunity once or twice a year, with possibly twenty officers attempting to promote. A larger agency may have 100 promotions available each year, with about 500 officers applying. Always look at percentages.

At LVMPD, a promotion from officer to sergeant occurred on average about three to five per month. If you are on a promotional list of, say 150 people, and that list is good for eighteen months, you get to ninety promotions very quickly.

Anyway, back to the application. In the United States you must be twenty-one years old to be a police officer. To be honest, I found twenty-one too young, but that's the law. It's a fickle balance between maturity and having the physical ability to defend yourself.

There are laws that can prohibit you from being a police officer. For example, if you are a convicted felon, you cannot be a police officer, or really any law enforcement official that needs to carry a weapon. Also, if you have a documented history of violence, more specifically domestic violence, it is likely you will not be hired, for the same reasons.

In the United States, you must carry a firearm to enforce the law. If you cannot carry a firearm legally in the United States, you are not getting hired. This includes non-citizens. I knew several officers who applied and became US citizens in order to be a law enforcement officer.

After you apply, you will be struck by the sheer number of people who apply. Do not allow this to scare you away. An average recruitment, depending on the jurisdiction, can be between 700 and 3,500. The numbers are very reflective of the population the agency serves. Currently, most larger agencies accept applications 365 days a year.

Finishing the hiring process is a chore, but those who drop out of the process are guaranteed not to get hired. Never quit any task unless you are dead. Understanding that quitting is not an option is taught to you in the police academy, but if you already have this in your mind, you will not allow anything to get in your way. You are the only person who knows if you will accomplish a task. You are the only person who can make you quit.

Choose not to quit, and you will likely advance far beyond the rest of the population. People who quit at the first sign of adversity will quit when things get rough on the street. These personality types are very undesirable. You must have the internal drive to accomplish your goal regardless of what it is.

If you can keep this in mind from the moment you type your name on an application, and keep it with you until you retire, you will succeed. Never give up, ever. Do not stop trying to get hired until you are hired or dead. When training, do not stop training unless you die. On the streets, if someone is trying to hurt you, do not stop fighting unless you die. The reason is simple: if you stop, you will die. So the only way to stop you should be killing you.

The academy was hard. I watched as people washed out. Some left due to academic issues and injuries. However, most just quit. It was just too much for them.

There was no way I was quitting. I was only leaving that police academy dead or under arrest, and if I was arrested, there was going to be a fight. I wrote a message to myself in my academy notebook. It was a three-by-five notebook you had to carry with you everywhere you went. It was always in your left breast pocket.

My message to myself said: "Body bag or jail."

This principle can be applied to many aspects of life. Not that this is a self-help book, but having this attitude is what separates defeat from success. Of course, there are exceptions, such as devastating injury; however, generally, never allow yourself to be defeated. The only person standing in your way in our great country is you. Never allow someone else to dictate your path in life.

Negativity is far more contagious than motivation. If the idea of quitting a process enters your mind, it will infect you. As you see others quit hard processes, these thoughts will enter your mind. If you allow them to take hold, they will never leave.

Try to remember that anything worth doing is hard. Further, processes that are designed to have a goal at the end are always filled with challenges. Try to remember that you are not the first person to go through the process, you will not be the last, and you will succeed. If you are tired, so is everyone else. If you are in pain, so is everyone else. If you are frustrated, so is everyone else.

It is important that you embrace the difficulties of life, even on something as simple as a job application process. Embrace the frustration and difficulty of the process and turn that energy into determination to win. Remember, I found that only 7 percent of applicants who apply to be cops are hired. If you quit mid-process, that gives you a 100 percent chance of not being hired. This 7 percent number is consistent nationwide also, not just in my agency.

Don't allow the numbers to dissuade you from applying. A very large percentage of those who apply do not show up to the written test. It's normal psychology: if you have a multiple-step process for really anything, people will drop out. People are inherently lazy and looking for the path of least resistance. Roughly 20 percent of people who are prescribed medication never take the prescription to the pharmacy. Just like anything in life, you will be rewarded for your dedication.

Realize that the hiring process for any police agency is very laborious. Stay with it. I promise police agencies need people to hire. Policing is hard; it's frustrating and emotionally draining. If you are not able to win the application process, you will not be successful as a cop.

The job application is the first screening instrument. It is designed to eliminate candidates. Again, don't be deterred. I promise you, if you are an average person, not a felon, it isn't hard to get hired. Most agencies will have recruitment information on their websites. Because police agencies need to hire officers, they have been forced to place how-to guides on the internet. It would be foolish to ignore this.

I would encourage you to know the agency website very well. There are a lot of reasons for this. In modern times, social media and internet presence is mandatory for public agencies. Use these resources to help you. A lot of public employers will use electronic sources to prove they are reaching out to minority candidates. I would encourage you to recognize this and get the electronic information.

If you are applying to a police agency, you should do some homework. You should be aware of everything that is available on its public accounts. Most agencies will list their core values, goals, vision, and mission electronically. These items could be something you are asked about during an interview. Also, there is basic information that you need online, such as dates and locations of tests. Most moderate to large agencies post study guides for their tests.

Most police agencies are small entities; however, I have yet to see one without an electronic presence. Further, the umbrella of law enforcement covers more than municipal police agencies. There are probation officers, parole officers, bailiffs. even investigators assigned to the district attorney and attorney general's office in your specific community. All these positions need to be filled.

Smaller agencies give you less opportunity to progress your career; however, there is also less competition. Larger agencies have more opportunities but increased competition. But as I have explained, the percentages do not change.

Try to embrace the fact that you know nothing of policing at this point. What I mean is that you do not really know for sure what you are getting into. I know quite a few people who realized they were not a good fit for traditional policing, but they ended up being great probation officers, bailiffs, or other nontraditional law enforcement officers.

Try to embrace the idea that you cannot over prepare for the application process. If there is a study guide (which is incredibly likely), use it. Stay away from the civil-service testing books you will find at bookstores and libraries. I find that these books will usually just explain things in generalities, whereas the website will give you specifics.

You are on the same level as everyone else, so make yourself a better candidate. You cannot over prepare. If the agency has a physical fitness test, ensure you can surpass the standards listed. If there is a study guide, memorize it. The most successful people in any industry have preparation on their side. If the physical test has a running portion, say a mile and a half in a specific time, push-ups, and sit-ups, do not waste your time on weight training. Work on running, push-ups, and sit-ups.

Again, the information on this will be on the website. If for some reason it is not, each state has Peace Officers Standards and Training (POST) standards. Look at the state physical fitness standards to be a peace officer in your respective state and follow them. If you have not been physically active since high school and are planning at twenty-one to run a mile and a half, that just is not going to happen. I once watched a candidate, an Air Force veteran who had taken a year off, attempt to run the mile and a half for the physical test. He was easily eighty pounds overweight and fell during his run. His injuries were so severe an ambulance had to be called.

Diversity

Before we continue with the specifics of hiring and getting hired, we must talk about diversity in hiring. It has been all over the news for years that police departments should reflect the communities they serve. I don't necessarily disagree with this, but I think that cops of any race can police any neighborhood so long as they are trained correctly. The idea behind officers being from the neighborhood they serve is that a person who grows up in, say, a poor, mostly African American neighborhood would be the best to police that area. This is usually justified by a person explaining different cultural issues within the various neighborhoods.

But creating a police department that is reflective of the community it serves is almost impossible to do. If it were possible, where would you feel comfortable drawing the line? Should only White officers police typically White neighborhoods? Further, how long could you retain this model? I explained how high police attrition is, and police officers promote or become detectives. Being reflective of the community is a great idea, but it just is not practical.

However, there is tremendous pressure from the Department of Justice (DOJ) for police departments to be reflective of the communities they serve. Every two years, each agency has to explain to the EEOC/DOJ what it is doing to fulfil this goal. To be fair, it does make sense, but from being involved in recruiting for so long, I can tell you that it is very easy to say but very hard to get there. It is almost impossible to have a police department that is an exact duplicate of the community it serves.

There are some cultures that do not accept law enforcement as an acceptable occupation. There are family, social, and community cultures, and some embrace specific career fields over others. I know this because I was responsible for managing recruitment in the final years of my career. I had long conversations at recruitment fairs, and people told me these facts.

With different races within the United States come far different cultures. Not all of a particular race will be part of a specific culture; however, a significant portion will be. There is a typical rural White culture. There are also typical cultures for any group. Identify the stereotypical culture for an urban African American teenage male, or a typical urban Hispanic male, and so on.

Again, it is improper to say that all urban White males or any group entirely belong to the same culture (that is a racist ideal), but most of them do. We identify it as odd when people of different races cross cultures. I have found that often when people see racist behaviors, or at least behaviors that they identify as racist, the issue is rarely the color of a person's skin. It is a cultural behavior they do not like. It is far more behavioral than physical.

This presents itself in occupations. How many White rappers are there? If you do find a White rapper, is that individual a typical member of the dominant culture of that occupation? There aren't many African American country singers for the same reason. Most psychologists are White females. Most schoolteachers are female, except for gym teachers, who are usually male. Is this because a skin shade or gender directs you to a specific profession? No, but your culture does.

Culture and race are related. It is uncomfortable, but it is true. The bottom line is that cultures will encourage some occupations and dissuade others. I have found this very common and, when I was recruiting for LVMPD, very relevant. However, I was exposed to it early in my career also. I was doing a foot patrol assignment with a Black officer who was from Barbados. We started a conversation with

46

a group of Black women. Midway through the talk, one of the women asked where he was from. He told them he was from the Caribbean.

The woman said, "I knew you weren't black-black."

I later asked him what this meant. He told me that there is cultural discrimination among the African American community. He told me that people who recently emigrated from Africa are treated as not Black, as are people like him from the Caribbean. I found this occurs in all races. White people from Eastern Europe are treated far differently from white people from Western Europe, and this goes both ways. It is not white vs. white; it is culture vs. culture.

What really troubled me about this was a situation I was involved in a year prior to my retirement. A local community activist group met with us to attempt to increase African American recruitment for police officers. The group was called Las Vegas Metropolitan Police's Multicultural Advisory Council (MMAC). The group was made up of members of many cultures and races; however, the primary focus was on African American recruiting. I was tasked with meeting with the group to assist in these efforts. This really is a great idea, as I have explained that there is a lot of racial disparity with the public sector. Efforts to increase minority applicants should, in theory, increase minority police officers.

One suggestion was a success video to attract African American men to policing. My bureau did research, and we found a police officer who was assigned to the Canine (K9), section. He had emigrated to the United States from Africa specifically to be a cop, and more specifically to be a K9 officer. We facilitated a very in-depth recruitment video that was very touching. The officer told a very compelling story of overcoming diversity, moving to the United States, and becoming a success. The story was truly touching.

When we showed it to the MMAC, the group's leader said, "I don't like it."

The police lieutenant who reported to me, who was African American, asked him why it was not liked. The only response we got was that it was not liked.

We went back to the drawing board, and my subordinate lieutenant suggested we find another officer who would relate to American-born

47

African Americans. We did, and that video was used in recruiting efforts. If you want more Black cops, their place of birth should be irrelevant.

The troubling thing about the MMAC group was that it started very strong, with many prominent members of the community, but by the time we were set to send the video out, only one member showed up to the meeting. As things got more difficult, members just stopped showing up. Further, the group's leader refused to return my phone calls a short time later when a candidate he was sponsoring voluntarily dropped out of the hiring process.

That was when I really started questioning the motives of the MMAC. Our goal was to attract more African American candidates for the job of police officer. However, it seemed like the group was more concerned with résumé-building than helping.

The problem is, cultures are hard to define and not quickly changed as you grow. You may drift between cultures. You see this when children of one race are adopted by a family of another race; they become the culture they are raised in. However, after they leave home, they may adapt to the culture of their race. Culture matters and will affect your career choice. Some cultures simply distrust the police and do not want their family members in these organizations.

This is apparent within the LVMPD. As an agency, we are unique in the fact that police and corrections officers are paid the same, and the testing processes are identical. However, there are significantly fewer White applicants for corrections when compared to police. There are also significantly more minority applicants for corrections than police.

When you look at the population of Clark County, the US Census has male and female almost exactly at 50 percent of the population each. However, the total population of LVMPD is about 67 percent male and 33 percent female. So, generally, as an employer, the agency is overrepresented with male employees.

When you analyze sworn positions (police and corrections), the distribution changes more dramatically. Remember that Clark County is about 50/50 male and female, but the total sworn percentages are about 86 percent male and 14 percent female. Less than 20 percent of the sworn officers in the agency are female. This is not the agency's fault;

this trend holds true for most municipal police agencies. This number is not statistically significantly different from the percentages of applicants for sworn positions by sex also, so the application process is not cutting out female applicants at a higher rate than male.

Corrections officers at LVMPD are distributed about 73 percent male and 27 percent female; however, police officers are distributed 90 percent male and 10 percent female. What factors are at play when 27 percent of corrections officers are female and only 10 percent of police officers are female? Again, the application percentages are about the same.

It would not be accurate to say the agency was intentionally hiring male over female. Law enforcement traditionally is a male dominated field. There really is no fault to be found here; like I said, I found that these numbers were not far enough from applicant percentages to be concerning. The percentages of applicants and percentages of persons hired was about the same demographically. Fewer women apply to be a police officer than do for corrections, and the corrections officer female population is not near the population distribution of Clark County.

Police officer racial distributions are the numbers that create curiosity and are the subject of many news articles and studies. However, in an agency that pays the same money, and has identical testing instruments for both police and corrections officers, racial and thus cultural differences become very dramatic. Racial demographics are always a topic of conversation within police agencies. Clark County's population is about 1 percent American Indian, 10 percent Asian, 13 percent Black, 32 percent Hispanic, and 42 percent White.

The total agency is about .5 percent American Indian, 8 percent Asian, 11 percent Black, 17 percent Hispanic, and 61 percent White. These totals are deceiving, as they include all positions, police, information technologies, mechanics, and so on. Sworn positions, those of police officer and corrections officer, have very clear cultural ramifications. When I spoke to applicants, they drew a hard delineation between enforcing the law and staffing a jail, and further, the difference between taking someone's freedom and supervising those whose freedom has already been taken.

The cultural issues really show when it comes to sworn positions. Both corrections and police having identical testing instruments and pay the exact same money, but at LVMPD, there are huge racial and thus cultural differences in staffing. Clark County's population is about 1 percent American Indian, with .1 percent of the corrections officers and about .5 percent of the police officers identifying as American Indian. This distribution is not bad.

The county is 10 percent Asian, with a corrections officer population being 9 percent Asian and a police population of only 4 percent. The distribution here indicates there is a higher likelihood of an Asian applicant working at the jail, but not on the police side. When I spoke to applicants, especially those who were first- or second-generation immigrants, they often cited a cultural distrust of the police. They further would discuss more acceptance culturally of working at the jail.

Clark County is 13 percent Black, with about 21 percent of the corrections officers being Black and 7 percent of the police officers being Black. The surprising issue here is that the corrections officers being 20 percent Black is an overrepresentation, where the police at 7 percent are an underrepresentation. These numbers are due to many factors. When I spoke with applicants, many cited the idea of supervising inmates over arresting people as more desirable. There seemed to be less of a stigma with the corrections officer job.

The county's Hispanic population is about 32 percent, with about 22 percent of the correction officers being Hispanic and 20 percent of police officers. Both police and corrections officer positions are underrepresented in the Hispanic category. First-generation Hispanic families cited language barriers, and I was unable to identify a significant reason for established Hispanic families.

An interesting fact was something I was taught in college. I had a professor who asked the class why police officers in cartoons of the '80s and '90s were stereotypically Irish. The professor said this was due to the civil-service test in New York being in English, and of the immigrants in New York, the Irish knew the English language better than Italian or Spanish immigrants. I have no idea if this is true or not.

Finally, 42 percent of the county's population is White, with 42 percent of the corrections officers being White and 63 percent of the police officers being White. These numbers are the most puzzling, as the corrections officer population is very close to the county's population, but on the police officer side, Whites are far overly represented. With some notable exceptions, such as Chicago, Baltimore, and DC Metro, I found that the statistical distribution was relatively consistent within most police agencies.

When I researched other agencies, I found that although population racial percentages do fluctuate in different municipalities, the LVMPD's distribution numbers are almost identical to the numbers of similar-size agencies. The distribution being similar, the interesting fact was that the overrepresentation of African American corrections officers as compared to police officers was also very similar. Understanding these numbers at a first glance can seem like a problem, but recruiting efforts to generate more minority interest is always ongoing. Each minority group has a recruitment counsel at LVMPD specifically targeting that minority for all positions. The above data is also shared with the various groups in order to attempt to generate interest.

If you are applying to a police agency, there is value in realizing the racial, sex, and cultural demographics of both the policing profession and the specific agency you are applying to. With LVMPD, exhaustive efforts are made to create an agency that reflects the community it serves. Recruitment councils and promotional mentorship programs are set up to allow minorities to succeed.

When I was the director of human resources, my bureau created a training program for all department members to prepare them for promotion and transfer competitive processes. This product was named Leadership Education Career Advancement and Development, and it was specifically targeted to the minority recruitment councils to ensure these transfer and promotion opportunities were made available to all equally. The program was a formalized mentorship, with a departmental orientation and career advancement trainings. It was well received but did not solve the issue of racial underrepresentation.

Recruiting specific races and sexes is very hard. Women do not typically pick this career field, and this shows in application numbers. Female cops are stereotyped as too manly or too weak. I can tell you also that female officers do face sexism within the industry. They are treated differently than their male counterparts.

When I worked with the female-specific recruiting groups, I found some interesting trends. Women employment candidates were far more dedicated than men. They showed up to practice physical fitness exams more often, they studied harder, and they showed up more consistently to various application tests.

The fascinating dynamic is that police departments are screaming for more applicants to fill positions they cannot fill; but they also receive so many applicants that they must cut the numbers very quickly. Another peculiar idea is that at the police academy, the idea, at least at first, is to induce people to resign. Prior to 2020, the issue was not application numbers at LVMPD; the issue was qualified applicants who could pass a background investigation.

The issue LVMPD had was finding qualified applicants. People's backgrounds are shocking. I reviewed them for a living for quite some time. Trends do occur; different drugs make resurgence in popularity (such as Adderall); and the advent of the smartphone brought to light an entire new world of sexual deviancy. Different behavior becomes acceptable one day and unacceptable the next.

Employment Standards

This brings us to employment standards. Each agency has a set of standards, and these indicate whether you will be hired. These standards come in two forms: published and confidential. Depending on the agency, its published standards can be as brief as a single sentence or as lengthy as pages upon pages.

Police officer is a civil-service position, and there is some value in explaining what that means. A civil-service position is a job that enjoys specific protections. These protections are based on established law and the fact that reasonable people would not do that job without some protections. Further, civil-service rules tend to ensure a fair and impartial testing process for the positions they cover.

Each jurisdiction has its own civil-service rules. CSR specify that the hiring agency must undertake to test for positions and hire you; further, they usually establish standards for continuing employment. CSR usually establish some sense of fairness, or at least an attempt at it. CSR may say what material a person can be tested on, what can be required, and what cannot be.

Most agencies will allow their CSR to be published and public. CSR are not the published job standards. Each agency has CSR, and these rules are more general than standards. Published standards are far more specific and are usually written for each specific job, whereas CSR apply at almost all positions.

CSR may establish what tests can be administered for a position, such as requiring a written test for a police officer. CSR can also cover discipline rules or probationary periods. Standards are different and specific to each position. A standard of being twenty-one years old would be a single standard for one job, such as police officer, whereas the CSR may require a year of probation time after academy graduation.

Now, civil-service jobs will usually require equal opportunity competition, but not all positions at a police agency are covered by the CSR. For example, 95 to 97 percent of police departments' established positions are civil-service positions. Not all of them are police officers; some are administrative support, mechanics, and dispatchers. The remaining 3 to 5 percent of positions are usually appointed positions, or positions that are not subject to CSR selection. These employees serve at the will of the head of the agency. It is very similar to how a newly sitting president appoints various persons to various positions. But with police agencies, there is no congressional vote.

Published standards are usually located on the agency's website, depending on how transparent the agency is. It is a good way to tell people what the agency will tolerate from an applicant. Often, standards are based on the CSR and state law. In Nevada, a person with a "documented history of violence" cannot be a peace officer. This is a state law and thus would default to being a published standard.

There is a need to keep some standards confidential. It is like stairs: confidential standards are more specific than published standards, which are usually more specific than CSR, which are more specific than state law, which is more specific than federal law. The agency's published standards are a good place to start. Things like age restrictions, personal history restrictions, and generalized rules will usually be published.

After you apply, your personal history will be compared to the agency's published and confidential standards. This will happen during the background investigation. The confidential standards are known only to the agency. These vary by agency but seem to be very similar across the United States. Confidential standards are very specific. For example, a confidential standard may be that you cannot have used marijuana for the past two years. It may also say that another agency's disqualification will disqualify you with this agency. Confidential standards are usually only known by the background detectives and those involved in the hiring process. Traditionally, these employees will sign a nondisclosure agreement to keep these standards confidential.

Back to the job application, your first barrier to membership. Usually, there will be knockout questions on applications. These are generally directly related to published standards. Questions such as "Are you a convicted felon?" or "Have you ever been convicted of domestic battery?" are asked because if the answer is yes, you can not possess a firearm, and thus you can't be a police officer, so there is no reason to process your application. Assuming you have not been convicted of a crime, and assuming you can fill in blanks, you should make it through the application process.

A high school diploma will usually be required, or the equivalent. An exhaustive exercise is to define what an *equivalent* is. It may seem obvious, but it is not. The general education diploma (GED) is one example of an equivalent, but if the candidate was homeschooled, then what? How do you establish equivalency?

The short answer is, there is no short answer. If you were homeschooled, some agencies may require proof that your curriculum was at a high school level; however, that is hard to evaluate. If your parents were your teachers, it is difficult to discriminate against you based on education level. If you were homeschooled or do not have a diploma, just make this process easy and take the GED test. It will save you a lot of time and frustration.

Many agencies have tried requiring college to be a police officer, and occasionally some politicians will claim that this would solve police abuse issues. However, the idea that there is a secret culture of police brutality within agencies is just ridiculous. Although most are very slow to change, a nationwide police corruption problem is nonsense.

The problem with requiring advanced education to be a police officer is twofold. The first is that racial demographics significantly change the higher up the educational chain you go. The candidate pool will skew whiter, as statistically more college graduates are not minorities. The second issue is that the more educated people become, the less likely they are to choose policing as a profession, at least initially anyway. When you consider the pay versus labor equation, money will usually win.

This comes with a curious contradiction. A high school graduate is charged with enforcing laws that are written by attorneys, defended by attorneys, and adjudicated by judges, who are usually attorneys. More agencies as time goes by require advanced degrees to hold supervisory positions; however, this creates further issues that compound police agencies' slowness to change. This is again compounded when you realize that police executives are appointed and subject to termination for any or no reason. Thus, there is rarely incentive to change. But this is the application chapter. I will return to the issue of change later on.

Back to the problem of recruitment: Most policing agencies, well almost all, hire the same people for the same jobs, under the same circumstances. So they are always in competition with each other. Larger agencies will often hire more applicants, thus robbing smaller agencies. However, smaller agencies tend to conduct the same theft, just later. The smaller agencies will usually steal well-trained applicants after they have served some years with the larger agency. You see that some larger agencies will require you to serve five years or repay the academy cost. If you are running a small agency, this is ideal. You get a tenured, well-trained officer for essentially free.

Testing

Police jobs are usually obtained after a testing process. After the application, the second barrier is usually a written type of test. Only about 50 percent of applicants will show up to the written test. This seems extreme, but it is a consistent statistic. Only half of those who apply will show up to the test. This is a huge loss of applicants.

We once called everyone who no-called no-showed to the written test, another MMAC idea. The 50 percent of no-shows had no good reasons for not showing up. Nonsense reasons were given. Some people cited forgetting the test, others said they'd changed their mind. Some were honest and explained that they had to apply for work to continue to collect unemployment benefits. Some cited negative media attention and policing having a poor public image. This is one of the many ways that negatively motivated media attention and ignorant politicians victimize those in high-crime neighborhoods.

Policing should be socially incentivized as the noble profession that it is. If a societal shift occurs, we may finally have departments that reflect the communities they serve. Before you blame police racism or corruption, I would encourage you to do research. Politicians, who are motivated by the next election cycle, will make claims to scare voters into action. Media outlets, motivated by clicks, have no incentive to be truthful, just dramatic. Like I have said before, the police are easy to blame.

Back to the written test. You have made it past the application and are sitting down to the written test. This test is made to measure your written intelligence, to thin the herd, and usually to comply with a competitive rule within the CSR. If you are a high school graduate, I do not see any reason you would fail the written civil-service test for police officers. I approved the test for my last few years at the LVMPD, and it's not hard. Further, we provided a study guide; most agencies do. The study guide is often used to show how we are attracting all manner of candidates and not unfairly testing them on, say, advanced mathematics or physics. Study guides are your friends. Most police tests consist of grammar, memorization, ethical, and moral questions. They are not hard.

Each state has Peace Officer Standards of Training certifications, usually abbreviated to POST. POST certifies state police officers and their training. POST usually requires a physical fitness test after the written test. Usually, the criteria of this physical fitness test is a published standard. Run this far in this amount of time; do this many push-ups. Each state is different, so I won't go into it much more. Just remember, physically work on what you will be tested on. If you run and do no push-ups, you will fail. Work on each exercise.

Interviews

Interviews are usually part of the process also. They are sometimes called oral tests, oral boards, or whatever title the agency uses. The bottom line is, come in and talk. During this phase, you will be evaluated on your ability to communicate. Further, the agency can ask you relevant questions, such as, can you kill someone? Believe it or not, some people who apply to be law enforcement officers are surprised that they may have to take a life. Well, you may have to, and if you cannot take a life, consider a different line of work. I will explain taking a life in my academy chapter.

Interviewers may at times ask you ethical questions or force you to remember details and recall them. At times, they can force you to make a choice between two seemingly equal options, to evaluate your ability to prioritize human life over property. Will you be able to testify in court? If you cannot get through a basic job interview, it's unlikely you will be able to reliably testify in court.

Make yourself look professional. Wear a suit. Sit up straight. Look the interviewers in the eye and shake their hands. Turn your cellular phone off. Do not carry a firearm into the interview. Other than this, I would say, prepare for a job interview. Be ready to explain who you are, what your motivations are, what experience you have, and why you want the job. Do not overcomplicate the issue; you are not expected to be an expert on police procedure. The interview is just meant to measure your communication skills and your basic understanding of things like integrity and ethics.

This is where reviewing the agency's website is a good idea. Bring up the agency's mission statement and values, and incorporate them in your answers. It is good to show a basic understanding of the agency and its goals. However, please remember, you know nothing about policing, so don't offer your opinions on crime-fighting strategies and how you would change the agency, or what they are doing wrong. Speak in a positive tone, answer honestly, and sound motivated.

Normally, you are being measured on motivation, communication skills, and integrity. I have failed a lot of candidates who, during their interview, chose to tell us how they would change the agency and began rambling on about some fictional idea they obviously saw on some television show. You know nothing about policing unless you are or have been a police officer. This is a tough concept, but I promise that policing is nothing like you think it is.

Background Investigation

After the interview comes the background investigation. These usually consist of a psychological test, a polygraph test, and a thorough investigation of background. The background investigation is usually covered by state law or agency standards. I will explain each aspect of this and the reasons each is done.

There are a lot of myths associated with these investigations. It is a result of ignorance of the law, confidential standards, and factors that are very hard to quantify, but I will try. During the application and testing process, you can be involuntarily removed for not cooperating, voluntarily removed at your request, disqualified, or hired. Occasionally, people can be deferred hired; this is usually due to a military deployment or injury.

A police agency, depending on its makeup or the city, county, or state managing hiring for it, has a very hard job to do. You must hire someone who will not run from conflict but will not create it; will have integrity but also has valid life experience; and will be aggressive enough to survive confrontation but be legally defensible if a life is taken. Essentially, hire someone who is good but not perfect; confident but not arrogant; aggressive but not vindictive; brave but not egotistical; and so on.

The agency that hires you will be required to defend the decision to hire you the day you are hired and be prepared to defend your actions both civilly and criminally, in some cases. You must be young enough to do police work but mature enough to do police work. Young enough to run, jump, and fight, but mature enough to try to avoid running, jumping, and fighting. This is a very hard balance. The entire person must be measured, but I will do my best to split these into individual parts to help you understand them.

Personal Background

The personal background will measure you as a person. Your personal background is split into segments, each of which could possibly knock you out of the process but is unlikely to by itself. I will go into each segment for you.

Job History

Let's start with the most obvious. You are applying for a job, so they measure your job history. Remember that police agencies are starving for qualified candidates, so it doesn't matter what your work history is, just that you have some and that it is consistent. You will read the words *consistent* and *reasonable* a lot in this portion of the book. I have found the only reliable predictor of future behavior is past behavior. I found that about three years of solid work history seemed to be key. Three years is both reasonable and consistent.

A person who had about three years of consistent job history, with no terminations or discipline, would usually make it through the police academy. When I say *discipline*, I mean documented or not. My expectation in hiring a police officer was about three years of consistent job history. I did not have the ability to discriminate on job history. What I mean by that is, I never cared if it was three years as a bartender or three years as a police officer elsewhere. I also found that it did not matter as far as completing the police academy. Three years of work was three years of work.

I also found that the same company for three years was not relevant either if it was the same career field such as a union plumber who worked for fifteen plumbing companies in three years because as jobs were completed, the plumber was laid off. Three years of work was three years. This worked for me. Good work history makes a candidate very attractive.

Including past work history, we had to figure out what you were like at work. Did you show up each day? Did you conduct yourself well? Did you do your job? If you were hiring people to do a job, you would naturally investigate their work history.

We found that around 2010, we had to deal with a huge increase of applicants, both male and female, masturbating at their prior workplace. It may shock you that we asked, but there are patterns of behavior that indicate poor performance as a police officer. This behavior is relevant to being a police officer, since a person with a history of sexual deviancy could be susceptible to power abuse. It is not the act of masturbation; it is the inappropriate location of the activity that is relevant.

Remember, police agencies are looking for reasonable applicants. Is this behavior reasonable for a responsible adult? Probably not. Masturbating or viewing pornography at work was a new phenomenon around 2010. It was a product of the smartphone. So, what is a reasonable amount of time you can look at pornography at work and this not be an issue? Well, it depends, and it is almost always flushed out in the psychological test. Keep your background reasonable.

I met with a candidate who had admitted to having sexual intercourse in public about twenty times. When he was asked why, his response was that it was thrilling to fear get caught. This behavior could be indicative of a bigger problem. But it also may not.

Patterns of behavior are the danger. When it came to sexual deviance issues, we always looked for a link to another issue. This is because what is sexually deviant to me today may not be to you. However, if we found sexual deviancy coupled with poor employment history, this could be a severe issue. Poor patterns are neither reasonable or consistent with a good candidate.

Credit History

Credit history matters also. Now, not as you would think. I never expected a twenty-four-year-old to have an 800-plus credit score. You would look for consistency. People in their early twenties in the United States are assumed to have some student loan debt, perhaps a mortgage or a car payment, potentially some revolving debt.

The way police agencies measure credit changed significantly after the economic downturn of 2009. Prior to 2009, a personal bankruptcy would knock you out of the hiring process, and if you were already hired, it would likely get you a healthy suspension. But the economic recession changed a lot of things, including how we weighed a candidate's finances. Bankruptcy was no longer necessarily seen as an indicator of a larger problem.

In 2010, I was a police sergeant. The new people we were hiring in their mid-twenties were more likely to have a bankruptcy or a divorce. If you have consistent or at least explainable credit, you will be hired.

For example, there was a candidate for whom everything else was within normal parameters. However, he had terrible credit with a bankruptcy. During his investigation, it was revealed that when he was in the army, he was deployed to Iraq. His wife left him, and he came home to thousands in debt. We hired that guy. The explanation was relevant, reasonable, and consistent.

Remember to ask yourself if this is reasonable. Two candidates who are the same age, let's say twenty-one, and each have a bankruptcy may not be equal. The prior candidate who served his country and received poor credit due to no fault of his own is very different from the candidate who has never held a job and claimed bankruptcy due to overextended credit cards.

References

References are checked, both personal and professional. References are great for the confidential standards. If the confidential standards say, "Must not have used illegal prescription drugs within five years of application," and your references reveal that you recently used their hydrocodone, you will be disqualified. The confidential standards are confidential, so you will not be able to fake your way around them. They are very specific; they must be.

References tell us who you are, where you have been, and most importantly, whether they trust you. If you are using people as a reference, let them know. Explain that a police detective will be contacting them and will ask them questions. Give them answers to give the detective, and explain why you are using them as a reference. Police officers are human lie detectors; they will identify if your reference is lying.

There are references you list and ones you don't. You may not list a prior coworker as a reference, but we may locate one and talk to that person. A vindictive ex-spouse will not hold much water; that individual's opinion is not great. Remember, there is a trained detective at the end of the investigation, one who knows how to get to the truth.

I remember one prior employer we called as a reference who revealed to us a pattern and practice of serious sexually deviant behavior; that was bad. One candidate had applied to be a police officer and an ex-spouse was made aware of it. She had not been listed as a reference; however, she contacted us. The ex-spouse was not vindictive, but she gave a very detailed account of the candidate's history. She explained that he was violent and prone to manipulation, and she was able to back up her claims with photos, dates, and times. The detective was able to use the information to prove the candidate was being dishonest in the process. Dishonesty will always get you thrown out.

Criminal Activity

Criminal activity is measured, both detected by law enforcement and undetected (you got away with it). Early in your background process, you will sign a waiver, known as a Title 5 waiver. It alleviates anyone who provides us with information from any civil liability and waives all your rights to privacy. It also compels some people and agencies to provide us with information. The document is great; it tells references there is no risk in talking to us, and it forces some agencies to give us information. Those who must provide us with information are law enforcement agencies and courts everywhere you have lived or been stationed. (Military people, we get all your UCMJ information.)

When you are asked about undetected or detected crimes, be aware of the big picture. You are telling a police agency about crimes you have committed. For the most part, no action will be taken. Most undetected crime is very minor, such as shoplifting as a child, speeding, or hitting a parked car and leaving. However, there are times when it becomes an issue. If you admit your role in a crime that is significant, it will be followed up.

Police officers are mandatory reporters. This means that if we are made aware of some crimes or actions, under some circumstances we are obligated by law to report the issue to the agency with jurisdiction. There was a candidate who was a law enforcement officer in another state and was applying to the LVMPD. During his background investigation, it was revealed that he was molesting his stepdaughter. When he flew home, he was arrested as he exited the airplane.

People assume that any arrest history will be disqualifying, and this simply is not true. However, lying about it will. The absolute most common reason people are disqualified from the hiring process is dishonesty. People get arrested; it happens. Very few people have no police contact their entire life. If you were arrested, don't lie about it. The agency will find out, I guarantee you they will. A DUI ten years ago is not going to stop you from being hired.

If you have been stopped, detained, talked to, cited, pulled over, witnessed a crime, or had any police contact at any point of your life, you may as well tell the agency; they will find out. Criminal history does include your citation history. Even speeding tickets that were dismissed will be evaluated. Everything now is electronic, and police departments, due to various social pressures, keep records for extended periods.

Your detective is a tenured cop who knows if you are lying. Many candidates were upset over being disqualified for crimes that were dismissed in court that they refused to admit to initially. If you are asked if you have ever had police contact, discuss it and answer the questions.

An incredibly frustrating issue is when we ask if you have been arrested for anything and you are dishonest and try to cover some embarrassing arrest up based on the faulty assumption that because you were not convicted, it doesn't matter. *Arrested* means just that. You are not going to manipulate your way around an arrest. Just bring it up if you are asked. Arrest history is released to us from the arresting agency anyway. We will get all the arrest reports and various pieces of evidence.

Drug Use

Drug use is another constantly evolving issue. Marijuana went from being a felony to possess to socially accepted over my time in law enforcement. As such, standards had to change. I found that daily use of any drug for up to a year, including marijuana, usually yielded a bad candidate. We identified behavioral patterns. Daily marijuana uses for a year or more did yield a troubling pattern and usually would be indicative of a larger issue.

Your drug use will be evaluated for frequency, severity, and variety. Most people are expected to have experimented with marijuana in high school or college, and this won't usually disqualify you. Remember, you're going to have to take a polygraph test, so don't lie. You are not going to beat the machine.

Drugs are an interesting fact of your background. The drugs you choose to use, and the reasons you indicate for using them, reveal quite a bit about you. Different drugs have different social implications. Like I said, a person who used some illegal drug daily for a year or more is likely a bad candidate for law enforcement. A person who experimented with drugs at sixteen, then at eighteen, then again at twenty-one, is also probably a poor candidate.

To dispel a few myths, marijuana possession is still a federal crime. It is illegal. If you are disqualified for excessive marijuana use, pleading its legality locally will not help. Further, people who experiment with overuse of over-the-counter medications, and people who experiment with designer drugs, are troubling. Taking a mass amount of cold medicine to get a high or using chemicals that are not approved for human use by the FDA for the same reason is a problem. It will be discovered.

Polygraph

At some point, you will be subject to a polygraph examination. When we get into the actual police work part of this book, I say to forget everything you think you know about policing, because unless you have physically been a cop, you have no idea. I promise, I haven't lied. Those of you thinking "Polygraphs cannot be used in court" or "Polygraphs cannot be used as a hiring mechanism" or "I can beat the polygraph," you are right and wrong. Oh wait, there is one more: "Polygraphs are only 85 percent accurate." Let's take these myths down.

First, a little about the test and the tester. The machine has very little to do with lie detection, although it does help. The machine can detect parasympathetic bodily functions. The machine along with the operator are very good at revealing deception.

The polygraph interview is best explained as a technique. There are many criminal interview and interrogation techniques. The polygraph technique only works if you have something to lose, such as your freedom, pride, or a job. If you have nothing to lose, and I place you on the machine, you will beat it. I could sit you down and tell you to lie to each question, you would, and the technique will fail.

The primary reason this technique works is that if deception is detected, the person being interviewed will see a consequence, such as not being hired or being arrested. So, based on this, if you have something to hide, you are being interviewed, and you are found to be deceitful, this would create a negative consequence for you. Thus the technique works.

Entire books can be written about this machine. Just realize that regardless of your upbringing, you know the difference between right and wrong, truth and lies. When you lie, and you are actively attempting to hide the fact that you are lying, your body reacts. This reaction is mostly involuntary. It is like the sinking feeling in your stomach when you are in trouble, or the butterflies in your stomach when you are nervous, or you have an unpleasant thought and your heart begins to beat just a little faster.

What most do not realize is that the polygraph has four parts: the machine, the interviewer, your answers, and potential countermeasures.

Countermeasures are when you intentionally try to alter the machine's results. Countermeasures are worse than lying, and quite frankly, are far more obvious. Usually if you attempt to employ countermeasures or alter the machine's results, you will be thrown out and likely will never be hired by any police agency.

There was a police candidate who was placed on the polygraph and was employing countermeasures. He was holding his breath and flexing his upper thighs during his answers. He was given several warnings, but he did not stop. He was then walked out and disqualified.

I received a phone call from an officer who had worked for me before, and he asked me to look over the report, because the candidate was his brother. I assigned the task to one of my subordinate sergeants. He met with the candidate. The candidate said that because he failed the test at another agency, when he was taking our test, he was trying to alter the results to pass. He will never be a cop.

The operator of the machine is the actual lie detector. This usually helps people understand these machines. Polygraph results are not used in court (there is no reason to), but the interview can be. Remember, the operator of the machine is usually either a current detective or a retired detective, usually in the homicide or sex crime arena, I have found.

Most state laws do prohibit hiring decisions made solely on polygraph results; however, almost every state has a public safety exception. If you fail the polygraph, in my experience, you have lied, or at a minimum you have something to hide. Thus, you are disqualified. I don't know where the "85 percent accurate" statistic came from, but it is simply nonsense.

Having said all this, there are people who ultimately *can* beat the test, even when they have something to lose. In my experience, very few people successfully do. There are so many factors to consider that it is quite a task to beat it. This goes far beyond just controlling your breathing. Breathing can be controlled, but when you control your breathing, it is incredibly obvious to the operator. Parasympathetic reactions things that you are not able to control, such as muscle contractions, heart rate, sweat glands, internal body electricity, emotions, and fear are all things that will expose your dishonesty.

I have seen people with various medical conditions have abnormal results, and I have also known people to be shown as deceptive due to another lie but not necessarily the one they are being asked about. When deception is indicated, the operator knows to investigate that category well. For obvious reasons, I will not discuss the entire process. However, I will talk about one aspect of it.

A person will usually lie to get out of trouble or rather, everyone has at least once. If you are asked the question, "Have you ever lied to get out of trouble?" how would you answer? You may think that the operator wants to hear you say, "No, I never lie." Well, you just lied. I know it, and so do you. Honest people will admit that at some time in their life, they have lied to get out of trouble. When a person admits that they have lied at some point in their life, this, ironically, is an indicator of honesty.

Polygraph operators are very interesting, and it took me a long time of supervising these professionals to truly understand their craft. During a preemployment polygraph, you will be asked to confirm all the information you have already provided everything from the initial employment application to the specific answers you gave during other parts of the process, such as your psychological exam. If you are serious about being hired as a police officer, just don't lie on these tests. The operators of these magical machines are absolute surgical experts at detecting deception.

Having said that, someone reading this may be thinking, "My friend is a cop, and he said he lied on his test." Maybe he did; maybe he beat the test. I will tell you, though, that it is very unlikely. Also, the more research you do into these machines, the more you realize that they are very hard to beat. This is the main reason that good attorneys will never recommend that their clients take a polygraph test.

The polygraph technique is different for each type of interview. Preemployment interviews are very different from criminal interviews. Each has a very specific industry-accepted technique. If I am asking you about a murder, the interview will be relatively specific. If I am asking you about your entire background, I will ask you generalized questions that have sub-questions. A generalized question could be, "Have you ever broken the law?" Within this category could be twenty specific questions, such as, "Have you ever driven intoxicated?" Or "Have you ever stolen property?"

These interviews are incredibly structured, just as a criminal investigatory interview between a detective and suspect are well structured. There is a lot of theater involved in deception detection. It goes far beyond the movie idea of good cop, bad cop.

If you take a preemployment polygraph, or if you are interviewed as a suspect by a police detective, the interview is very structured. Details such as the temperature in the room, introduction, tone of voice, handshake, and multiple entries and exits from the room are all structured. Early in my police career, I took several advanced interview and interrogation courses of instruction, some even having specific certifications based on copyrighted techniques.

There are a couple of theoretical ideas that helped me understand the polygraph. First, imagine a disinfecting wipe. You wipe a surface and kill 99.9 percent of bacteria, then if you wipe again, you will kill 99.9 percent of what's left. Your background detective is the first wipe, and the polygrapher is the second wipe. Get the picture?

Second, imagine placing yourself in a room with a doctor. You are in that room with a doctor who specializes in and has extensive experience at identifying a specific disease. Further, that doctor has a machine that measures the symptoms of that disease. When the doctor tells you that, based on your symptoms, his experience, and your condition, you have the disease in question, very few people would doubt this, especially when a second opinion is built into the scenario. The polygraph operator is the doctor, and your background detective is the second opinion. Does that help?

Another point to consider is that this is your first time trying to defeat this process. The polygrapher has seen thousands of people try the same tactics that you are going to try. Predictable human behavior is a hard concept for most to understand. The idea is that most people, when placed in a specific scenario, will behave in a similar manner. Predictable human behavior is culturally specific. Various studies have shown that this concept is over 90 percent accurate.

The concept of fight or flight is an example of this. People will choose to either fight and overcome a threat or flee it. Fear of public speaking is another predictable example for most of the population. If you consider this within the concept of using deception, it can help you understand. Polygraph exams rely quite a bit on predictable human behavior. As individualistic as we all like to think we are, we in fact act very similar. Because deception is so antithetical to your psychological baseline, these interviews are very effective.

You will be seated in a very specific chair, on a pad that measures muscle contractions. Sensors will be placed on your palms and around your chest. The exam will almost always be recorded from several different angles. The equipment will be plugged into a computer that will monitor your body. Your baseline will be measured as you listen to instructions, usually before you think the exam has begun.

You will be asked questions that you are asked to be truthful on, and some you are asked to lie to. Your body's reaction to these questions will be evaluated. Then you will be asked preemployment-specific questions. Usually, question categories will be mixed to effectively measure your results.

For example, you may be asked a question to be honest on, then one to lie on, then the actual preemployment question. Your answers will be recorded as you go. Depending on the technique being used, you may be asked the same question several times, or your examiner may leave the room for a brief time to measure your response to being alone.

You will likely have a practice run. This is an attempt to expose you to the questions in advance so there are no surprises. It has the effect of calming the applicant down, and regardless of what you are told, it is being measured.

Another great reason for you to know what will be asked of you is the buildup. Great for the test, that is. If you know that you are about to be asked, "Have you ever used illegal drugs?" the fact that you know what will be asked is a great opportunity to measure your reaction to it. If you are planning on being deceptive, seconds before the question is asked, you will be thinking about it. As that anticipation builds, your body will react. As the examiner says, "Have you ...," your body has already started to react to the question. Your body's response will be measured prior, during, and after the question is asked, then prior, during, and after you provide your answer. Because of this, answers must be kept very short.

Questions will be asked in a manner that will elicit a yes/no response. You will be given the opportunity to explain complicated answers. For example, let's say you are going to be asked, "Have you ever lied to your parents?" You may want to explain that you told a minor lie to your parents about coming home late or a bad grade. You will be given the opportunity to explain all these issues, and then the question will be worded in a way to consider these issues. The question may be changed to, "Other than what we have discussed, have you ever lied to your parents?"

Psychological Test

The psychological test is a critical part of the testing process. It is usually split between a written product and a verbal interview. The written test is about half a day, and the verbal interview is about an hour. I am not going to go into specifics on this for obvious reasons. However, just be aware that the psychological written test is very well made. It measures various personality types, and it does this dozens of times.

This is why it takes so long. You will be asked the same questions many different ways, as well as some irrelevant questions to measure your truthfulness. In Nevada, the test measures conscientiousness, emotional stability, extraversion, openness to experience, and agreeableness. Your state may differ, but not by much. See your state's POST standards for more information.

The psychologist who evaluates your written test and interviews you will be a specialist. These professionals are licensed psychologists who make their career out of preemployment exams. They will usually have contracts with many different police agencies. Just like the polygraph examiner, these professionals have tested thousands of applicants and will identify any potential red flags early on. They will also work with your background investigator to dig into any specific identified issues.

Most of the data needed to be established is found within the written portion. I am not a psychologist; I just supervised them. Patterns are developed and used. They are easy to identify and very easy to see. If you are being deceitful, it will show. If you are overly aggressive, it will show. However, most fascinating, if you are trying to falsify your results to make yourself look better, that will show also. This art is very complicated, and there were times I had to have the psychologist walk me through his results. However, I can share that those potential issues are identified very early.

LVMPD's psychologist was very good at analyzing these results. The great thing is, he has all of your information from your background investigator and your polygrapher, so if you are dishonest, that can be identified almost immediately. To pass, I would say be honest, reasonable, and consistent.

There are red flags. I will not list them all; however, I will mention one. Anytime anyone is fascinated by fire, examine their background for animal cruelty. If you find both a fire fascination and animal cruelty, it is usually an indicator of a very dangerous person. However, most patterns are very subtle. Just be honest. If you are honest and you fail, maybe policing is not for you. Perhaps another career is for you.

The Results

Finally, all your results will be evaluated and compared to the agency's confidential standards. At that time, you may be offered employment, permanently disqualified, or temporarily disqualified. Temporary disqualifications are usually due to a time standard. If you were recently terminated from a job but the rest of your background was good, you may be given a one-year disqualification. If you return a year later, with good employment history for the prior year, you will likely be hired. The hiring process is exhausting, but the process itself is a method to measure your commitment.

7

The Academy

The academy is peculiar in the fact that it is very well structured to find your breaking point. It is strange because up to this point, the agency has spent about $3,000 on you. That was the approximate cost of the background investigation. A police academy is made to teach and certify you. However, the beginning portions are designed to encourage resignations.

I found that nationwide, academies mostly follow the same format. Each academy must provide a specific amount of training in various areas as per your state's POST laws. It's puzzling to me when people think they have identified a policing problem and decide "more training" is the answer. More training is almost never the answer. The real answer is to review existing training and hold agencies accountable for their staff.

Throughout my career, I learned a few law enforcement facts that I will share with you:

1. If you have never been a cop, you cannot accurately understand the position. It sounds harsh, but would you hire a lawyer with no experience? Your opinion on policing matters becomes valid once you are a cop.

2. There is bad everywhere. There are bad teachers, doctors, and mechanics. The problem is that you cannot identify the bad ones until they do bad stuff. That is how you define bad—by comparing it to ideal.

3. It is very easy to blame the lowest-paid person in a chain of command for a mistake, as it is always easy to blame the police when something bad occurs. When you blame the police, you have a few advantages. They will not defend themselves, because they will not jeopardize an investigation or their job.

The police will usually offer no opinion to the media, or to you specifically, especially if the issue is part of a larger investigation. Further, they are obligated to tell the truth, so you can lie, and they can't, or shouldn't. Very few people are willing to wait for all the evidence to come out and to work through an entire investigation. We saw this in 2020 and 2021 very often, as various politicians and pundits would offer opinions or even publish stories based on partial information or actual falsehoods. There is nothing wrong with not offering an opinion on an issue until you have received all of the information; in fact, it is wise.

4. Cops do make mistakes. They are young, overworked, and usually underpaid. A cop is twenty-four years old on average, has a high school diploma, and is a human being. Cops make mistakes, and we as a society just seem to be very unwilling to accept this. We understand that other occupations make mistakes; however, for some reason, we tend to hold police officers to a very high, at times unreasonable standard.

Academies' structures and curriculum are different based on jurisdiction; however, most follow a similar format. When you go through a police academy, the first one to two weeks, you will be bombarded with video after video, story after story of cops being murdered. You will be told to quit, and you will likely be placed under immense stress in order to make you quit. This eases up a little afterward but is still a large part of the entire academy. Each state is different, but all need to figure out who is going to quit and get them out of the way fast.

I found that live-in or live-out academies have about the same attrition rates. An average police academy will lose about 10 percent, and then that group will lose another 10 percent in field training. Once you get to the point where no one else will quit, the humbling process begins.

It is imperative to absolutely humiliate recruits. This is done for several reasons. The most important thing, I think, is to get rid of anyone who is there to abuse power. There are people who become cops to abuse power. The great thing is that people who abuse power are usually very sensitive to humiliation. So, when they are humbled, they will usually resign. It's like the abusive husband who is confronted by a stranger who is not scared of him. Traditionally he will cower in fear, because he is a bully and is being stood up to.

My police academy experience was in 2001. Policing was much different then. The first four weeks were designed to make me quit, with lot of yelling, unrealistic expectations, running, and academics. During the first four weeks, you are offered the opportunity to resign dozens of times. It is hard to understand the logic from the ground level. However, imagine the scandal if a cop walked off the job during a critical incident. At two a.m., in an alley, with some guy punching you in the face, are you going to quit? Or are you going to fight and win?

The academy does what it can to create an atmosphere of stress to see how you will respond to it. Some people respond well to stress, and some don't. I found that I personally, for some reason, function very well, almost better than normal, under stress. I think this is why I spent such a long time in patrol.

Police academies in the United States are all about six months long. Some require you to live there; most do not. They all take private citizens and make them police officers. The transformation process is usually well structured and modular in design, each step building on the last. I will do my best to offer you an idea of what you will learn in a police academy.

One thing I have failed to mention is the job title. *Police officer, sheriff's deputy, constable,* and *trooper* are often used interchangeably. There are some minor differences, but for our purposes I will lump them all into the title of *police officer.*

Until the 1990s, most agencies hired you as a police officer and then trained you in the academy. This was changed in the 1990s; you will now see people hired at an introduction rank, like recruit or cadet, while they are in the academy. This accomplishes a couple of goals. First, it makes it easy to terminate you. If you are a police recruit and it is a probationary rank, the agency can terminate your employment for any or no reason. Also, the title of a sworn police officer brings with it some benefit and responsibility, such as the ability to carry a firearm across state or county lines, conceal firearms, and make arrests. It is best not to give people such powers until they are properly trained.

Most police academies are of a paramilitary nature. There are a lot of basic training or boot camp ideas like inspections, marching, rank, and structure and for good reason. As the military is creating soldiers, the academy is creating a strange hybrid of citizen and soldier.

I found that police academies were more aggressive or more militaristic on the east and west coast. There is a culture shift as you get toward the Midwest. This is where you see more academic police academies; however, they all do the same thing. Police academies form the people you trust. The purest form of law enforcement is the line-level police officer who wants to make a difference.

Resignations

Before we get into what you are taught, I want to just go over resignations quickly. It's hard to understand, but police academies must find your personal weakness and exploit it. The idea is to induce you to resign. Your weakness cannot be left to be exploited by a suspect when you are on the street.

If you do not have the mental toughness not to resign, you should consider another career field. Everyone has a weakness, whether physical or mental. It is wise to teach people how to overcome their weakness and not allow them to encounter it on the street when their life is in the balance.

When you are a police officer, you may be confronted by someone trying to hurt or kill you; a hurt child; provide devastation; or the most stressful situation you have ever experienced. The issue is that quitting in the field is not an option. If you quit in the field, you will likely be killed, or an innocent citizen may be killed. The academy places huge stress on you in order to expose your weaknesses. The idea is to weed out those who will quit under stress.

If your family members were taken hostage, you would want a police officer to save them, one who will not quit under any circumstances. Great stress is placed on the recruit to induce the types of stress that may be met with in the street. Police academies have a great deal of psychological structure to identify people's weakness and offer solutions.

Learning the Law

So, let's talk about what you learn: first, the law at its varying levels of intensity and categories, be it criminal, civil, or constitutional. Your job will be to enforce the laws of the jurisdiction in which you are employed. We will stick to the levels I just spoke of to break it up: constitutional, civil, and criminal.

Constitutional Law

We will start with constitutional law. The United States Constitution gives you specific rights. These rights are primarily to protect you from the government. As a police officer, you will become the enforcement arm of the government. You will be the executive branch of government.

Just a quick review: the United States government is split into three categories, legislative, executive, and judicial. The legislative branch creates the law. These are elected officials at the local, state, or federal level who write the laws which you will enforce. They are usually attorneys, and they love to write them some laws. At times, it seems they write laws with no regard as to whether the law can be enforced.

I was involved in a, well, spirited conversation once with a local legislator who could not understand that just because a law is passed does not mean that every police officer will arrest everyone who violates it. This conversation was about passing a law to make it a criminal violation to feed the homeless. I tried to explain that you cannot simply pass a law like this and expect it to be enforced citywide, immediately, thus solving the issue you are having with churches feeding the homeless in your local area of responsibility. Yes, he wanted to make it illegal to feed the poor.

The legislature really should at least consider the constitutionality and, dare I say, the commonsense aspect of the law. However, it seems that they at times simply write a law, usually along party lines, and then essentially move on. The issue is, there is no accountability, or at least not immediately. If a legislature passes a law, and you are arrested for violating that law, then through various appellate avenues you make it to the US Supreme Court, which declares the law unconstitutional, there is no accountability to the legislature who wrote the law except to voters.

Please don't be an ill-informed voter. Make your vote count. Remember my point earlier that it is very easy to blame the police officer, but try to keep in mind that police officers don't write the law; they just enforce it.

Legislation should always be the final attempt to solve a given problem, not the first. Further, no matter how hard you try, you cannot legislate to force people to think with the same values that you do. You cannot legislate morality; people will violate the law if they wish to. Legislatures should be considering the long-term ramifications of the laws they are passing, and I think some do. Some are only thinking about four years away to the next election.

Legislation is a very powerful tool. Try to keep in mind that it is not just criminal laws they are passing; they are also deciding how to spend tax money. Regardless of your political affiliation, I would ask that you become an informed voter. I have seen the ramifications of bad law. If you are basing your vote entirely on a preferred news network, or your specific labor union's endorsement, you really should do a little more homework.

Back to our review of the United States government, the legislative branch of our government creates the laws, and the executive branch enforces those laws. The executive branch consists of the police, the president, and government officials. As a police officer, your job will be to enforce the laws passed by the legislature. It is a powerful job, and you will either arrest people for violating the law or force them to follow it.

The executive branch of government is the intermediary between the lawmakers and the courts. The executive branch is made up of all kinds of people, including police officers, lawyers, and elected officials. It is important to understand that there is a difference between those who make the laws and those who enforce them. I say this because the conflict occurs when a citizen disagrees with the law being enforced.

The issue is that the executive branch is not the place to argue your point. That comes next, in court.

Most states allow police discretion. That is, the law allows for police officers to evaluate whether an arrest, citation, or warning is necessary. Discretion is essential to policing. Laws do not cover every eventuality, and further, a law may be broken by a citizen and it is completely justified. Police offices must be given the authority to make these distinctions; further they must receive adequate training to properly identify these scenarios.

At times, people are the victim of a crime, and they do not wish to pursue charges against the suspect of the crime; this is another example of the need for discretion. There are some laws that have mandatory arrest statutes. These laws completely take the discretion away from police officers and obligate them to make the arrest under every circumstance. At times, police agencies make some laws mandatory to arrest, again taking discretion away from the police officer. Every state has different laws; however, I will try to explain some of these mandatory arrest laws.

Domestic violence tends to be a mandatory arrest and mandatory prosecution. The intent is to prevent domestic violence victims from being further victimized. Domestic violence almost always escalates and becomes more and more violent as time goes on. Another example of a mandatory arrest is usually driving while intoxicated. Issuing someone a citation for this crime and letting the individual drive away does not solve the problem at all, so an arrest is usually mandated.

The judicial branch of government is the branch that evaluates and interprets the law and how it is applied. This branch is made up of the local, state, and federal court systems. Local and federal judges are almost all exclusively attorneys. The judiciary will evaluate your methodology in enforcing a law, and it will also correct any wrong it identifies.

The issue we have is that our current legislatures use the judicial branch as a second legislative branch. I say this because judges, almost exclusively the US Supreme Court judges, will make a ruling on a case, and said ruling now becomes the law, or more appropriately, the correct way to interpret that law. The judicial branch is where you fight a wrong. If you feel you were unjustly arrested, this is where you seek relief. You do not argue the constitutionality of the law on the side of a freeway while getting a speeding ticket. Cops make mistakes, as do legislatures. These mistakes are often corrected in the judicial branch.

Constitutional law is a huge part of how you will be a cop. Through various court decisions, the judiciary has established the rules for policing in the United States. The Constitution is in place to protect you, the citizen, from the government. It establishes rules for the government and protections for citizens. You enjoy a right to privacy. The government can invade this right; however, it must follow certain steps prior to invading your privacy. You have the right to freely travel; however, the government can stop this if it takes certain steps.

As technology changes, or if the Constitution is challenged by a particular situation, as the courts apply the Constitution, this affects policing. Policing as a general profession is evolving all the time. The founding fathers would not have known of the advent of smartphones and the advanced technologies we enjoy today. Because of this, at times, the Constitution may require further definition and explanation. When this occurs, police must abide by these rules. Those entrusted with enforcing the nation's laws must have guidance. Answers to questions such as when can someone be arrested or when can someone be searched will be answered.

Constitutional issues are rarely simple. When a protest is deemed unlawful, that must have a definition that is clearly written and understandable. When the government seizes evidence from you or your home, it must follow rules. If it does not follow the rules, the individuals responsible will punished. If they follow the rules and obtain the information correctly, it can be used to arrest and possibly convict you.

The Constitution manages far more than just how to police. However, it is important to remember that the police, whether a municipal police officer or a Department of Justice special agent, are the enforcement branch of the government.

Law enforcement is an ever-evolving profession. It learns from its past, or at least should, then applies those lessons. So, what are the rules? They are easy to understand. Remember that the US Constitution applies to you everywhere in the United States. Each state has its own laws, but the Constitution applies in all states.

When can your freedom of movement be limited by the government? This is a very funny area to explore with people in their late teens or early twenties who have not yet realized the world is a very grey place and not as black and white as it really should be. Based on this, there are many ways your freedoms can be restricted, evidence can be gathered, and you can be imprisoned.

Contact

To start, we should talk about the contact, as this will usually occur first. The police must follow rules when they contact you. When they follow these rules, they are rewarded with successful enforcement of the laws, and in theory keep you safe. But there is a fine line between freedom and privacy. Your right to privacy should not be able to infringe on another's. Further, your actions should not infringe on someone else's freedoms. This seems simple; however, it is incredibly complicated. The basic premise is that all people are equal, and no one's rights are more important than another's.

When the police initiate contact with you, they have to follow specific steps to initiate that contact and continue it. There are three levels of police contact, each more invasive than the last: consensual encounter, reasonable suspicion, and probable cause. Each of these requires a different level of justification, and the three are not exclusive. What I mean is that the police can start at one level and graduate to another, either going up the ladder or down. We will talk about each, but very briefly, a consensual encounter is a conversation, probable cause is an arrest, and reasonable suspicion is right in the middle of the two.

Consensual encounter

The first level of contact is a consensual encounter. These are the least understood and most abused, intentionally or not. A consensual encounter requires consent on the part of the citizen being encountered.

It requires no justification or steps to follow. It is merely a conversation. These types of encounters with police are the only ones you can walk away from.

If a police officer approaches you and asks to talk to you, you most likely feel compelled and curious to find out why. Therefore, these encounters can be very effective. The citizens involved may feel a genuine obligation to speak with the police, or more realistically, a need to defend their actions and convince the officer of their innocence. These contacts are incredibly effective because of these concepts. If an officer initiates conversation with you, unless you are educated on the facts, you may not realize that you can decline the conversation and walk away.

The issue with these encounters is that they are sensitive and can become de facto arrests regardless of the officer's initial intent. Citizens must reasonably think that they can leave at any time. If I, as a police officer, approach you and say, "You have to talk to me," reasonably, you will think you cannot leave. This would not be consensual; you would reasonably feel obligated to remain. However, if I say, "Do you mind if we speak? You are free to leave at any time," this creates a different dynamic.

The trick here is that even when you tell people they are free to leave, they often will not leave. People have a natural tendency to speak, and at times people can talk themselves into jail. Next time you are having a one-on-one conversation, stop speaking and see how long it takes to feel awkward. News reporters have developed this technique very well. During an interview, a reporter may just remain silent after receiving an inadequate answer, and the person being interviewed will feel psychologically obligated to fill the silence.

Consensual encounters are a great way to speak to someone you cannot force to speak with you. Perhaps you can see both how valuable and how easy to abuse these are. The Supreme Court has found that these encounters are a necessary part of police work. However, they must be used carefully. Something as simple as asking a person to come back or turn around can invalidate this contact.

I could write for an entire chapter on these encounters. These contacts require citizens to participate of their own free will. If you ask a police officer for directions to a destination, this is a consensual encounter. If you ask a police officer a legal question, this is also consensual.

Reasonable suspicion

Next is reasonable suspicion. This is midway between the casual nature of a consensual encounter and an arrest. These encounters have some rules the police must follow. They are sometimes called Terry Stops, due to the source of their authority, which is Terry v. Ohio, 392 U.S. 1 (1968). Some states add provisions to these stops or require the police to take additional steps. However, federally speaking, the issue at hand is, can police forcibly detain you but not arrest you? The answer is yes. A reasonable suspicion stop can take place.

If police officers observe you and have reason to believe you have been, are currently, or will be involved in a crime, they may detain you. Books have been written on this case and its ramifications. I will keep it very general for us. You could be a witness, suspect, or victim of a crime. If the police have reasonable articulable facts that can link you to a crime past, present, or future they may detain you in order to identify you and investigate your involvement in that crime.

Most states provide a sixty-minute time limit on these types of stops. It is important for you as a police officer and a citizen to understand that the detention here is done to identify you and figure out what your involvement is in the crime at hand. Once that is done, the detention must stop.

Before I move on to probable cause, we should go over some real examples of both a consensual encounter and a terry stop. If I am at a red light, stopped in my police car, and you pull up to the same red light next to me, so far, no contact has been made. Other than the red light, nothing is really stopping you from driving away. If your window is down, and so is mine, and I strike up a conversation, this is purely consensual. We are two people having a talk, waiting for a traffic light to turn green.

At times, I would do this and ask the simple question, "Do you have a driver's license?" At this point, nothing stops citizens from putting their window up and ignoring me. However, often, I would target vehicles I suspected were not being lawfully driven. As soon as the driver admitted to not having a license, or it being expired or suspended, now I had a reason to investigate. I just went from a consensual encounter to reasonable suspicion. Now I can stop you and investigate your involvement in driving that car with no license.

Probable cause

Finally, probable cause is an arrest. Police can stop you to arrest you based on establishing probable cause, or as a result of a previously obtained arrest warrant. Citations are also types of arrests. In order to arrest you, the officer must take some steps to establish probable cause or have an arrest warrant for you.

Now, each state has different laws and generally different rules. For example, in Nevada, a police officer cannot make an arrest for a misdemeanor crime that was not committed in his or her presence, with some exceptions. Some states delineate when you can make an arrest for an attempt of a crime, such as attempted burglary.

To begin this talk, we must generally establish what a crime is, then what an arrest is. Remember that in our legal system, things must be definable. If you cannot define a term, how can you possibly detain someone or defend yourself from it?

Misunderstandings of definitions of crimes are a common source of conflict. For example, the definition of a car can vary. A car and a motorcycle are very different and need definitions to indicate this. A motorized wheelchair should not have the same definition as a car. Definitions are what make the legal world spin.

So, what exactly is a crime? A crime is an act or failure to act that is forbidden by law, something you did or did not do that is illegal. People often get hung up on how a failure to act is a crime. Car insurance is mandatory; thus, failing to get it is a crime. Failing to feed your children is a crime; failing to stop at that red light is a crime.

What is an arrest? How do citizens know when they are under arrest, and how does the arresting officer know? It is not as obvious as you would think. A police officer may have all the evidence in the world to arrest you, but he or she may choose not to arrest you, or may choose to arrest you later. Usually, police officers know they are arresting the person, but not always. Sometimes a consensual encounter can cross the line into arrest without the officer realizing it.

An arrest usually involves lawfully detaining someone, requiring a physical touching, after obtaining the necessary facts to establish probable cause. Arrests are the ultimate in detention. You are not free to leave, and further will be going to jail, or will receive a date to appear in court. When under arrest, you enjoy specific Constitutional protections. You have the right to remain silent, for example.

People tend to become confused when these three levels of contact move from one to another. A consensual encounter can become a reasonable suspicion stop that can ultimately result in an arrest. If you are ever under arrest and the officer tells you that you enjoy the right to remain silent, it would be in your best interest to not speak at all. If you are under arrest, there is almost no way you are going to talk your way out of it. Further, there is a huge chance you talking will make it worse. Most defense attorneys will advise you not to speak to the police, with your best interest in mind.

Searches

Searches are another aspect of constitutional law that you will have to understand as a police officer. When can you search people or their car? What can you search for? Again, books have been written on this subject. There are many types and scopes of searches. Generally, if you have enough to arrest, you have enough to search, but not always. Generally, if you have enough information to detain someone, you will have enough information to perform a pat-down or frisk.

Pat-downs

There is a difference between a pat-down for weapons (frisk) and a search for evidence. You can pat people down or frisk them with consent, or if you can articulate the need. A pat-down is when you use your hands to feel the outside of a person's clothing to check for weapons. Obtaining consent could be as simple as asking, "Do you have any weapons, and can I check?" This would be enough to establish consent.

Of course, the person could decline. If an individual declines, and you cannot articulate the need, you are not legally able to touch them. Articulating a need for a pat-down can be incredibly simple, or as complicated as you need it to be. If I am speaking with you and I clearly see the outline of a weapon on your person, that is enough articulation. If the person tells you they are armed, that also is good enough.

Those are relatively easy to explain. Sometimes it is not that easy; most of the time, it is not that easy. If you are in an area where you frequently take weapons off people who are dressed similarly to the person you are talking to, or perhaps you can see a bulge that is where people often carry weapons, like a waistband area, you can pat down for weapons. This would be *articulation*. All articulation means is explaining the facts and circumstances.

Pat-downs or frisks are always for weapons, not evidence. However, there is a concept called *plain feel*. This is a little complicated. If you are conducting your pat-down (I am assuming you are doing it legally; either you have consent or you can clearly articulate the need), and you plainly feel what you immediately identify as an illegal item, you can immediately seize the item.

The most common way this applies is when a police officer is doing a pat-down and feels a glass smoking pipe. These pipes are used to smoke methamphetamine or crack cocaine, and when you feel them under clothing, with training and experience, there is no doubt what they feel like. Location can help you also. If you are patting down a woman and you feel the glass pipe tucked under her armpit, where her bra strap is located, that is plainly a pipe. What else could it be?

Search for evidence

Searches for evidence can get very complicated very quickly. When it comes to searches, you can ask for consent. "Can I search you for drugs?" Searches are location- and item-specific. In order to gain consent or a search warrant, you must establish what you are searching for and where you are searching. For your search to be legal, your consent or search warrant must be valid. Indicating you are going to just search a house is not enough. You must indicate what you are looking for and where you will be looking.

A consensual search is very straightforward. First, the person must have *standing*. In this context, a good way to define standing is that the person has the ability to grant consent. Is the item that individual's to control? I have no standing over my neighbor's house, so I cannot offer you consent to search it. Because I have no standing, if you find something illegal in my neighbor's home, you can't arrest me for it. People with standing can object to the search also. The item being searched must be under their control, such as their car, their home, or their jacket. A person with standing has an expectation of privacy over the object.

Second, the person with standing must consent to both the scope of the search and the object of it. The scope of a search is how invasive it will be. Such as, you could consent to only allowing police to search your left pocket but not your right. Or they may search your entire car, except for the trunk. The object of the search is what they are looking for. You must consent to both what they are searching and what they are searching for.

Search warrants must indicate the probable cause the police have to make the search, or the reasons they believe there is evidence of a crime in a place where a person has an expectation of privacy. Also, the scope and object must be explained.

A brief example would be if undercover officers have purchased illegal narcotics from your home on several occasions. Each time they purchase the illegal narcotics, it is from the same person at the home. Via investigation, they establish that you have standing over the home. This can be done by viewing utility bills or rental contracts. The home must be described to establish the scope of the search, and then the object would be illegal narcotics.

Before I move on, it is important to establish the scope of the search, which must be valid or reasonable. In either consent or a search warrant, the item or items being sought must be assumed to be in a reasonable place. If you gave me consent or I obtained a search warrant to locate an illegal rifle, my search would only be valid if I searched places that rifle could be. I could not search your glove compartment for the rifle; rifles do not fit in glove compartments.

Small amounts of illegal narcotics can be located almost anywhere, thus the scope of a narcotic search is immense. Searches are incredibly complicated, and I could literally go on for chapters. Especially with digital searches, data is the new evidence. Your browser history or thumb drives can be used to implicate you in a crime. If you are going to get consent or a warrant for a search, always attempt to get it for the smallest possible item, such as narcotics, so you can search anywhere they may be.

If you are going to be an enforcer of the law, it is important you are aware of what the rules are. If you plan on being a career criminal, you should probably look up the laws too. However, most criminals will not do the research and do silly things to get themselves in trouble. For an average citizen who is just trying to get by day to day, just remember, if you don't have to speak to the police, don't. If they ask for your consent, say no.

Even the most inept criminal defense attorney will tell you to not speak to the police and consent to nothing. I used to find it very amusing when a person was arrested for some crime and was able to talk or consent themselves into a conviction. This works both ways; if you are a good cop, you should always be asking questions and getting consent.

We covered consensual searches and searches based on a warrant. There is also a probable cause search that applies mostly to cars. If police stop a vehicle and establish probable cause that there is evidence in the car, they can normally seize it. There are rules connected to these searches, and they vary by state.

If you must conduct a search of a vehicle, and you don't have time to obtain a warrant, you can search it. This is usually based on the fact that the car is mobile and can be driven away from you at any time. You can also inventory a vehicle that is being impounded without a warrant in most states. There are a few more searches, but for our purposes, this will work.

You can search someone you are taking to jail. A search of a person going to jail is called a *search incident to arrest*. The intent of the search is to establish that you are not allowing contraband into the jail.

The scope of these searches matter. If you are not allowing a bag to go with the arrestee into the jail, there is usually no reason to search it. However, if the arrestee is wearing a jacket into the jail, you should search each pocket.

I am going to stop the search rules here, I could literally go on for chapters on the subject, and many constitutional scholars have written books on searches, but for our purposes in this book, I think we have covered the basics.

Rules

There is an incentive for the police to follow the established rules. The courts in the United States are very quick to remind you that, as the police, you must follow the Constitution. If at some point in the interaction you are found to have violated a rule, anything you obtained as a result of the violation will be inadmissible as evidence. So, there is incentive to follow the rules.

If you violate a rule and discover evidence, the legal term for this is known as "fruit of the poisonous tree." If you break the rule, your case is thrown out. I have found that it is rare in modern-day policing for these errors to occur intentionally. If they occur at all, they are usually either unintentional or procedural in nature. Even if you are investigating a homicide and you find what is obviously the weapon used, if you find it illegally, you cannot use it as evidence.

I will end our constitutional law portion here. I could go on for chapters on this subject, and I would lose most of you. Some of you have read what I have written and want to know more. I have covered the basics here; it is enough for us to move on.

Criminal and Civil Law

Next to constitutional law are criminal and civil law. Police are often involved in civil law disputes; however, they normally have no jurisdiction in these areas. Civil law is usually mediated by judges. Civil law includes things like divorces, lawsuits, child custody disputes, and evictions. These issues can create a dispute that involves the police; however, people are rarely arrested for violating a divorce decree or a civil case violation. They may be found in contempt of court for the violation, however, and be penalized via fine.

Criminal law changes state by state. However, it usually requires intent and action, and there are some federal constants. Criminal law is split between crimes against property and crimes against people. Crimes against people are almost always more serious. Each law enforcement agency is required to report crime statistics to the Department of Justice. This process is called *uniform crime reporting* (UCR), and because of it we do have some consistency between various states.

Most crimes are obvious in the legal world. The obvious crimes are called *illegal per se*. These crimes are inherently wrong. They are illegal because they are wrong. Things like stealing or killing fall in this category.

Mala prohibita is a term used to describe crimes that are illegal because the law says they are, such as tax evasion or traffic violations. Most UCR crimes have consistent definitions throughout the United States. This helps with crime statistics.

Because each state is different and can create its own laws, there must be some consistency within definition. If you are trying to measure murder rates from state to state, you must have a similar definition of murder from state to state. I use murder for this example because it is probably the most misunderstood crime.

Each crime statute has what are called *elements*. All the elements are needed to convict someone of a crime. Elements are like ingredients for a cake. Each individual ingredient is needed for the cake. However, each ingredient by itself is not a cake.

Think of the crime of burglary. A generic definition of burglary would be, "any person who enters any structure or vehicle with the intent to commit another crime is guilty of burglary." The elements of this crime are:

- *any person* (an animal cannot commit a burglary)

- *who enters any structure or vehicle* (the person must physically enter the structure or the vehicle; entry can be the entire body or just a hand)
- *with the intent to commit another crime* (the person at the time of entry must have established the intent to commit another crime); so, if the person enters the structure and then establishes intent to commit a crime, it is not burglary)

Homicide is the killing of one person by another. Not all homicides are illegal. If you kill someone trying to kill you, you have committed a homicide but not murder. If you run a red light and kill another driver, you have committed a homicide but not murder. If you are in a physical fight with someone, and you punch them, and they fall and hit their head and die, that is a homicide, but not necessarily a murder.

Murder usually is defined as the intentional killing of one person by another, with malice aforethought. You either through intent or negligent intent took actions to take a human life. It is important to understand the difference, and why police officers are not charged with murder when they are forced to kill someone in the capacity of their jobs.

Theft or a crime of property is an easy one to understand: don't take or break things that are not yours. Theft usually means to permanently deprive someone of property, which means you may have taken it or destroyed it. There is usually a financial threshold to separate a misdemeanor theft from a felony. Twenty-two years ago in Nevada, it was $250. Anything under $250 was a misdemeanor, anything over was a felony. As the years have gone by, it has risen to about $650 in Nevada.

Some items are automatically a felony, regardless of their value. This is based on two categories, either tracking or their inherent value to the victim of the theft. Vehicles, firearms, and livestock usually fall into this category.

The method of the theft matters also. If a theft occurs due to an intentional entry to a building or a vehicle, this is a burglary. If property is taken from you by force or threat of force, this is a robbery. If you take small items, say $5 in value, from the same person numerous times, each theft can be totaled to get to the felony mark. If you are entrusted with property by your employer and you take it, this is embezzlement. A theft will almost always require a victim, a person who was wronged.

Person crimes require a victim also, but at times a cooperative victim stops cooperating. This will necessitate a constant victim to complete a prosecution. Domestic violence is a good example of this. Victims of domestic violence who call 911 are usually initially cooperative, because they need help. However, at times, they become uncooperative. Unfortunately, this happens quite a bit.

The traditional scenario is a woman who is beaten by her boyfriend and calls for help. He is then arrested, and between the time of the arrest and trial, they work out their problems, and the victim refuses to testify. In these cases, the State can become the victim, to ensure a prosecution. This is done to ensure the safety of domestic violence victims. The State will, or should, always prosecute.

Person crimes can be a simple battery, one person using their body to hurt another. This is usually a punch or slap and is a misdemeanor. There are criminal enhancements that can create increased punishment. Enhancements are usually the reason you committed the act, the nature of the victim, or the amount of damage you do.

If you use a weapon to hurt someone, we move into felony territory, such as if you stab or shoot someone. If you use your hands to create the same type of damage expected from a weapon, this can be a felony. Substantial harm or death is usually in the same category. Some jurisdictions call it *aggravated assault*.

There are criminal enhancements that will cause you to receive more punishment for your crime. Usually, the reason you chose the victim is relevant for an enhancement. If you target a family member, or if you are furthering the cause of a criminal gang, or if you pick a victim based on a protected class like sexual orientation, you will likely get an enhanced sentence. I will end criminal law here. Your local jurisdiction could differ, but really, if it is not yours, don't touch it, including someone else's body. It is that simple.

Policies and Procedures

Policies and procedures will be a large part of any police academy. State-run academies will usually have specific classes for each agency that is sent there, to teach its own policies. The police department's policies and procedures are the law of that agency and are vastly different from agency to agency. There are some consistencies, such as constitutional principles and use of force, which I will talk about shortly. Agencies tend to overwrite and over-analyze their policies. Policy manuals can get into thousands of pages very quickly. As police agencies evolve, their policies will change, and usually grow.

In my years in this trade, I only ever saw one police leader actively try to consolidate policies. This was Clark County Sheriff Joseph Lombardo, sheriff from 2014 to the 2022. Sheriff Lombardo identified that policy manuals tend to garner the opposite result than they are intending. When agencies attempt to policy their way out of problems, they tend to create a whole new subset of problems.

Usually, the problem is the sheer size of the manuals. With so much information, it is easy to either show that no reasonable person could possibly know all the information contained therein or create the issue that a reasonable officer cannot go through a shift without violating a policy. When you create an environment like this, you invite misconduct.

Police executives reading this, be agents for change. Make policy manuals easy to understand and follow. Realize that you cannot policy your way out of every eventuality, just like legislatures cannot create laws to solve all problems. Further, realize that decades of writing often create repetitive hard-to-read policy. Further, the policy that your Office of General Counsel writes has to be understood by the high school graduate in the academy.

Use of Force

Use of force is probably the most misunderstood category of policing knowledge. The interesting thing is that use of force does not have to be complicated. Police use of force is governed by the standard set forth in Graham v. Connor, 490 U.S. 386 (1989). This case was heard by the United States Supreme Court, and it decided how police use of force should be evaluated. This case developed the *reasonable officer standard*. This standard is a nationwide standard that all law enforcement agencies must follow. I will tell you what the case says, then we will discuss its application.

The case specifically says that police use of force must be evaluated from the standard of a reasonable officer, one who was in the scenario and had the same amount of information and training the original officer had at the time force was applied. If the officer found out the force was not needed after it was applied, this factor cannot be used to evaluate the reasonableness of it, because the officer who used force did not know it at the time the force was used.

The case also finds that force used by the police must be evaluated by a three-prong test. The prongs are:

1. The severity of the crime at issue
2. Whether the suspect posed an immediate threat to the safety of the officer or others
3. Whether the suspect was actively resisting arrest or attempting to evade arrest by flight

A very brief application of this could be a scenario where a person is stopped for walking across the street out of a crosswalk. At this point, the crime at issue is very low in severity. There is no risk to the safety of the officer, and the offender is not resisting or evading. Based on this, very little force can be used, no more than the officer's physical presence. An officer's physical presence is a level of force.

If, during the stop, the offender attacks you and attempts to kill you by taking your pistol from its holster, this changes everything. The offender is now trying to commit a murder. He or she is posing a severe threat to you and is physically resisting you in an attempt to flee. A lot of force can be used in this case.

Graham v. Connor heavily added to the previous court case for police use of force that was Tennessee v. Garner, 471 U.S. 1 (1985). When you examine the actual practical application of these cases, some simplification may occur. I do not mean to oversimplify this issue, but recent events have so overcomplicated police use of force that some simplification is needed.

Most agencies unnecessarily impose unattainable steps on officers making use-of-force decisions. Further, the US Supreme Court found that police use of force must be evaluated by a reasonable *officer* standard, not a reasonable *reporter* standard. The issue is, if you have never policed a community, you cannot realistically place judgement on an officer's actions.

To be clear, there are times where an officer's actions are clearly excessive. However, the shift we have seen to blame the officer must be stopped. With the addition of body cameras, two things have occurred. Officers are often being shown to be justified in their use of force, and the public is being exposed to how brutal policing can be.

First, we must acknowledge that force is sometimes needed. People try to fight the police and kill the police. Police officers are taught to physically defend themselves and to physically defend the public. If you are struggling to get away from the officer but you pose no threat to the officer or the public, the police can use force to restrain you. This force is limited to the force used to place you under control. It could be physical force, pepper spray, or an electronic device such as a stun gun.

If you are trying to harm either the officer or the public if escape occurs, then the officer can use force to stop your threat. If you have shown by your actions that you pose a threat to the public, actions can be taken to stop you. For example, if you have a pistol and have shot at police indiscriminately, a police officer may be justified in shooting you in the back to stop your actions.

This is a hard reality, but it reminds me of a story one of my field training officers told me. He gave me a scenario and asked what I would do. The scenario was as follows:

> You are dispatched to a robbery at a local convenience store. The clerk claims he was robbed by a White male wearing a red shirt and blue jeans. The suspect was armed with a rifle and fired a shot at the clerk but missed.

When you arrive on the call, you are walking up along the side of the store. When you go around the corner you see a White male about thirty feet from you wearing a red shirt and blue jeans. He is kneeling down behind a concrete barrier and pointing a rifle at a police car that just pulled into the parking lot.

The suspect has not seen you yet. However, you see that his finger is now on the trigger, and he about shoot and probably kill the officer who is driving into the parking lot.

When we break this down, we have an armed suspect who has already shown he is violent by robbing a store and shooting at the clerk. When you arrive, you see him pointing a rifle at a police car. A rifle has enough power to penetrate the windshield of the police car and kill the officer. Further, the suspect's finger is on the trigger about to kill the officer.

Unfortunately, you do not have time to give any warning, and the suspect is too far for you to stop him physically. The only real course of action is to shoot the suspect, probably in the back, to save the life of the officer. Generally, the public becomes very suspicious when a police officer shoots a suspect in the back; however, based on my scenario, was there another option? Reasonable people do not point rifles at police cars.

A quick side note: never bluff force. The problem with bluffing force is when your bluff is called. The most common bluff of force is usually used by a friend or family member of the cop. During an argument, a relative will say the magic phrase, "My son-in-law is a cop." The person uttering this phrase is doing so based on the assumption that the person hearing the phrase will yield or give up. The problem is when the person hearing the phrase doesn't care.

Another very common example is the unloaded pistol. If you have the legal authority to point a gun at someone, it should be loaded. If it is not, and your bluff is called, you now have nothing left. You have bluffed that you are willing to shoot, but now you are exposed to be holding a heavy useless piece of metal.

If you are going to represent yourself as an authority figure, be prepared for the person you are presenting it to not to care. You see this often in newer police officers who tend to transition from speaking to screaming to shooting. They have not prepared themselves for someone who just doesn't care that they are the police. So, when they give a lawful direction that is ignored, they scream, assuming the raised volume of the direction will persuade compliance. When it doesn't have the desired effect, and the new cop is not prepared for this, you see shootings occur.

Never bluff, and always be prepared for people to not care if you are the police. Bad guys tend not to care that you are the police. If you bluff and it works, that's great; however, if it doesn't work, you have backed yourself into a corner.

Firearms Training

Police academies should provide introductory to intermediate firearms training to students. This training should contain marksmanship skills, which should include qualification exercises. Police officers carry pistols, and pistols are very inaccurate firearms with very short barrels. If an officer is forced to shoot someone, the shot should count and take only the minimum number of shots to stop whatever the threat is. Thus, the targeting area should be the center of the target presented.

This is another hard issue for people. Even now, in 2022, people are still asking why police do not shoot someone in the arm or leg. First, pistols are very inaccurate. Aiming for a small object like an arm or leg, which moves very rapidly, will likely cause you to miss your shot and probably hit an undesired target. Because of this, police officers are trained to shoot the center mass of whatever target is presented, because it is incredibly likely that you may miss. If you aim for the center, the likelihood of missing reduces.

Further, we should really talk about arm and leg wounds. I have seen many fatal arm and leg wounds. Further, I have seen people survive being shot in the abdomen and head. A police officer's pistol is there to protect the officer and you. Its job is to physically incapacitate the person who is causing harm. There is no shooting to wound or to kill; there is only shooting to stop. This is something I was forced to unlearn from the corrections academy and learn in the police academy.

Other Topics

Physical fitness, policies, tactics, role-playing scenarios, emergency vehicle operations, and a lot of other topics of training are covered in the academy. There is in-depth instruction on dealing with people in mental crisis, as well as understanding your limitations as a police officer. You will be taught about your specific agency's policies and procedures. As I have explained, a great deal of training is dedicated to your survival. Understanding that your mind can make your body do just about anything and that you can survive any encounter is key. Your mind is so powerful that even if you are shot, if you are not dead you are still able to fight.

This is a common thread in police academies and various military trainings: realizing that when you are alone, shot, bleeding, tired, and psychologically drained, you can still reach very deep in your soul and push forward. This is what keeps us from burying officers daily: the will to survive. We were subject to many drills where we were set upon by multiple attackers, essentially no-win scenarios, to make sure we would not quit during a fight. You fight until you think you cannot fight anymore, then you find the power to fight more.

One such drill, which we called the "fight for life," was particularly brutal. Toward the end of the academy, you are escorted into a room. The room is pitch black and has several strobe lights flashing. It has music playing at such a loud volume that you would be unable to carry on a conversation. At that point, various members of the department begin to, well, beat the crap out of you. Your job is to fight them off, survive, and leave the room. If you quit, you will likely be terminated or, at a minimum, you will be exposed to the experience again to pass.

I fought off two attackers until one placed me in an ankle lock, and then I began kicking him in the head with my other foot. He then transitioned into a position where his legs were wrapped around my waist and he was punching me in the face. I was so mad, I just wanted him to die, and I knew he was a cop.

I decided something that I remember to this day. I realized that the face punches were not going to stop, so I accepted them and thought about how to incapacitate him. I gathered the strength to force myself to a squatting position. I stood up, but he refused to unwrap his legs from my waist and now wrapped his arms around my head. It was like I was carrying a very large toddler.

I then just fell face-first to the ground, landing on him. When I did, I heard the very satisfying sound of the air in his lungs escaping his body and his head bouncing off of the padded floor. When this happened, I stood up and walked out of the room.

To be fair to police academies across the country, I am not going to go into much more detail. The problem is that each agency is different and each state has different laws. However, what I have explained here gives a good general idea of what is taught.

De-escalation and simunition training is usually also part of academy training. *Simunitions* are bullets fired from a modified weapon that are made from a soft wax. However, they hurt and leave very large bruises wherever they hit you. They are a great training aid.

Generally, police agencies do a very good job at initially training officers, usually because initial police officer training is codified in state law. I have found the weakness in law enforcement training is in advanced, post-academy training.

8

Field Training

I went through field training as a student and spent about five years as a field training officer. I will try my best to combine both experiences in order to teach you what to expect and what can be changed. Police academies do a good job of teaching the black-and-white of policing. Field training is where the rubber meets the road.

Field training is where you are taught to apply the teachings of the police academy. Application is strange, as even after extensive training by a police academy, there can be an attrition rate of 10 percent. I think it is the same as understanding what you are taught in a technical school and then applying it. Anytime you have had trouble applying instructions or directions to a situation, you are in the application grey area of things that simply cannot be taught and must be experienced.

Field training officers (FTOs) are usually three-year police officers. Any newer, and you risk an ineffective trainer. Police officers tend to go through three stages that I have noticed. The first is the humility phase. This is usually the one-to-three-year officers. They are still learning how to apply their craft. It takes about three years to see everything and for the types of calls for service to start repeating themselves.

During this humility phase, you are very aware of your liability. You are unwilling to make unilateral decisions, and you take many steps to ensure your decision-making is sound. It's a necessary stage to get through. As you draw closer to the three-year mark, you rely less and less on your supervisor for guidance, and you start being independent.

The second phase is a mastery phase. This phase lasts from about three years to six years. During this phase, the officer is working at a journeyman level. He or she is developing routines and interests. During the mastery phase, officers will decide to remain, to either train, become a detective, or plan for promotion to sergeant. They are looking long-term. After five to six years, an officer has a well-established career and usually develops long-term career plans. These phases tend to change with the people, but for the most part, they are consistent.

Trainees who resign in field training, I've found, usually come to one of two realizations:

1. Police work is dangerous, and they do not wish to do it.
2. They do not want the responsibility of solving other people's problems.

These are usually masked with stories of sick family members or lack of familial support, but I found these are comprehensive.

Statistically, police work is not as dangerous as many construction-related jobs, so I found it troubling when people used danger as a reason to resign. I discovered that it wasn't the danger that bothered them, because I would often point out how construction was a dangerous profession. The issue wasn't the danger, it was the *type* of danger. Some people could not deal with the fact that they were being attacked or physically fought. Any police officers who make it through field training have likely had to defend themselves at least one time or have been involved in some kind of a critical incident. Almost all your activity will be non critical, but a small portion will be.

My first call for service was a 911 hang-up call at a pay phone. It was not exciting. I found that field training as a trainee for me went very fast. It seemed to be over very quickly. The application of knowledge is a problem for some people, but it wasn't for me. When I became an FTO, I was able to identify very quickly those who were not going to be successful. I found that confidence was a key factor in success, as was life experience. People who had significant life experience, especially those who had gone to war, seemed very successful.

Field training is a lot like theory and application. The academy is the theory, and the field training is the application. By the time a person is in field training, having passed the hiring process and graduated from a police academy, the agency has invested close to $500,000 in the person. However, there is still attrition. People just, at times, cannot apply what they are being taught. Trainees are unpredictable. I had trainees point guns at me and lie to me. Several quit.

Field training is a structured program, with measurable goals that you must meet. It is usually around six months long. The LVMPD uses the San Jose Model of field training, where trainees are evaluated daily. You will typically have a minimum of about seven FTOs throughout your training. Toward the end of field training, trainees are scrambling to get their goals done. Perhaps they never had the opportunity to take a burglary report, and they need that box checked, or maybe they need to make a DUI arrest. It was always great to hear a trainee get on the radio and take a call from another officer, to get it checked off their list. It showed heart and willingness to work as a team.

Over my career, I saw a lot of tragedy, heartbreak, and horrible circumstances. As new police officer, I experienced culture shock. Maybe there is something in my law enforcement career that can help someone else. I saw quite a bit and learned quite a bit.

The interesting thing about working in patrol is you have your finger on the pulse of the city. You see the results of poor political decision-making on those who are purported to be helped the most. I can think of no other job where you are exposed daily to the real world. No filter, no theory, no actors, just real everyday life.

Very early on, I saw the horrific costs of drug addiction, poverty, and homelessness. I quickly saw the political divide that is prevalent in real-world inner cities. Politics really do play a significant role in people's daily lives, I think more of a role than people think.

As I get to this portion of the book, I find myself wondering what a reader would want to read. Policing is a very pure profession; you speak to people when they are at their absolute worst. You see people when they are at the crossroads of their lives.

PART TWO
My Career

Part two of this book will attempt to expose you to police work through my eyes. Whether it was academic classes, cooperate security or generalized life experience, every life event impacted how I policed. I attempted to take over two decades of experience and condense them into the second half of this book. Because of the size of this task, I necessarily had to eliminate quite a bit. I was forced to stick to the most memorable events, and further, I had to keep detail to a minimum. I spent a great deal of time policing Las Vegas, based on this, there is no way I could possibly fit everything into one book.

I tried my best to remain neutral, accurate, and to be honest, entertaining. Policing is a peculiar occupation. It fills movie plots, television shows, nonfiction books and novels. At the same time, it is incredibly divisive, as people attempt to provide explanations based on their personal experience, opinions, and 20/20 hindsight. In the second half of this book, I offer you a firsthand account of the reality of police work in the United States. Policing is an incredibly noble profession; officers place their lives in jeopardy to protect all of us. At times, cops do go bad. Sometimes the cop goes down a bad road, sometimes their supervisors contribute to this decline. Regardless of the cause, the human element of policing will always ensure mistakes are made.

Cops are humans, and due to their humanity, mistakes occur. Police misconduct has many contributors. The police, legislators, and the citizens of the community have some culpability. I offer you an unfiltered, pragmatic reflection of my experience policing a major urban, metropolitan city. I hope you enjoy our journey.

9

Officer in Training

So I suppose we will start at the beginning. I graduated from the police academy and entered field training in 2001. I was at the end of my police academy time on September 11, 2001. I was standing in the parking lot of the firearms range when I heard about the terrorist attacks. Throughout the morning, we were being updated through dedicated police networks.

Midmorning on the west coast, midday in New York, I was seated in a set of bleachers with my academy class. About every hour, we were taken off the range and given updates on what was happening. At one point, we were told that we were going to graduate from the academy that day, and we were going to be placed on sensitive infrastructure security.

I had done security before, and I was going to graduate from the academy early. However, the country had changed. We were all entering a new world. No one knew what was going to happen. Anyone who was an adult on September 11, 2001, and who says nothing changed was not paying attention before. It was a strange time, and it was a scary time.

The day crept by, minute by minute. By the end of the day, calmer heads had prevailed. We were not going to graduate from the academy early. We were going to graduate on time, but we were going to be the police academy that graduated after September 11, 2001, in Las Vegas. Policing changed that day, another change of many.

First FTO

My first FTO, Officer Brian Harries, was a veteran cop of the 1990s. He had very strong opinions on Rodney King and the changing climate of policing in the 1990s. Officer Harries was a twice-divorced, chain-smoking, gravel-in-his-voice, get-your-hands-dirty cop. I can honestly say I never saw him do anything wrong. I can also say that policing was very different in 2001.

He explained things to me in a very pragmatic way, and by explain, I mean *yell*. He explained how to sit at lunch so you could win a gunfight if you were ambushed. He told me not to talk about work with my wife; she wouldn't understand.

If you are a new cop or looking at a career in law enforcement, do not hide details from your spouse. I promise you will end up a mess. Cops often use the adage that their spouse would not understand, or they would be scared. I have found this to be nonsense. Your spouse's imagination is far worse than what you may tell them.

I spent my entire time as a line-level police officer policing very violent neighborhoods. My first assignment was my introduction to inner-city violence. I spent my first phase of field training in a violent neighborhood just east of the Las Vegas Strip. The area I was responsible for had seen a legitimate police officer, off-duty, murder a citizen in the 1990s. Not a use of force, or a horrific police fight, but the murder of a citizen by a police officer. In 1996, a police officer murdered a private citizen in Las Vegas. Two officers who were off-duty and patrolled the area returned to the area and preformed a drive-by shooting, killing a local citizen. Well, here I was five years later, right after September 11, 2001, working patrol in the same neighborhood.

Brian spent very little time explaining the incident, and I was glad, I just wanted to learn policing. He witnessed my first bad search, when I missed a crack pipe. He was there when I attempted to make several bad arrests out of naivete.

Brian was rough, mean, loud, and abrasive. He was a great cop and a better trainer. He was incredibly impatient and had no compassion for me at all. He yelled, screamed, and only accepted a mistake once. After that, I was obviously not responding to training. I never once had a problem with him; he taught me a ton. I have come to learn that not everyone learns from this type of trainer, but I have never cared about being yelled at. I would rather be yelled at than die.

I stopped a car for running a stop sign, and Brian seemed happy. I greeted the driver, and he was enormous. He had somehow forced himself into a small Volkswagen. Then he ran a stop sign and was thrust into my life.

I greeted him, told him why I'd stopped him, and returned to my car with his driver's license. I ran him, and the gentleman who I knew at that time was six foot six and weighed about 290 pounds had significant violent prior felonies that he had been to prison for. He had a valid arrest warrant, so he was a wanted fugitive. His crime was significant: battery with substantial bodily harm. He had beaten a person almost to death. He was running from justice, and I had just met him.

The correct thing to do was to call for backup, then safely remove him from that car from a distance, using high-risk criteria: point a gun at him, order him from the car, place him on the ground, and put him in handcuffs. I knew all of this. I knew how to handle a dangerous person, and they did not get much more dangerous than this guy.

Preparation prevents use of force. If you know someone to be dangerous and properly prepare for every dangerous eventuality, you will likely live. It is important that you do a thorough investigation and prepare based on what you know.

Brian had seen the warrant and the gentleman's size. He also knew what I was supposed to do. But in fact, I did not do anything right. I walked back up to the car and asked the nice gentleman to exit. He did. I looked up at him, while standing about two feet from him. I told him he was wanted, I was the police, and he was going to jail. He could have killed me, but he did not. He did what I said. He let me arrest him and take him to jail.

I placed him in two pairs of handcuffs, because one pair was just too small for this man. I then, with great effort, placed him into my police car, very proud of my first felony arrest. I closed the back door and glanced over at Brian, who was holstering his firearm.

I briefly wondered why his pistol was in his hand. Then, like a ton of bricks, I realized what I had just done. He then taught me a lesson.

He began screaming at me and asking me if I was Superman, if I was invincible, if I wanted to die. He told me how stupid I was, and how I should just quit that day. I deserved every word. I never treated another violent person like a speeding tourist again. I learned my lesson.

A lot of people cannot deal with being yelled at, like I said. They say things like, "I am not a child. Don't yell at me." I never understood this. If you are my boss, and you need to yell at me, go ahead. I can take it. Especially when I just placed my life in danger and placed you in a position where you could have had to kill a man to save me. Yell away, I say, yell all you want, and then yell more. I promise you I will learn my lesson, and I did.

The rest of my time with Brian was relatively mundane. I learned a lot. In the three weeks I was assigned to him, we managed all kinds of events. After my first week, I learned that Brian moved at one speed, one hundred miles per hour for everything. I would go home and study laws and policy for hours to make sure I could keep up with him. I never wanted not to have an answer to a question or have to ask him for help. We responded to a lot of calls, a few homicides, and various other boring disputes, including a comical one over a bicycle between a vagrant and the twelve-year-old who the bike belonged to.

Second FTO

After my time with Brian, I moved on to my second FTO, Larry Kilver. Larry was the exact opposite of Brian. He was quiet, reserved, chose his words very surgically, and never yelled. Larry moved slowly, but very deliberately. He approached policing like a chess game, always looking a few moves ahead. He was very reserved, spoke little, and was very patient.

It was weird to go from Brian to Larry. At the end of my first week with Larry, I received an unintended integrity check. It came out of nowhere and could have cost me my career. I was convinced up to a point that I was being set up.

During field training, we took several written tests to check our ongoing learning. The tests covered policy, law, and procedures. The day of one of these tests, I arrived at work early. The squad I was assigned to had two members of my academy class with me as trainees. Trainees are always early, because, well, you are a trainee. It was up to you to have your car ready, all equipment checked, and be prepared to drive out of the station at 3 p.m. precisely.

I walked into the locker room about two hours before my shift was to begin, and like a scripted prerehearsed scenario, my fellow trainees both told me that they had obtained a copy of the test we were to take that day. They were cheating. It wasn't hard to do; the tests at the time had not changed in years and were simply recycled. However, easy does not mean it was all right to cheat.

I could cheat too, they said. It would be easy. I glanced down at the form they handed me, and it was titled, "Phase 1 test." It seemed legit; I handed it right back and walked out.

I declined to cheat and left the locker room. I got ready for work. Preshift, I was greeted by Larry. He asked me if everything was OK, and I said I was fine and expected him to leave it there. I had planned on telling him about the test after we left the station.

However, Larry saw straight through my cover and pulled me outside. He demanded I tell him what was wrong and tell him that second. This was very out of character for such a calm guy. The only way out was to tell him the truth.

It was time to enter my line. "Sir, I was offered the opportunity to cheat on the test today. I declined."

Now, based on the size of the agency, and the fact that these tests were recycled so much, I expected him to just make some comment, and we would move on. I thought I was being tested. I knew then that some police agencies have Integrity Enforcement Units (IEU) that often set cops up to see how they would respond.

I knew an officer employed by the Los Angeles Police Department who was approached by an undercover IEU officer who wanted to report a stolen bicycle. The officer was working overtime and working the perimeter of a parade, and the IEU was expecting him to blow off the report and refer the "victim" to the police station, apparently violating LAPD policy at the time. However, the officer told the undercover officer that he would take his report, but he needed to ensure the victim was not armed. When he asked if he could pat down the undercover officer, the undercover officer ran. The officer working overtime later found out that he ran because he was wearing a recording device and was concerned about being discovered.

Knowing all of this, I assumed this was a test. Larry would say, "Good job, kid," and we would go to work. However, that is not what happened. His face turned white as a ghost, and he called our sergeant. It was at that time I realized this was not a set-up; it was real. I was a probationary officer, in my fourth week on the street, and I was caught up in a cheating scandal.

I was introduced to my first Internal Affairs investigation. For those of you who haven't realized it yet, my academy mates were cheating on the test. I had just reported their cheating. This was real, not the integrity check I had thought it was. They both received discipline, and I did not. It was surreal, and very strange. I was questioned and was thanked for my integrity. The other two officers went on to receive further discipline later in their career. One was terminated, and one resigned in lieu of. I retired many years after they left.

My remaining time with Larry was very quiet and uneventful. Larry was big on proactive stops. We made a lot of traffic stops. His leadership style was very subdued. I found I preferred being yelled at to having a quiet supervisor. When your boss is quiet, you don't know if you have done something wrong, I found myself asking if everything was OK about once an hour.

Larry and I became friends later in our careers. I tried to recruit him several times for various positions as I was promoted. He spent twenty-seven years in patrol; he never left patrol or was ever promoted past police officer. He was part of a lost generation of policing. You would be hard-pressed to find a career patrol officer currently, especially with the anti-police sentiment dispatched by politicians and members of the very vocal minority of 2020 and 2021.

Would you remain in patrol if you did not have to? Would you allow yourself to be placed in positions of immense liability that could cause you to lose your job or your freedom? This is unfortunate, because just like any other job, a person gets better with time. Therefore, the best street cops I ever knew were career patrol officers who have since retired. They knew everyone's name, they knew fathers and cousins and family members of victims and suspects. They were aware of crime patterns and suspect behavior. They were the officers movies are based on the cop who overhears the frustration of a detective who cannot find a suspect of a crime and interjects into the case a breaking fact or name.

The terrible thing is, these cops were the ones who even the bad guys trusted. They got information no one else could. Now that officers are being vilified for their actions, being branded racist and murderers, no one would remain in patrol longer than absolutely necessary. There is simply too much liability.

Third FTO

After Larry, I was assigned to Derick Serome. Derrick was a mountain of a man at six feet seven inches. He had a special police car with no prisoner cage because he could not fit in a car with a prisoner cage. He was more of a moderate; he was not quiet, nor did he yell. Man, he liked to walk. We would do foot patrol for hours, in the most violent apartment complexes, until crime fell into us.

He taught me how to be stealthy. Everything from light reflections to jingling keys was addressed. He taught me to walk with a large flashlight in my left hand. This was an old cop trick that will likely disappear with technology, as big heavy lights are not really needed with LED bulbs. The big and heavy lights we would carry were about eighteen inches long and were heavy. With the advent of technology, a light the size of a pen now could outshine these relics. You walk with the long heavy light in your weak hand. If you are attacked, you already have a heavy thing in your hand to defend yourself.

When we walked, we walked in complete silence. We developed hand signals to communicate. We would very often just walk up on a crime. It was very common for us to walk up to people in the middle of drug deals or drug use. It was odd, because criminals at night seemed to be attracted to lights, streetlights, porch lights, all manner of lights. They really had every reason to stay in the dark shadows. However, when they wanted to hide, they never hid in the shadows; they would seek out dumpster enclosures or covered parking stalls. Both choices limited their exit points, so it was easy to trap people.

If you are a criminal, attempt to hide in plain sight. If you can use the shadows to hide your location, you will go undetected, because we did. We walked in the shadows. It was a great skill to learn.

Because we spent so much time walking in the dark, our eyes were already adjusted. It was strange how close we could get to someone before they saw us, and then I would see how close I could get before they realized who I was. No one ever ran; well, some tried, but by the time their eyes realized who we were, we were so close to them that running was just silly. By the time they took one step, we would have tripped them to the ground.

I have never used night-vision goggles, but I would imagine that they have a similar effect. When you are comfortable with the dark, you can see all you need. The ambient light of a city, combined with moonlight, gives you plenty of light.

I will share a dark urban policing trick … well, it's more of a myth. Cities have a large amount of ambient light. This light allows people in the dark to see things they normally would not. Turning off a police car's lights before approaching a group of people just generates a foot pursuit. I learned this early. However, you would be surprised how many experienced cops would shut off their lights to be unseen, only to make themselves stand out like a beacon.

As soon as your lights turn off, your black-and-white police car can be identified. Ambient city light shows your police car like it is highlighted. It is far more stealth to pull up with your lights on. Because your lights are facing the suspect, they cannot even see the make or model of the car you are in until you are quite literally two feet from them. You see them shield their eyes from the lights and try to identify what kind of car you are in, only to realize it once you have already gotten out of the car.

I would watch police cars turn off their lights, be identified, and generate foot pursuits often. Just go outside at night and have someone drive toward you with their headlights on. Then do it again, and have the lights turned off about fifty feet from you. You will see that when the lights are turned off, there is no doubt what make, model, and color the car is. It is just ignorance of light sources. Work in the dark enough, and you will learn these things. Lessons from Derrick.

Derrick loved to fight; it was like a hobby to him. When you are in a police car, and you are driving to a call, it is a strange thing when you realize you cannot get there fast enough. Imagine you are in a police car, you know a person is being hurt, and it is about a mile from you. You are the only person who can help. You have lights and sirens to attempt to clear traffic, but the frustration hits very hard when you just cannot get there fast enough. It really hurts when you get there and a life is lost.

Derrick would sit in the passenger seat, and when we were going to a fight call, especially a bar fight, he would scream "Faster!" while punching the passenger-side airbag cover on the dashboard. Not that I was going too slowly, but he wanted to get to the fight before it was over.

Field Training, Phase II

After Derrick, I transferred into Phase II of field training. Whether intentional or not, the timing of graduating from one phase to the second and final phase had an impact on me. I had to move to another station. I also realized that my training was progressing at a rate slightly faster than most. I came to the realization that I was going to graduate field training and be a cop soon. With this revelation came many others. They were profound for me, and I will try to explain them to you.

First, I realized that I was willing to die for someone else. I certainly did not want to die; however, I realized that if I had to die to protect someone, I was willing to do that. Another realization was that I had seen the absolute depravity of mankind. I had seen the terrible things people will do to each other. People are not inherently good. Human beings are terrible people who inflict suffering upon each other for enjoyment. Anyone who sincerely believes that humans are inherently good has no idea what a human being is capable of. We are a depraved race.

People do terrible things to each other, and not just physical things. People are vindictive and narcissistic. Power is abused, and the weak are taken advantage of. With this understanding, I realized that if I had to kill to save a life, I could. I did not want to kill, nor was I looking forward to it. However, I understood that there are some people who will continue to victimize others until they are stopped. The most committed of these people will continue hurting people until they are physically unable to.

Realize that all people are not you, and just because you would not do something does not mean that everyone won't do it. You cannot expect all people to act like you and respond like you. There are people who will murder, maim, or seriously victimize the weak, and they will not stop unless they are physically unable to continue. This is the strange dichotomy of policing: to save a life, you may have to take a life.

Another realization I came to was that I was capable of extreme violence. I had never been violent in my life; however, on several occasions, I had shown that I was capable of matching and overcoming the level of violence that I was presented with. The further stranger issue was that I was able to control this trait. I found that I operated best when I was under extreme stress. I seemed to be able to function well, far better than most, while under tremendous pressure and stress. It was a strange realization that I could physically devastate someone and be in complete control of myself.

Perhaps this was due to training, or some previously dormant portion of my mind. As I will explain, I spent far more time in patrol than most cops do. Until injury put me into an office, I found that I thrived outside.

The unpredictable nature of patrol makes you develop this skill. You must function appropriately even when you are placed in the most life-threatening situations. When these events occurred, I never panicked, I never froze, and the strange thing was that I had clarity. These events became very easy for me. As I will explain, I saw cops panic, freeze, and lose control. For some reason, this was never an issue for me.

Back to field training. I transferred to the historic west side of Las Vegas. This area was just as violent as the previous one. It was historic in that it was the neighborhood where the African American Hoover Dam workers were allowed to live during dam construction. Since the 1950s, gang violence had overtaken the area. It had become a very poor and violent part of Las Vegas.

First FTO, Phase II

My first field training officer for this second phase was Darren Linx. Darren was by far the smartest cop I had ever met. By the time he was an FTO, he had obtained a master's degree and was quite literally attending law school at night while training me. He would study while I investigated. He gave me a long leash.

We did a tremendous amount of follow-up. We submitted arrest warrants and served search warrants. Darren taught me to investigate, really investigate, not just a patrol basic investigation. Every call for service needed to be solved. By that, I mean I had to identify the cause of the original issue and resolve it.

We sometimes took days solving issues that a traditional patrol officer would have solved, at least symptomatically, in minutes. We would arrive on a call and ensure there was never another call for the same issue at that location again. This style of policing is not bad, it's just very time-consuming. We would always ensure our squad mates were not in need of us, and then we would begin our follow-up on whatever we were working on. I submitted my first arrest warrant during my time with Darren.

Second FTO, Phase II

When I left Darren, I transferred to Aaron Welsh. Aaron had been cop in New York. He was able to figure things out so quickly, he was hard to keep up with. He would figure out someone's motivations or someone's ideology in minutes. He established very quickly that I was close to graduating field training and needed very little further training. He would push me and expected far more of me than a trainee at my phase.

I do have two stories from my time with Aaron. The first was a call for service we received from the Clark County School District police. They had received reports that when a particular school bus would let out that afternoon, two feuding gang members would fight. These fights in this neighborhood turned into shootings regularly.

The entire squad arrived and waited for the school buses to offload their violent passengers. The bus stop was located at a four-way stop sign. We had very specific descriptions of the combatants, with names and clothing.

We were all standing outside of our cars when the bus pulled up. The two combatants exited, saw us, and started to fight. It is a fallacy that seeing a cop will prevent crime all the time. Sometimes, the fighters knew the fight would be broken up, so they started it quickly.

I ran up and pulled one of them off the other. I spun him around and lost control of him for a second. I then readjusted my grip and slammed him down into the hood of a police car ... with a red hood. Police cars don't have red hoods. However, some lady stopped at the stop sign that day did have a red hood.

Realizing my error, I looked up at my trainer, who was standing next to our sergeant laughing at me. To be fair, it was funny. I had fought a kid, thrown him onto the hood of a car, and was now a comedic item. I arrested the kid for something and never saw the lady who stopped at the worst stop sign in Las Vegas that day again. Once I lifted him off the hood, she simply drove off. I promise you, with how hard I threw the kid, I had to have dented her car hood, but she was not interested in sticking around apparently.

My second Aaron story was slightly more embarrassing. I had stopped a car for not having operational brake lights. I was writing the ticket and was very proud of myself. I had discovered several other equipment violations during the stop. The gentleman had no brake lights, no license plate light, and no working seat belts.

I was not used to traffic enforcement, so I had to look up various statutes and codes. I wrote this gentleman about five citations, and it took me about thirty minutes. During those thirty minutes, I had neglected to control the driver of the car. During those thirty minutes, he pulled out a toolbox from his trunk and began repairing his vehicle.

By the time I looked up, his trunk was open, there were tools scattered around the travel lane, and his upper torso was under the rear of his car. My ever-vigilant trainer was laughing so much that to this day, I have no idea how I did not hear him laughing. I voided the tickets in the name of training and let him go. The vehicle was repaired by this point.

Aaron and I still see each other now and again. He tends to tell people how I should be dead, stabbed to death by a screwdriver-wielding mechanic.

Graduation

My final trainer was a gentleman named Eric Warner. Eric was very down-to-earth and spent his days sitting in his car while I managed his calls for him. It was my job, after all.

I graduated field training on time, with no issues. I was trained well. On my last day of field training, I was at an apartment with my trainer. We were in separate cars, and he was watching me from a distance. It is a rite of passage known as *solo beat*. Everyone remembers it, because it is the first time you are alone in the car.

That morning, we were dispatched to a domestic disturbance. When we arrived, the wife answered the door, her face swollen, and told us her batterer was upstairs. This complex was strange and had three-floor apartments. While we were walking up the stairs, the male jumped from the third-floor window and ran. I took the report for domestic battery, humiliated at what had occurred. A suspect had gotten away.

Later that day, I was dispatched to the hospital to follow up. Don't get ahead of me here. He, the guy who jumped, was in the emergency room, the victim of a stabbing. She had waited for us to leave, found him at his mother's house, and stabbed him with a kitchen knife. I arrested both of them that day, my last day of training.

10

Junior Officer

It is common just after field training to be placed in a limbo status. You are finished with training, but your permanent position is either unknown or not ready yet. When this happens, you essentially remain on your training squad for a few weeks.

For us, being new, it was great. We were the most junior officers in the agency, and we were holding a day-shift spot with weekends off. Temporarily holding it, anyway.

During this time, you are not a trainee, but you're not really a cop yet either. You are a floating semi-cop. You spend your time relieving senior cops so they can go to lunch and doing the jobs nobody wants to do. I did not mind. There is a hierarchy, and I was at the bottom. It is what it is.

Vehicle Pursuit

In one event, I was taking a stolen-vehicle report. It was me and a senior officer who later went to SWAT. I was taking the report, and my partner on the call was covering me. There is a concept known as *contact cover*. When you see two cops, and one is off to the side doing nothing, he is the cover officer. The one talking is making contact. It is a simple tactic that helps you get the job done without people sneaking up on you, or crime suspects returning to the scene to attack you or the victim.

On the radio, we began to hear the beginnings of a vehicle pursuit. Cops on my channel were chasing a stolen car. We used to chase stolen cars. My partner said, "You got this?"

I said, "Go."

He left me to my report. I continued the report and started listening to the radio. The stolen car had crashed, and the suspect had just carjacked a person at a red light. I told the stolen-car victim I was writing a report for that I would be back, and I left him.

As I drove toward the pursuit, the suspect had crashed a second car and was attempting another carjacking in a parking lot. An officer assigned to search and rescue had attempted to physically stop the suspect, who produced a pistol. The officer shot at the suspect and missed, and the suspect successfully carjacked his third stolen car of the day. Cops were chasing him, and he was headed toward a very heavily residential area.

He predictably crashed his third stolen car and began running toward a group of cars that were stopped for a red light. As he was running, a homicide detective, who had been trailing the pursuit, had a clear shot. She accelerated her vehicle and ran him over. His crime spree stopped.

He actually thanked the detective as he was being placed into an ambulance. Suspects like this must be physically stopped. They will continue to victimize until they are stopped. Several times in my career, I encountered people like this.

We stopped chasing stolen cars around 2007. This was the result of a suspect who ran a red light while being chased and killed several people. We went through various tactics to see what would work; we had to still get the bad guys.

We went through a policy of helicopter surveillance. The helicopter would locate the stolen car, increase altitude so it could not be seen or heard, and broadcast the suspect car's location. The theory was that if the suspect was unaware he was being chased, he would not drive so recklessly. We quickly learned that even though the suspect thought he was not being chased until he was home, he continued driving recklessly and carjacking people when his vehicle became disabled.

Anyway, the officer from search and rescue who attempted to shoot the suspect was getting promoted to sergeant. He became my sergeant a short time later. He and I never talked about the pursuit, not realizing each of us had been involved in the event.

After I had worked with him for a few months, he told me the story of how he shot at the suspect of a carjacking and missed, his bullet striking a car door. I asked him where this was, and that's how we discovered we had been on the same call a few months before. He explained that the suspect was running, and when he shot, he missed the moving target and shot the door of a parked car.

The next time we were at the range, I covertly took a large marker and drew a vehicle door on his target. When the targets were presented to shoot, he saw a large car door he was to shoot at. No one talked, and he never knew who did it ... well, until now.

Downtown

After field training, I was assigned to downtown Las Vegas, I worked for a newly promoted sergeant named Kevin Mcmahill (his real name). He went on to be a public figure, promoting quickly and leading our agency for some time.

New sergeants will traditionally be promoted to undesirable squads with bad days off. This is because when you promote, you start your seniority over again at the bottom of that promotional level. So new sergeants with no seniority at their rank supervise new police officers with no seniority at their rank. This generally creates a strong bond, as sergeants learn how to lead with new cops who are learning how to police.

New cops just out of field training are ripe for abuse. They are selected for the bad jobs no one wants. They are forced to work overtime. They are junior, and they pay their dues. I never had an issue with this and was prepared for anything.

Kevin saw us as family and did not like us being abused. He was very protective of us new cops. Don't get me wrong, I paid my dues. I worked bad shifts, with bad days off. I worked mandatory overtime and put in my time as a new guy. However, Kevin did a good job of filtering the garbage, so we were relatively left alone.

Undercover

When narcotics came asking for new undercover faces, Kevin asked me if I wanted to do it. I jumped at the opportunity. I spent about one day each week, usually our designated training day, working with the narcotics section. As I have said several times, and will say many more, you must forget everything you think you know about policing; if you have never been a cop, you have no idea what police work is. Undercover work is intense, as even regular cops have no idea how it works. Unless you have worked undercover, you have no idea what it is like.

Forget what you have seen on television, the lone undercover operative wearing a "wire" and operating by his own set of rules. That was a process that ended in the 1980s, mostly the result of a lot of misconduct and dead cops. There are some details that I am just not going to share. However, I will talk about some generalities of undercover work.

Undercover work is done as a team. Usually, only one or two members of the team will be the operational undercover person. They are rarely ever known to be police officers to the defendants, even after prosecution. Undercover officers have an entire second identity. Another driver's license, passport, vehicle, false job, everything you would need. It's quite involved. Portions of the team will be assigned to surveillance, undercover protection, and case management. The case manager ultimately does the arrest and all the reports.

Officers selected to work undercover must be very average. They should not be significantly taller or shorter than average. They should speak very average and not have a distinctive accent. Visible tattoos that are distinctive are usually a deal breaker; they must be liked but forgotten about. Vehicles must be plain in all ways. No distinctive stickers, customizations, or anything that would make it memorable.

I must admit, I was not cut out for the work. I tried it and had fun, but I found I just wasn't a good fit for long-term undercover work. There are many kinds of undercover work, too many to write about in this short section. Generally, you have the following:

- daily undercover work, people who buy drugs and pick up prostitutes
- long-term undercover work, people who work cases like drug interdiction and human trafficking
- hyperspecialized undercover work, people who are sent after bad cops, politicians, high-level organized crime cases and such

The latter type is the most dangerous. It requires a huge commitment from the officer, as it takes over a large portion of your life. Remember that cops, undercover or not, are just like you, with wives, kids, baseball games, and front yards to cut. If you're out to dinner with your wife and that corrupt mayor calls you for drugs, you must leave, no excuses.

Undercover work is not healthy. Officers who enter highly specialized undercover work really should rotate out to a regular assignment around the two-year mark. The problem is that no one can maintain a dual life for an extended period. Police departments across the country fail to recognize these issues frequently. The result is high levels of alcohol and drug abuse by officers who have never been around these substances.

I knew an officer (one of many) who spent a huge amount of time in a highly undercover role. He had never taken a drink of alcohol in his life. However, by the end of his career, he had received three DUI arrests. The issue is, when you live two lives for so long, you begin to confuse the lives. Imagine being a good father and husband during the day, and then at night you are forced to put on the persona of a criminal drug dealer, pimp, or fence. The problem is the day and night jobs begin to merge.

That same person who is a good father and husband plays a role at night. You are given almost unlimited money, and there is little accountability for the money, as people you are buying drugs or stolen cars from do not provide receipts. You are frequenting bars and clubs that are infested with crime. If you drive too fast and are pulled over, you will be let go quickly to not jeopardize your cover. If you commit a crime in the performance of your role, you will likely receive immunity from prosecution. You are assigned a false identity and have access to a fleet of cars to use as you need.

Not all undercover cops go bad, but some do. It rarely hits the news, because there is rarely any video, as they are not in uniform. You are a rock star at night and a father during the day, but these roles start to combine quickly. Agencies should monitor their high-profile undercover officers.

Back to my first year. So, narcotics is looking for new cops to help. I was asked, and I went. I learned how to buy drugs, surveil dealers and users, follow the money, and serve search warrants. It is difficult, because you must change everything you have been trained to do. You cannot talk like a cop or even carry yourself like a cop.

Cops do carry themselves far differently than the rest of the population. I promise you, if you put me in an environment, I can usually pick out the career cops in the group. Cops stand and walk in a very unusual way. If you have met someone who seemed very overconfident and totally disinterested in you because they were looking through you, it was probably a cop. Cops have a demeanor and hold themselves in a very peculiar way. It is a mix of hypervigilance and misdirection.

Cops are trained to see through what you are telling them and are usually five sentences ahead of the conversation. If you are lying, they know it, and if you are exaggerating, they know it. We were taught early how eye movement can indicate deception, and the conversational patterns of people who are being dishonest. Further, cops walk very erect in order to see above the crowd. They will usually walk with their arms just a tad farther from their waist than you would. It is because they are so accustomed to wearing a duty belt. Cops do everything they can to turn off their cop persona off duty, but it is almost impossible.

I will never forget the first time I bought crack cocaine. I was put into the passenger seat of a pickup, then driven to Fremont Avenue and Las Vegas Boulevard. The driver of the pickup I was in was the experienced narcotics detective who was training me. He pulled up to a lady who was simply waiting for a bus, rolled down my window, and told me to "ask for a slice."

By this time, I had been embarrassed enough, and I learned to do exactly what I was told. Field training has a way of humbling you. I realized I knew nothing about this policing thing, and I was to learn from the experts. So I leaned out the window and said, "Let me get a slice."

This lady, who was just waiting for the bus to take her to work, presumably, walked up to me, spit a piece of rock cocaine into my hand, took my twenty-dollar bill, and returned to her seat at the bus stop.

Have you ever had anyone spit a piece of crack into your palm? If you're reading this, probably not. It took every ounce of will power for me not to say, "What the fuck?" My driver, I think realizing this, quickly pulled away. The arrest team moved in and arrested her.

We did not arrest everyone that night. We did exchange a lot of freedom for information. I bought a large amount of crack my first night, and my head was spinning. It is hard psychologically shifting from uniformed officer to undercover and then back again. I'd only had a similar experience one other time in my life. I had played Santa Clause at school. I went in and spoke to a kindergarten class. I left, changed into my regular clothes, and spoke with the teacher on the way out. The way the children responded to Santa Claus versus the way they responded to the strange man talking to the teacher was very dissimilar.

Search Warrant

My training detective on that first night kept referring to a search warrant he had to serve before we went home. He must have brought it up about a dozen times. He did this in the same way you or I would say, "I have to get milk on the way home": mildly annoyed, with a hint of urgency. After my first night of buying drugs, he remembered the warrant. He literally said, "Shit, let's go serve this warrant." I didn't care. I was having fun and experiencing an entirely new version of policing.

We drove to a nondescript alley behind an apartment complex. We met up with the narcotics team I was with that shift. I recognized them all from our initial briefing and from throughout the shift. I was expecting to cover the back door, or maybe sit in the car, or some other junior-guy assignment.

The team had obviously done this thousands of times, and this was twenty-one years ago. These factors both led to the issue of this seeming very impromptu and thrown together at the last minute. They put on yellow shirts that said *POLICE*. My trainer threw me one, and I put it on. The actual undercover officers wore face coverings.

I must make one thing clear: search warrants are not served this way today. It was incredibly dangerous. However, policing evolves and grows as time passes. Today, this warrant would never have been served in the manner it was. Further, it would likely have been served by Special Weapons and Tactics (SWAT).

I continued to expect to be assigned some garbage job and would be thankful for it. My training detective was second in the line, and I was third. I got no further training; the train then left the station. My trainer's partner was first in line, and he produced a ramming tool to smash in the front door. The front door was smashed in, the officer smashing it moved out of the way, and my trainer entered the home followed by me.

We then entered a small apartment, with a small living room/kitchen, a single bathroom, and two bedrooms. I remembered some brief search-warrant service training in the police academy, so I started yelling, "*Police*, search warrant!"

We cleared each room. At the end of the initial clearing of the apartment, which took about ninety seconds, we had three people in handcuffs on the living room floor. Then the search began.

When I say *search*, I am implying that we searched the apartment, which we did. However, remember, this was a long time ago. We destroyed that apartment. I helped break open dressers, cut open the back of couches, removed light switch covers, pulled down wall coverings, and just committed generalized destruction. We destroyed that apartment.

I began to feel a little guilty. However, the warrant yielded a large amount of methamphetamine, as well as ingredients to make more; a lot of cash, presumably made through drug sales; lists of clients and monies owed; and a very small amount of nine-millimeter ammunition.

Toward the end of the search, I think my trainer saw my guilt. He said, "It's pretty destructive. Do you want to read the warrant?"

I said I did, and my guilt flew away as I read. The three individuals who were now headed to jail had been selling large amounts of the drug to one of the undercover officers. The three were members of a criminal gang, and because of the sheer amount the police had been buying from them, these three had stopped selling the drug at a local high school because the undercover officer was able to purchase larger amounts of product faster than high school students.

The initial meeting was the result of a fifteen-year-old girl who these three were selling the drug to in exchange for sex. The child had reported her addiction to her parents, and the address was passed on to the narcotics section. I remember thinking we should burn the apartment to the ground, but we didn't.

11

On-the-Job Observations

As I was getting off probation, I had been out of the police academy for eighteen months. Usually, police officers are on probation for two years after they are hired. During my first eighteen months in law enforcement, I had done quite a bit. I had worked patrol, undercover, and generalized policing. I learned a lot about my trade and a lot about life in general. There are a lot of psychological phenomena that you can only experience via policing.

Right around the eighteen-month mark, I found that I was acclimating to police culture. I was growing increasingly intolerant of the criminal defense attorney and criminals. The defense attorney's job was to undo what I did. Their job was to reverse the progress I was making.

During what I call the *humility phase*, one to three years, police officers tend to think they are going to save the world. As they master one task they move on to the next, all to make a difference. I saw some very specific personality types begin to develop. I don't know what came first, the personality or the job, but I noticed a lot of similarities. I was able to categorize cops based on their personalities. Before you enter what I call the *mastery* or *journey* phase, three to six years, you are still dependent on help. Help comes in the form of supervision, training, literature, and senior officers.

When it comes to personality development, there is a large representation of obsessive-compulsive disorder (OCD). I noticed that the personalities were not permanent; they tended to shift, and some people had them more severely than others. This OCD seemed to come in two categories. The first was equipment obsessions. People would spend thousands of dollars on new ballistic vests, firearms, and hundreds on flashlights. The second was routines, people who had to follow the same routine each day preshift.

It's very strange to see this, but I knew cops who would be legitimately mad if their routine was disrupted. I knew one cop who would leave the station daily and drive straight to the car wash. He would have his car washed, and then he would go to the same gas station and get his preshift snack. After these rituals, he would begin taking calls. Precisely one hour before his shift ended, he would go back to that convenience store and fill his car with gas, and read magazines. It was odd, but so is policing.

De-Policing

When you spend forty hours a week driving around a city, things tend to happen in front of you. Patrolling is really split into two areas: what you see and what you are called to. What you are called to is always what takes up most of your time, and it is unfortunate, because you will not create any crime reduction by only going where you are called. When people call you, they know you're coming. When people know you're coming, they have the advantage. They tend to hide their drugs and guns, or they prepare to ambush you.

The real way to reduce crime in a given urban area is self-initiated field activity (SIFA), the *what you see* part of patrol. Take the fight to the criminals, stop them when they have their guns and drugs, surprise them, and make them guess your intentions. Some cops saw themselves as call-for-service cops, and some saw themselves as hunters, looking for work.

De-policing is a real phenomenon that I have personally witnessed. It occurs when police are afraid or refuse to act on what they see. I was involved in an initiative to test the broken windows theory. It involved identifying the traditionally high-crime areas and not allowing any crime in those areas go unaddressed. This includes jaywalking and parking violations.

I offer you only a synopsis of the theory. A gentleman named Theodore Moody was running this initiative. He later ran for sheriff in

Clark County. I don't have the specific data, but I can tell you anecdotally that we saw a significant violent crime reduction in downtown Las Vegas. The areas that did not receive this intensive policing saw no crime reduction; the areas that did saw a reduction so large that property values increased. Flooding an area with cops and enforcing laws very judiciously does make a difference. However, people always want the law enforced on others, not themselves.

The broken windows theory was used by Rudy Giuliani to clean up New York City when he was the mayor. The basic idea is that if people see a building with one broken window, they will not hesitate to break another, or they will not see an issue if another is broken. As windows are broken, and time goes on, the neighborhood destroys itself. Meanwhile, when police enforce even the smallest crime, larger crimes won't occur. Further, people who commit larger crimes cannot commit them if they are in jail. Controversial or not, more police enforcing laws does make neighborhood safer. I saw it.

As various police scandals arose, SIFA was reduced. It is only natural: if you look across the country at times when police officers have been vilified and prosecuted, it was almost always after they acted on something they saw rather than something they were called to. I saw in the early 2000s a tide shifting to the police officer being guilty until proven innocent. I used to joke that we would one day have cameras following us around. I had no idea they would be attached to us.

It is foolish to think that cops won't hold back if they think they are in danger of being hurt. To be clear, hurt in the public eye. I never met a cop who was afraid of being hurt by a suspect, but I met plenty who were worried about being prosecuted for doing their job.

The fact that cops are human beings is lost in the political argument. Anytime a cop is involved in a use of force that is deemed excessive, or is accused of racial profiling, there are ramifications. Let me be clear: any cop who breaks the law should be prosecuted. Bad cops need to be fired. However, I have noticed that the most vulnerable population to criminal activity are those living in poverty. If you couple this with the idea that intensive policing reduces crime, the solution is always more policing, never less. The problem is, it becomes politically expedient to prosecute police at times.

Another issue is asking "Why?" Why do cops go bad? Police agencies have a duty to be transparent, but then the media has a duty to also be transparent. LVMPD is by far the most transparent agency in the United States. I attribute this to Sheriff Joseph Lombardo. What other agency livestreams video from the scene of officer-involved shootings (OIS), then in three days shows you all the camera footage, discusses policy, and answers questions; then even tells you if a policy violation occurred?

Policing can be dirty. It requires people to insert themselves into dangerous situations. Policing is a violent task that involves, at times, killing. Cops know this; however, uninformed politicians live under the shield of this protection and attack it without understanding how filthy it is. When conflict occurs, it is almost always at the hand of the suspect. You are not going to hear me say, "If he just did not resist, he would be alive," although I don't necessarily disagree. The issue with police uses of force, controversial shootings, and poor police tactics is all the same: it is the human element.

Remove what you think a cop is from your mind. Now insert this idea: a twenty-five-year-old man with a spouse and a young child, making just enough money to pay the mortgage or rent. On top of this, if he is terminated for cause from his employer, he will never be hired by another company in the same field. Now add to that the fact that the job is of such danger that he must wear a ballistic vest and carry a firearm. One more point: everything you do is news. If you make a mistake, it will be on the news, and it will be spun to be either your fault or the fault of your profession.

Now that you have a real idea what a cop is, put him in a fight, a physical fight for his life. What happens during this fight, a real fight? Your blood pressure rises, your adrenaline increases, you become tunnel-visioned on the threat at hand. You become emotional, you become scared, and you make decisions based on that emotion and not on logic. The logic centers of your brain have closed because of your fight-or-flight mechanism.

When you consider this, you understand that cops are human beings, not robots or computers. You expect perfection from no other profession but demand it from this one. Considering all of this, would you aggressively police if you could be the next national police scandal? De-policing occurs, and it hurts the most vulnerable of our population, because it creates a rise in crime.

Those living in poverty know crime, heartache, and tragedy. Their only hope is the cop who drives down their street. When vocal politicians feel the need to vilify cops and tell the public that the police "acted stupidly," the cops are not going to act. When a politician plays into the idea that police are bad, it emboldens those who wish to victimize the police or the public. If politicians were held to the same standard as our police, our country would be far better.

If your job consisted of two parts, what you are assigned and what you find, you time would be naturally split. If you discover that you see far more results with what you find, rather than what you are assigned, you will likely gravitate to this type of labor. If you garner better, more potent, and more valuable results from the labor you discover, rather then what you are assigned, you will begin to occupy your time with what you find rather than what you are assigned. Now imagine that a few of your coworkers are terminated, possibly arrested, or maybe are simply disciplined internally for actions that took place while they were working on something they came across rather than assigned.

As I have explained the police see far more desirable results during SIFA. Bad guys carry guns, drugs, and a plethora of other paraphernalia when they think they are not going to have police contact. They transport kidnapping victims, money, drugs and weapons when they think they will have no police contact. A career criminal who anticipates police contact will sanitize their person to avoid detection or criminal persecution.

As a cop, you know that you are far more likely to yield drugs, guns, and large evidentiary hauls when you surprise the bad guys. However, you also run a risk. You run the risk of ambushing an active criminal in the middle of some criminal activity when you seek out SIFA. However, when you surprise a bad guy, they are far more likely to be armed, and thus are more likely to harm you. Unarmed suspects will not be able to produce a weapon. Further, fight or flight only applies when you generate a surprise to the suspect.

If as a cop, you are willing to accept these risks based on perhaps your skill level, or perhaps you really feel that you will be able to protect the citizens of the city you are serving by actively and aggressively seeking out and arresting bad people by surprising them, you will likely yield good results. Now place the risk of a potential shooting in the scenario. Perhaps an officer involved shooting that may result in you being prosecuted. Is there a risk that you will be the next example, that a politically motivated individual uses to further their career? Perhaps you will be labeled a racist, or a bigot. Your employment threatened or severally scarred based on the contact. Now when you balance the risk reward are you willing to take the risk?

Balance the fact that you are not required to perform any SIFA. How would you proceed. When police participate in de-policing those who suffer are those who live in high crime, lower income areas. I never participated in de-policing, but only a fool denies that it occurs. There is only one true way to prevent crime, increased police deployment. De-policing results in the most vulnerable of our population being victimized.

Prostitution

Early in my career, along with narcotics purchasing, I did some limited work undercover with prostitution. Prostitution is a very peculiar crime. From the outside, it really seems that the prostitute is the violator. To be fair, as a new cop and even as a more senior cop, I thought this also. I did not really learn the truth of prostitution until very late in my career.

The truth about prostitution from a police aspect is that is incredibly complicated. Prostitution has a very unique world; it is a world that exists parallel to our world and at the same time perpendicular with it. These worlds tend to collide when a family member is involved, or when you see news of a large prostitution sting.

If you examine it in a very cursory way, it looks like the prostitute is engaging in a crime and is choosing to engage in this crime. I found that this is simply not true. The problem is, it is very hard to explain the victimology of the prostitute. An entire book could be written about it. Prostitution has its own language, with a unique culture.

The issue with prostitution is that the true suspect, or the true criminal, is often hidden from sight. The other issue is that the prostitutes are usually consenting adults, at least they are by the time they see police. The real situation is that the prostitute is trapped. This seems very strong, and people will usually say overly simplistic things like, "They should just walk away from that life." This is just not a very educated understanding of the issue.

The writing that follows will be a summation of my learning on this issue. I will include my personal experiences and attempt to really try to explain this strange world.

In my entire law enforcement career, I never met a male prostitute. I am not saying they don't exist; I am just saying I never met one. I learned very early that this profession is female dominated, which is peculiar, because most criminals are male. The typical dynamic is a woman who is the prostitute, with a handler. The handler is often called a pimp, panderer, or daddy, (yes, daddy). So, let's enter this world.

From very early in my career, I found that there was a pattern with prostitution. The pattern seemed, like I said at first, to be the woman who was the problem. However, I promise the women in these cases are the victims.

Before I was involved in any undercover work, I only saw these women from a patrol officer's point of view. The interesting thing is that the uniform you wear as a police officer turns off productive conversation with these women. Prostitutes are all very similar. There is a pathway they seem to follow. Some start at strip clubs, where they usually begin serving cocktails and progress into dancing. After dancing, they progress into prostitution itself. Prostitution is not legal in Clark County (the county Las Vegas is in).

The other pathway I found was women who were brought into the world of prostitution through drug use and manipulation. I don't have much experience in the human trafficking area of prostitution; however, I can say that typically prostitutes follow the same pattern. They are all imprisoned. The technological advancements that took place in the early 2000s have exacerbated this issue. I found that technology has created another pathway into this world: that is, internet pornography.

Prostitution is a journey of absolute devastation and destruction. Early in my career, I only encountered women in this field very late in theirs. That is common; the patrol officer will usually only see prostitutes very late in the prostitute's career. In field training, the prostitutes I encountered were almost always drug-addicted. Usually, I found that crack cocaine–addicted women were Black and methamphetamine-addicted women were White. I will give you the caveat that I did meet White women who were addicted to crack cocaine, but I never encountered a Black woman who was addicted to methamphetamine.

There are really two crimes that are enforced most with prostitutes: solicitation or loitering for the purpose of. Loitering for the purpose of prostitution requires a fair amount of investigation on the officer's behalf. One thing to remember is that in order to make an arrest, the officer needs to have either probable cause to believe the individual has committed a crime or an arrest warrant, which is also based on probable cause. Conviction, however, requires a much higher standard of proof, beyond a reasonable doubt. This is far more advanced than probable cause.

Probable cause is difficult to define. A good frame of reference is to think of 51 percent. Probable cause usually exists when the facts and circumstances known to the officer would lead a prudent person to believe a crime was committed and that the defendant committed the crime. Proof beyond a reasonable doubt is 100 percent. So, to arrest an individual, the police must establish probable cause; to get the conviction, the district attorney must be able to prove it beyond a reasonable doubt.

For loitering for the purposes of prostitution, the officer must establish probable cause (51 percent) that you are committing a crime. People often point out that a case was thrown out in court. This is not uncommon; when the standard for arrest and the standard for conviction are so different, this is to be expected. With loitering for the purposes of prostitution, officers can use reasonable facts and circumstances that would make you think that this person was loitering or staying in an area for the purposes of prostitution activity.

So, how do you enforce prostitution crimes as a uniformed patrol officer? Some ways that this can be established is clothing. If it is winter, thirty degrees outside, and there is a woman wearing a mini skirt and a halter top, this could draw your attention to the woman. It is very basic advertising. The woman is advertising her services, and the person paying for sex will be attracted to the clothing.

To be clear, a woman's clothing is not in and of itself proof of prostitution. Skimpy clothing is not the sole area to focus on here. Evening wear and attractive dresses are common. When women traditionally go out on a date, they may wear revealing clothing or a miniskirt, but there are differences. Women out on a date typically wear shoes that they can walk in; prostitutes often wear five-inch-plus heels. Further, purses are an indicator. Traditionally, when women go out on a date, they don't carry large purses. Prostitutes will carry large purses, and if you can search the purses, the contents will help you prove your case. A purse containing sexual lubricants, sex toys, or dozens of condoms can help your case.

Think it through. When I went out with my wife, she usually carried no purse. I carried her driver's license. So a woman who is alone, wearing very revealing clothing and five-inch heels, and carrying a large purse could draw your attention. Clothing is not enough, though.

Another factor is the neighborhood. Prostitution is very geographically restricted. Prostitutes and their customers usually stick to a specific area, mostly to attract and conduct business. This is not just a prostitution thing. If you think about your cities, there are areas that are residential, commercial, and retail. If the area you are patrolling is high in prostitution, coupled with the above issues I explained, start to build your case.

How do you know that the area is high in prostitution? Things to ask include, have you contacted a lot of prostitutes in this area? Is it an area known for prostitution? Have your colleagues made a lot of contacts in the area related to prostitution? In Las Vegas, "Is the area frequented by tourists?" is a valid question, because in Las Vegas, prostitution and tourism are linked.

We have addressed neighborhood. Now, look at activity. Is the woman walking alone, along the sidewalk, facing traffic? Remember, no single fact will get you the arrest; you must build on multiple facts. Prostitutes walk facing traffic to see the drivers of the vehicles that are driving toward them. Now keep looking. Are they waving at cars? If they are waving at cars, is there a commonality to the cars? Are all the cars they are waving at driven by lone male drivers?

Based on clothing, neighborhood, walking, and waving at cars, you have at least enough to perform a reasonable suspicion or Terry stop. If you choose to stop the woman, or if you choose to conduct a consensual encounter, find a way to search the purse. Also, ask questions. Why is she there? Where does she work? Isn't she cold?

She may actually tell you she is a prostitute and is working. Now you have plenty to arrest her. Loitering for the purposes of prostitution is hard but not impossible to establish for a patrol officer, because they tend to stop the activity when they see you.

Soliciting prostitution usually requires some mutual conversation. Statutes vary, but generally, it involves the prostitute either offering or agreeing to a prostitution transaction. This usually requires an undercover officer, but not always. You would be surprised what people tell the police. Lies are very common in this world. The prostitutes are very well educated on how to deal with you, especially if you are in a uniform. They have been trained. It is unlikely they will engage in a consensual encounter with you.

If you do stop them, they are likely to tell you a very brief story. They want the encounter to end as quickly as possible, and this is due to several issues. One is, they don't want to get arrested. The other is, they may get beaten for talking to you. They will likely want to call for help. They may tell you they need to talk to their husband or boyfriend. *Husband* or *boyfriend* means pimp.

Dealing with prostitution undercover is a very eye-opening experience. The interesting thing is that all kinds of men hire prostitutes. Therefore, undercover work in this area is easy. I was shocked that as I worked my way into this world in an undercover capacity, prostitutes would offer or agree to engage in prostitution regardless of how I looked. What I mean is that there were days when I was clean-shaven, hair cut short, looking like a cop, and I had no problem picking up a girl. One time, I was able to pick up a girl in uniform, in my police car, by convincing her I was a bad cop. It worked.

What this taught me was that all kinds of men hire prostitutes. Regardless of what you look like, they will engage you in conversation. The myth that only bad men participate in this world is just that: a myth. When I was arresting the customers, this was reinforced, as I arrested men from all conceivable professions, firefighters, teachers, physicians, carpenters, and of course, the unemployed. Prostitution is pervasive and infects all worlds.

I interacted with a mentally ill prostitute many times. She was very obviously developmentally disabled; however, she still worked. She would often wear fairy costumes. I found this puzzling at first, until I interacted with her. I arrested her dozens of times, and I don't know where she ended up. It was sad, but there was no solution.

Traditionally, the women in this field are "turned out" or made into prostitutes at a very young age, around sixteen years old. The pimp will create a hook to keep the woman in the life. Although the woman is not physically restrained, she is mentally restrained, whether through drug addiction, manipulation, or sheer fear.

I met a seventeen-year-old prostitute who had been transported to Las Vegas from the Midwest. When I saw her, I immediately noticed she was young. She was wearing regular clothing, but she was walking against traffic and waving at lone male drivers in an area that was heavily affected by prostitution. I also noticed that she was utilizing a push talk phone. It seemed she was reporting each car to someone. It was very odd behavior.

I drove past her while observing her activity. The neighborhood was very violent and plagued with drug use and prostitution. The area has changed somewhat now but is still a high-crime area. Fremont Avenue from Las Vegas Boulevard east was a very high-crime area. Mayor Oscar Goodman changed the western tip of this area, making it a tourist attraction, but if you head east enough, you will end up in the area I was in.

I turned around, got out of my car, and began talking to her. At first, the conversation was pleasant. But once I started asking where she lived and where her parents were, she started walking away from me. Also, she was using her push to talk to ask for help. Who was she calling? She was calling "Daddy." For those of you who literally think she was calling her father, she wasn't.

I really was puzzled as to why this child was walking away from me. Regardless, until I found her parents, she was not staying in that neighborhood. I walked onto the sidewalk and reached out to grab her. She proceeded to try to punch me several times. I am embarrassed to admit this, but I felt very perplexed. It didn't hurt, but was I going to punch a little girl?

As she kept punching me and trying to walk away from me, I told myself, *Do something.* I literally went through my options in my head and eliminated most of them. *Punch her back?* I was not going to punch a little girl. *Pepper spray? Baton?* No to both. This was a child.

Finally, I grabbed her by the back of the neck. She kept using that stupid push to call for help. I started to push her down to the ground, and once she was forced to her knees and then onto her torso, I took that stupid phone and put her in handcuffs. She was immediately very confrontational with me, screaming and shouting for the phone that was in my hand.

It took a while to calm her. Once she was in a condition to talk to me, she tried to tell me her parents were on the other side of that phone. However, and I am not making this up, on the other end of that phone was her pimp, who kept saying, "White girl, hey white girl" repeatedly.

I was able to get the phone and put it in my car. Once it was out of listening distance, she told me her story. She had come to Las Vegas to become a professional dancer, and that was her manager on the phone. She was only prostituting herself to get to her audition. She explained that her manager had all her ID. All of these are red flags.

The thing with juvenile prostitutes is, they are incredibly susceptible to manipulation. Even interviewing them can create a bad atmosphere. It is like interviewing a child victim of abuse. The interview itself can create a block that cannot be overcome.

In child-abuse cases, a forensic interview is required. These are very specialized interviews that use very specific language that allows you to extract the correct information from the child victim. You cannot conduct a forensic interview on the street in uniform. You also cannot properly interview a child prostitute on the street in uniform. It just doesn't work.

I called the vice section, which responded and took over the case. I never followed up, but I can tell you that after waiting for vice detectives to arrive, we were out with this little girl for about an hour. I unlocked my car to get to the girl's property. Still on the phone was her pimp. "Hey, white girl." I gave the phone to the vice detectives with a warning of how irritating it was.

When you stop juvenile prostitutes, you have the best chance of getting them out of the life. In this case, the girl had answered an advertisement in a local newspaper somewhere in Ohio looking for dancers. She ran away from home with her "manager," who brought her to Las Vegas, took all her identification, and began pimping her out. It was a tragic story of manipulation.

This was the first time I was forced to see the prostitute as a victim. As the years went by, I began to learn the inner truth of this world. The girls or women are almost always turned out at a very young age. Usually, their pimps hook them with drug addiction or heavy manipulation, like holding her child hostage or hoarding all her identification so she cannot leave. This occurs as he begins to build his harem of girls.

As the harem grows, the pimp gets very good at identifying the girls who are susceptible to being turned out, either at a young age, or an already damaged girl who is stripping. The manipulation is applied, and his income grows.

I learned late in my career that these girls are victims, and it takes a very dedicated hand to try to get them out of the life. As they grow up in that world, they become accustomed to its perks, like quick money, nice gifts, drugs, and expensive purses. It is a glamorous life that is very alluring. I have a friend who has been a vice detective for some time now. He told me that the life they enter becomes an addiction, and it is almost impossible to pry them from the life after the age of twenty.

Imagine yourself an impressionable child who may have been abused. You make a stupid decision and end up addicted to heroin or cocaine, and now you are cut off from your friends and family. You become trapped. Women who start their career going into stripping usually already have some mental baggage they take into the job. As the issues are not addressed, they are exacerbated, and the pimp is waiting in the wings to scoop these women up. I remember early in my career asking undercover vice detectives where the "high end" girls were. They always gave me the same answer: "There is no such thing."

As I progressed through a brief time of working undercover, doing vice activity, I found that I did not like it. I took all the classes and put in the time, but it never took hold on me. Vice detectives told me very early on that either you can do it or you can't. I found out that I could not. Mechanically it was not a problem, asking a woman for sex, but the repetitiveness is what killed me on it. As I matured in policing, I began to understand that the people who actually make good vice detectives are the cops who early on recognize that these women are victims.

I have worked undercover picking up girls on the street. I have worked undercover picking them up in casinos, and I have worked undercover in hotel rooms using a call-out service. I noticed a few things. First, all the women are the same. All are victims who have been forced into this life by some means or another. They are all led by a pimp, who is usually very good at manipulation and usually extremely violent.

I have encountered prostitutes at the beginning of their career, mid-career, and toward the end. I have found they are all very similar. The public assumes that they are consenting adults, and they don't see themselves as victims or criminals. I probably am not doing their situation justice, as I only know the world very superficially. However, I promise that it is tragic, and the women are horribly treated.

Later in my career I noticed a trend, or rather a shift, in this line of work. The trick roll became far more pervasive. *Trick roll* is when an unsuspecting prostitution customer is robbed by his prostitute. I saw this first when I responded to an apartment where a man had been drugged and his car stolen.

When I became a police lieutenant on the Las Vegas Strip, I found that these crimes are so frequent that it has created a new culture within the prostitution world, a culture of enchanting your customer then robbing him. It is a perfect crime.

Imagine you are in Las Vegas. You think prostitution is legal, or perhaps you don't care. You hire a prostitute and take her back to your room. She then creates a distraction, and you have now lost $5,000 and your Rolex watch, plus no sex! I have interacted with experienced prostitutes who memorize the sounds that the room safe makes with each number pushed. So, if you think your valuables will be locked up in the safe, they won't be. She heard you punch in the combination, and she knows it now.

When these crimes occur, they are rarely reported. Imagine going back to your wife at home after being robbed by a prostitute in Las Vegas. Are you going to tell your wife what happened? Are you going to return to Las Vegas to testify? Or are you going to come up with some crazy story about a bad blackjack hand and a lost watch?

At one Las Vegas property, these crimes became so common that as a lieutenant, I began responding out of frustration. Statistically, there is no way to know, but I would say that only about 1 to 5 percent of these case are reported. When you do catch one of these women and ask her the obvious question, "Why?", she will normally tell you that her pimp forced her too. It has become a financial race to riches. The woman who can bring back the most money in the shortest amount of time is usually rewarded. Coupling this reward with the crime not being reported and society in general seeing these women as criminals, these crimes almost always go unsolved.

12

Patrol Work

Back to my policing career. The days turned into weeks, and the weeks into months. I gained an extensive amount of experience in this time. I was partnered with an academy mate of mine, and this helped us both as we learned the job.

Patrol work is very monotonous. It is about 97 percent repetitive and 3 percent absolute terror. The 3 percent always takes you by surprise.

As I have said, policing is evolving. It is an ever-changing job that requires quite a bit of adaptation as the years go by. I took as many training classes as I could my first three years in order to master my craft. I became a defensive tactics instructor, and I was one of the agency's first taser instructors.

Tasers

When we first received tasers, we had to check them out each day. We were told to take them out and attempt to use them—yes, *attempt to use them*. The science behind tasers at the beginning was very murky, and we were unsure how the things worked.

We were using these things on everyone. We were like a child with a new toy. I found out by speaking to some of the more senior cops that it was the same when we first got pepper spray. I have several taser stories, but I am trying to keep this as chronological as possible.

On one event, my lunch partner had been dispatched to a suspicious person call at a local shopping mall. As our lunchtime grew closer, I started to head that way. I pulled up to the mall and parked behind his car. The call was in a shoe store, and I slowly began walking that way. He had said nothing on the radio, so I assumed he was all right.

However, he had made a tactical error. The suspicious person was seen stealing shoes and instead of waiting for backup, he had approached the shoe thief alone.

I opened the door to the business and was greeted by a store employee who spoke very little English. She was pointing toward the back of the store. I walked where she pointed, and as I did, I saw a uniformed leg sticking out from the bottom of a shoe display. This was puzzling to me. When your mind sees things that it is not expecting, you begin to think of and eliminate possibilities until you get to the correct one. This process takes milliseconds, but it occurs nonetheless.

My mind dismissed possibilities as I walked closer. Then I turned the corner and saw my partner in a wrestling match with a sixteen-year-old boy. I noticed that it looked like the boy's family was looming over the two. My partner, I knew, had wrestled in college, so my attention was on the family. They were not making any threatening gestures, so my attention went back to my partner as I continued to now jog toward.

When I reached the two, the boy threw a pistol under another shoe display. I grabbed it, secured it on my belt, and returned to my partner. With the contraband pistol no longer in his possession, I thought the combatant would stop. However, he did not. The fight intensified as he began to try to land punches on my partner.

So, having no choice, like a diver into a pool, I joined the two on the ground. We struggled for a few seconds, and then I remembered that I had a taser. These things were supposed to stop fights in less than a second.

I was too close to deploy the tool with the cartridge, which has wires that are twenty-one feet long. So I removed the cartridge and began driving the device into the suspect's back. It did nothing, and he started punching at me.

I ended up deploying the taser fifteen times into the suspects back and neck. I finally gave up on the tool. The three of us struggled more, and the teenager was finally taken into custody. We dragged him out to our cars, and I searched him. He was under arrest and going to jail. In his right cargo pocket, I found the reason he did not stop fighting when he threw his pistol. He had another pistol. He had been stealing shoes while concealing two pistols.

Tasers were not always useless. I found, however, that if you deploy them with the cartridge on, they are far more effective. I have deployed the weapon on several people, and I found that at best, they had a 50/50 success rate.

In one event, I was dispatched to a man with a gun. He had entered a local auto repair garage, became involved in an argument with an employee, and produced a gun. When the call was dispatched, I was very close.

There is a response-time myth that we should talk about at this juncture before we get deeper into this story. In movies, you see that during robberies, the crooks have police response time down to the minute. If police worked like firefighters, responding from the station, this might be plausible. However, when you call 911, it is likely forty-five to fifty seconds before a police officer is dispatched to respond. This may seem like a short time, but go ahead and start stabbing yourself for forty-five seconds and let me know how much damage you do.

After the 911 call is answered, and information is relayed, the call-taker will now send the information to the dispatcher. The dispatcher will then dispatch an officer to respond, assuming of course all officers are not already assigned to events. If an officer is dispatched to the call and happens to be ten minutes away, that's ten minutes on top of the forty-five to sixty seconds.

However, on this call, I was quite literally right around the corner. I pulled my car around and saw the suspect, who then saw me and ran. As he ran, I drove behind him. He finally ran through an alley, forcing me to get out of my car. He ran up to a self-locking door on an apartment complex entrance. I had him; it would take him time to pull out his keys and open the gate, or so I thought.

As he approached the gate, a gentleman walking on crutches opened the gate from the inside and held it open for the bad guy. The bad guy entered the complex, and the gate began to close behind him. I pulled out my taser and deployed it. I missed him and hit the crutches guy. He went down like a ton of bricks. Very embarrassing.

Gangs

As time went on, I began to be reminded just how violent and depraved mankind can be. While I was working early in my shift, an anonymous caller reported that there were four dead bodies in an alley that was known for excessive drug use. When a single person calls 911 and remains anonymous, the likelihood of the call being legitimate decreases. However, not in this case. The neighborhood around 21st and Sunrise was infested with Hispanic gangs; I say this so you understand the culture. As unpopular as this is to say, criminal gangs are usually broken down by race. There are Black, White, Asian, and Hispanic gangs. Gangs populate neighborhoods that they are comfortable in. This is very consistent.

Las Vegas did experience a phenomenon known as *hybrid gangs*. These gangs were a by-product of ill-conceived ideas on urban improvement. The theory was that if a gang identified with a specific housing project, if you eliminated that housing project, the gang would disappear. In the early 2000s, politicians in Las Vegas were bulldozing government housing complexes to eliminate the gang problem. Unfortunately, gang members are gang members. There is no code of conduct here. If their housing project is bulldozed and they move, they don't reform. They simply create a new gang with their new geographic friends.

Hispanic gangs will traditionally occupy poor Hispanic neighborhoods. There is the organized crime aspect; however, there is also the street-level drugs and prostitution. Poor Hispanic neighborhoods are traditionally populated by immigrants from Mexico and South America. For the absolute most part, illegal or not, these families are very hard-working people. The gang as it establishes control places the population in fear. This fear is exacerbated by a fear of immigration issues. Crime will usually go unreported, and families face retribution for interacting with authorities.

So I arrived in the alley and was greeted by four dead bodies. We locked the crime scene down and later found out that while the call came in at about three p.m., the homicides occurred at around noon. There had been a breakdown in a narcotics transaction at the trafficking level, and these homicides were a result of this high-dollar deal going bad. The horrific nature of the event was made worse by the fact that the crime went unreported for an extended period. The neighborhood had always been known for violence, but this placed the street on another level.

A Bizarre Event

Chronologically, if we move further into my career, we enter my second year of policing. I have a lot of stories, and they are worth telling. At a later event, I was dispatched to a call of a suspicious situation. It was early in the morning, just past sunrise. The detail I was sent to investigate was a large amount of expended rifle cartridges in the street.

When I arrived, I noticed just that. The street had four lanes, two north and two south. The northbound lanes were littered with expended rifle cartridges. There were thousands of them. There were so many shell casings in the lanes that cars had made tracks in the lanes, and the casings had settled where the vehicle tires had not been. Very similar to when cars drive in the snow, and you can clearly see the tire tracks.

I got out of my car and was trying to understand just what had happened. As I looked around, I tried to understand what had been shot at. Then I looked up and saw an apartment, and the front of the apartment was quite literally completely covered in bullet holes. I walked up to the apartment and saw that the front door had been shot so many times, the hinges were broken into pieces.

I broke down what was left of the door and saw a dead body just inside the apartment. After an extensive investigation, I found that the shooting had occurred around two a.m. This shooting was called in. However, the officers that investigated it did not see the shell casings or the apartment, presumably because it was dark. They reported the call as being unfounded. It was a bizarre event.

Suicides

Death is an immense part of policing, and it is something that you must learn to deal with. Over my career, I have responded to and seen death in all its stages. Homicide is tragic; robbing people of their life is tragic. I found, however, that suicide was usually far more destructive to families. I have seen suicide in so many ways, I also identified quite a few trends.

I can tell you that I found out suicide is a very discriminate phenomenon. I noticed that the Caucasian race was far more likely to commit suicide. Methods were also very specifically discriminatory. I found men would use far more fatalistic methods, like gunshots and jumping from large heights. European men seemed to hang themselves more often. Women almost always used pills. Asian men use swords, I literally watched a Japanese man push a sword through his chest to kill himself. It was very strange to notice these trends. Suicide is a hard thing to study, because both your victim and suspect are dead.

I was waiting at a red light next to a popular Las Vegas casino property. I had a feeling, and I looked right. You end up trusting these subconscious feelings as you go through your career. I have read studies that indicate that your brain processes items and your body responds to stimuli, and at times you are not aware of why you respond. Such as the time I made a car stop on an older luxury sedan. I passed the rear doors and began to greet the driver. Then I realized my pistol was in my hand. I did not remember pulling it out. Later in the stop, I found an illegal gun placed in the rear pocket of the driver's seat. I realized that I must have seen the handle of the gun and not realized it. After such a long career, I am convinced that God does guide you through life, and I think that He is heavily involved in intuition.

Anyway, back to the red light. I looked right and was about to dismiss my feelings, then I saw him. A homeless man had jumped from the fifth floor of the parking garage. My eyes contacted him as he passed the third floor. I watched him hit the ground. He hit the ground with his face and chest first. The rest of his body curled backward, like a scorpion, then unfolded as he came to rest.

As I investigated his death, it was a suicide, and there was a huge twist. A week prior, he was standing on the fifth floor of the same garage. A police officer saw him and drove into the garage. The officer talked to him, literally off the ledge. He was committed and talked the medical staff into releasing him. He walked to the same garage and jumped. His hospital papers were still in his pocket.

Suicide is terrible. The family and friends who are left behind are always filled with questions. They wonder what they could have done to save their loved ones. But there is usually nothing that can stop the event. I have found that the only way to even come close to preventing this is to provide your loved ones with love and support.

People in general need very little positive affirmation. Very small comments, showing your love, and letting people know they are doing well goes miles. People don't need billboards taken out; they just need love and support. Supporting your loved ones takes so little.

Many years later, when I was an FTO, I responded to probably the worst suicide call I ever experienced. Two brothers owned homes across from each other on the same street. One of the brothers had a weekly poker game as his home that the other brother attended. The two were involved in an argument, and during the argument, police were called. The brother who did not live there made a suicidal statement and left for his home.

He was pursued a few minutes later by his brother. As my partners and I arrived, the brother who lived across the street was entering the other brother's home. No more than a second went by and we heard a gunshot. We ran into the home, and the brother whose house we were in had blown his head off with a shotgun. The other brother was now holding the shotgun.

It was obvious what had happened. We were in a very small living room, and the brother holding the shotgun would not drop it. So we fought him over it. We fought him over the shotgun while slipping and falling in blood, skull, and brain matter from his brother. It was horrific.

Families are very important; family structure is also very important. A full family really does stop a lot of problems before they start. I found that fatherless homes, broken homes, and people with no support systems really did create immense tragedy. Children who came from established two-parent homes seemed to do better. I also found that domestic violence and general familial violence seemed less prevalent in solid, established families. Not absent, but definitely less prevalent.

Domestic Violence

The only problem with having an established family is that it is easy to hurt each other. Homicides are usually committed by a domestic partner; you hurt the ones you love. When people learn how physically and mentally vulnerable they are, they also learn how vulnerable others are. Thus, they now know how to hurt others.

There was a 911 hang-up at a home. I responded to the home and knocked at the door. I knocked and waited a few minutes. I really considered walking away, but something in my head told me to stay. I waited a very long time and just kept knocking. Normally, I would have left, but again, something told me to stay.

I stood to the side of that front door for about five minutes. The front door had two vertical windows, one on each side. They were about a foot in width, and spanned from the bottom of the wall to just over the top of the door. The windows had blinds. I looked down at the bottom of the right window. I saw between two of the slats of the blinds the very tips of a small child's fingers.

Now, 911 hang-up calls happen for many reasons. Prior to smartphones, home lines would auto-dial 911 if they were left off the hook too long, or if there was electronic trouble on the line. Back then, mechanical 911 hang-ups were not uncommon. I had convinced myself that this was just that until I saw those tiny fingertips.

I then began to absolutely pound on the door. I was about to force the door open when it slowly opened. I was greeted by a woman who had three very young children, two of whom were clinging to her legs, and she was holding a baby. I heard a man inside the house screaming. I looked past the woman who answered the door, but I saw nothing. Then I looked at the woman and saw the blood. She was bleeding from a head wound.

The blood was not pouring, but it was actively streaming from her head. I have seen many people pass out, and I have noticed a few commonalities. I have also seen people fake pass out. When people pass out, their eyes are what tells you if it is real. I noticed that it starts with a stare. They look directly forward at nothing, then their eyes seem to roll back. Once the color of their eyes is no longer visible, they are going down.

In the time period of about three seconds, she fixed her gaze, and I watched her eyes roll back. I jumped in and grabbed her. I was able to grab her around the waist so that when she fell, the baby she was holding fell onto my chest. I held her with my left arm and the baby with my right. I lowered her to the ground and walked into the home.

I placed her in the entryway, which was also a living room. She almost immediately woke up, saw me, and began crying. There was blood all over my uniform. I attempted to see where she was bleeding from.

We were in a living room with very high vaulted ceilings. The living room was about sixty feet long by forty feet deep. It had a single couch, and on the rear wall was an open sliding-glass door, with the screen door closed. In the back yard, I could see a pile of gas cans.

The floor of the home was flooded. I wasn't standing in inches of water, but someone had obviously either flooded the home and the floor was still wet or there was some leak. It was far too much liquid for just having mopped to be an explanation.

Because the front door was open and the rear door was open, there was a draft coming through the home. A man presented himself from the kitchen, and he was irate. I only speak what I call emergency Spanish so I can work my way through a life-threatening situation; however, I cannot have a Spanish conversation. This gentleman was screaming in Spanish at me.

I asked him to sit on the couch. He did not immediately sit down, but after a lot of yelling, he finally did.

I was trying to speak with the woman who answered the door; however, she was Spanish-speaking and obviously injured. She kept pointing down a hallway and saying a name. I looked down the hallway and saw what was obviously debris that was floating in a pool of the liquid we were all standing in. The debris appeared to be broken parts of a door. I knew that my backup was on the way, so I just had to maintain the quasi peace. I saw a broken statue that was on the floor. It was broken into several pieces, and there was blood on the pieces.

The man who was seated on the couch tried to light a cigarette. I told him not to do it. He understood English. However, as I was attempting to calm this woman who was bleeding, he continued trying to light his cigarette. The gentleman tried to light his cigarette five additional times. Each time, I was able to stop him before his lighter sparked.

My backup arrived, walked in, and greeted me. I asked him to see what was at the end of the hallway. He walked down the hallway and returned two minutes later with a teenage boy. When my partner walked up to me, he said, "Get outside now." He took the teenage boy and my attempted smoker from the couch into the front yard. I was able to bring the woman and her young children there as well.

Once outside, my partner explained that the flooded floor was a result of gasoline being poured throughout the home. We worked our way through the call as the fire department made the home safe, and when all was said and done, I found out what happened. The husband and wife had been involved in an argument. She had threatened to leave. He had hit her over the head with the statue, knocking her out.

He then left and went to the local gas station. He filled about ten five-gallon containers with gasoline. While he was doing this, the middle child, who was about five years old, called 911. The husband returned home and was pouring the gasoline on the home's floor, and while this was happening, the teenage son locked himself in a back bedroom.

When the husband was finished pouring his newly purchased gasoline on the floor, he attempted to kick in the bedroom door, and that is when I knocked at the door. Eventually, the wife made it to the door, and now we are caught up.

During interviews, all members of the family who could manage answering questions confirmed the story. The husband admitted that he was hoping that he could initially kill his family. Then, when I arrived, his goal was to kill me and his family.

About three months later, the case went to Justice Court for the preliminary hearing. The husband in this case was charged with various person crimes as well as some arson crimes. Police and fire department personnel all showed up to testify. The assistant district attorney who was assigned the case got my attention and met with me in a side office.

He explained that the wife was uncooperative and was refusing to testify. The two had reconciled, and the couple wanted the case behind them. The array of public safety witnesses who arrived that day watched as this man received a sentence of five years probation.

13

Community Oriented Police

Right around the three-year mark, I was asked to join the Community Oriented Police (COP) team. I had caught the attention of the sergeant of the team when I served a search warrant on a smoke shop. Laws have changed, but at the time, smoke shops could sell glass pipes as a novelty only. I was able to establish that the owner was selling to people who were asking for drug pipes. It was a small warrant, but it worked.

COP teams usually were tasked with community events, various school and charitable activities. They really are the social portion of policing. McGruff the Crime Dog, National Reading Week, and various other community events are usually done by this team. Their mission is very specific depending on the station to which they are assigned.

Where I was assigned, we focused on business licensing and problem apartment complexes. Business licensing was easy; the laws are very straightforward. Serving alcohol without a license and those types of violations are very easy to enforce. When I was able to shut down the smoke shop, I was taken to the COP team.

Problem apartment complexes are very complicated cases. You would have a complex of, say, fifty to a hundred apartments. The owner tended back then to be either out of state or a corporation. The apartment manager had no authority, usually, to act on behalf of the owner and was often threatened with unemployment if occupancy goes below a certain percentage. This created incentive to rent apartments.

In order to maximize occupation percentages, there was an incentive to lower prices. Cheap rentals were very attractive to bad people ready to do bad things. In addition, there were statutes that prevented managers from discriminating amongst renters for past arrests and convictions. Wherever you stand on this issue is not relevant; anyone can see the problem arising. Some even started renting by the hour to raise money. Before we cast judgement. The apartment manager was wrong, but she was simply trying not to lose her job. She maintained the percentage the owner wanted by lowering rent. She was not able to discriminate and thus was caught in a feedback loop.

As complex crime rose, my job was to meet with the manager, try to identify the owner, and take some sanctions on them for operating a dangerous business, or a *chronic nuisance*, as the statute is written in Nevada. The law basically said that if the police were called to a complex an excessive number of times, the owner was operating a chronic public nuisance and could be prosecuted.

When owners are out of state or unreachable, and managers are willing to just resign in order not to deal with police pressure, it is very hard to maintain peace in problem complexes. The problem is the people this issue hurts the most are the poor. Those people on some sort of housing assistance are plagued with violence.

Complexes are very willing to rent to those using government vouchers, as this is easy, secure money. There is nothing wrong with this; however, the poor are then placed in apartment complexes with very undesirable people. If you are a gang member, and you realize that an apartment complex is renting very cheap, with no regard for your criminal background, it attracts you and your friends. A program called Crime Free Multi Housing began to combat this; however, like most federal programs, it did little to solve the issue.

There was one such complex with about fifty units. Crime was rampant in this complex. Shootings were very common, as was property destruction. One time a gang took over the complex and spray-painted "Fuck the police" and "Police stay away" on several walls.

Crime in the complex began to escalate. I was driving by the complex once and a gentleman who was about eighteen walked out from an alley and waved me down. I got out of my car and saw that his right hand was very deformed. He was a dark-skinned Black male, but his hand was grey.

As I began to process what I was seeing, he told me that he had been shot in the hand with a shotgun. It made sense and explained his missing fingers and the blood dripping from his hand. This unfortunately escalated to a feud between two gangs fighting for control of the complex. I began applying pressure to the manager, who gave me assurances she would take steps to improve the complex. She took no such steps; she just kept renting units.

After about ten contacts, I arranged a meeting with her and her lawyer at the station. I explained to her that I was going to hold her criminally liable for any more crime in the complex. I also threatened to have their business license revoked if the crime did not subside. She assured me it would; she would take steps to improve conditions for her renters.

About three weeks after this meeting, I was following up on a previous night's call of a pit bull running at large, scaring residents of the complex. I was able to identify the apartment where the dog had come from, and I walked up to it and knocked. The problem was, I was alone. I was very aware of how dangerous this was, but my frustration with this complex had grown to levels I cannot explain. It was like I was telling the manager that if she did not improve the conditions, I would.

The apartment was on the second floor, and the front door was right at the top of the exterior staircase. I knocked, well, pounded, on the door to try anything to stop the violence in this complex. The renter answered the door, and I began to ask him about his dog. Apparently, he was not comfortable with the line of questioning, as he shut the door behind him and walked toward the stairs. For all of you aspiring cops, do not stand at the top of a flight of stairs when talking to a suspect.

A dog running at large is a misdemeanor; however, in the city, this gave me leverage, as I could ask about vaccinations and potentially arrest the owner. It's petty, but I was tired of people dying at this complex.

The predictable happened. He pushed me down the stairs, or at least he tried. I was able to grab him and start a vicious fight as he continued to try to throw me down the stairs. I had called for help and was now fighting with this guy as we both fell down the stairs. I had the presence of mind to ensure he was under me each time we rolled over a step, and I was under him in the spaces between each step, causing him quite a bit of pain.

When we landed at the bottom of the stairs, I assumed he would try to run away. He didn't, and the fight continued. The thing about close-quarters fights is that you cannot get to any tools, no pepper spray, no batons, because your hands are occupied with protecting yourself. So, we fought. We rolled into a nearby parking lot, and then I heard a glorious sound.

When you are a cop and in a fight, there is something that happens to you when you start to hear the sirens headed your way. You begin to think, *Well, my friends are coming; this will be bad for you.* Still, we fought and fought. He landed some hits, but I landed many more. He was clearly untrained and out of shape.

Finally, my partner arrived, and we arrested the guy for fighting with me. My partner then asked me what was wrong with my gun belt. I looked down and saw that my hips were not properly aligned. Right around then, the pain set in. I had severely injured my spine, and the pain began to be so intense that I started to lose vision. It was very strange.

At that time, I was introduced to a sergeant who was probably the most uncompassionate person I ever met. His name was Blake Mirum. Blake was a jerk, he was a supervisor on a patrol squad, and he arrived because my sergeant was off that day. He was there to do his job, to investigate a fight a police officer was in. I was lying on the ground trying to figure out what was wrong with my spine. He walked over to me and told me to get up and write the arrest report. I was puzzled, as I was clearly injured. He just did not care. This would be my first confrontation with Blake, but not the last.

My partner explained that I was injured, and Sgt. Mirum told me in no uncertain terms that I was to finish the arrest report, and if I felt I needed medical attention, I was to drive myself to the hospital. I realized the only way I was going to get medical attention was if I got that arrest report done. I drew out a three-paragraph report, threw it at my partner, and got in my car. Then I realized I could not bend correctly. So, partially seated in the passenger seat, I turned on my siren and drove myself to the hospital.

I arrived at the hospital and could not navigate exiting my vehicle, I told my dispatcher to have a nurse come and get me. A few seconds later, a team of nurses came out, pulled me from the car, and got me into the emergency room, where I was treated for a variety of spinal injuries. My wife was called, and my partner ended up meeting me at the hospital and getting my police car back to the station.

It took years to recover from that injury. But the good news was I was able to force my doctor to release me to full duty about six months after this incident, when I absolutely lied to him and said I was no longer in any pain, and I did not need a back brace or any more physical therapy or surgeries. I paid for that decision later in my career.

14

Field Training Officer

After about a year working in the COP section, I was selected to be a field training officer. An FTO is a real first-line supervisor. You are responsible for new officers who have no idea what they are doing, but this is not a police supervision book.

I was called and told I would be an FTO, and I would be assigned to Sgt. Mirum's squad. The hits just keep on coming. It was an 8 percent raise, though, so there was that.

Off to a Bad Start

In the locker room on my first day, I spoke with my new partner, Shane Romney. Shane was a great partner, a very aggressive cop who had been a cop for two years at another large police department. He and I had worked together off and on, and we knew each other well.

Cops normally get dressed at the station. They drive their personal cars to the station, wearing the bare minimum: socks, white T-shirt, and usually some kind of shorts. They walk into the locker room and put on their uniform. At the end of the week, they have five pairs of socks, five shirts, five pairs of underwear, and one pair of shorts to wash. It is very hard to drive your personal car with a gun belt on, and normally you don't want people knowing what you do. So, leaving your home in uniform is out.

I was often confused when people (usually from other agencies) would brag to me that their entire neighborhood knew they were cops, probably out of some nonsense bravado. I always responded with the same thing: "So, they know when you're not home and when you are asleep?" The conversation usually ended there.

For those of you who are not in the field, or for those of you starting a career in law enforcement, when you are a cop, you must hide this as much as possible. It's hard to understand this unless you are in the role. The fewer people who know you are a cop, the less of a target your home and family will be. Further, the last thing you want is an arguing couple to knock on your front door to mediate their dispute.

So, I was getting changed at work and talking to Shane. I knew that I had been selected to come to the squad because Shane's previous partner had chosen to transfer to swing shift. This squad was day shift with weekends off. Shane's former partner transferred to swings with Tuesday, Wednesday, and Thursday off. I made a joke to Shane that his partner must not have liked Sgt. Mirum. I said something like, "I guess your partner and the sergeant just did not get along." I had no idea what had happened, and it was just a joke.

The first issue was, Sgt. Mirum was in the locker room and heard me. For a reasonable person, you may be thinking that this is a harmless comment, but his immaturity and tyrannical supervision style was far from reasonable.

Further, Shane's previous partner (I found out later that day) had transferred off the squad due to a terrible argument he had gotten into with Sgt. Mirum over a day off. It was not a vacation or any kind of discretionary leave issue; it was sick time. He needed the day off to transport his children to a doctor appointment.

For some of you who need context, our sick-time allowances are specifically meant for illness of either you or a family member, and for you to go to doctor appointments or to transport and care for a relative who has a doctor appointment. The issue was, Sgt. Mirum disagreed with the officers' employment contract and felt that sick time could not be preplanned. It must only be used for unexpected illness, in his opinion.

The argument ended with Shane's partner saying something like, "Well, I will be off tomorrow. If you don't like it, write me up."

Sgt. Mirum did just that, and the two were not on speaking terms from then on. Shane's partner moved on shortly thereafter, and I replaced him. The fault was shared by both somewhat. However, the sergeant should have known better. And I had just unknowingly placed my foot squarely in my mouth.

We had a heavy day of work ahead of us. The first four hours were taken up by a course of instruction in landlord tenant laws. We had to be in uniform because we were headed to the streets after the class. Text messaging was relatively new at the time, and during the class, I was checking my flip phone, as my wife and I were texting back and forth.

Let me assign myself some blame. I should have been paying attention and not looking at my phone. However, I did look at my phone, and the issue was I had embarrassed the instructor. This was a retired police sergeant who had been elected to the office of constable, and his job was to manage landlord-tenant issues and eviction-type laws. He was giving a course of instruction on the issue.

He has asked a question about a specific issue. I heard the question and knew the answer; however, I waited for someone else in the classroom of about fifty students to answer it. I took the time to look down at my phone.

He then called on me to answer the question. I closed my phone, looked up, and answered the question. The instructor, assuming I hadn't been listening, was caught off guard by my correct answer and made a very slight comment about me paying attention to the class. Fair enough. I should have been paying attention. That was my fault.

After the four-hour class, I got up to walk out, and Sgt. Mirum asked me to talk to him outside. I went outside and waited. About fifteen minutes passed, and I began to get curious to see what was taking him so long. Standing outside, I looked through a small window in the door. I saw Sgt. Mirum obviously yelling at another officer on the squad. I had no idea what he was yelling about, so I returned to my waiting position in the parking lot.

About another five minutes went by, and Sgt. Mirum came out of the building. His eyes found me quickly, and he asked me to follow him around the corner. I walked behind him and followed him to a small landscaped area that was out of sight of everyone, surrounded on one side by a building and two sides by a fence.

Once around the corner, Sgt. Mirum turned around and faced me. He then began yelling at me. His argument was that I had embarrassed him during the class by not paying attention. This portion of his rebuke, I understood. I should have been paying attention.

Then the locker room conversation was brought up. He felt that I was making fun of him because I made a joke about Shane's partner leaving the squad. He went on an escalating tirade about how I was embarrassing him, and I was making fun of him. He really felt that not only had I known about the disagreement the two had but that I was making fun of him for the event.

At this point, a very odd thing happened. He said, "If you think you are going to come to my squad and embarrass me, we can handle this right now."

What did he mean by that? Well, all doubt was alleviated when he turned so his body was totally facing me; took a step forward, so he was about three inches from me; and like a thug, raised his hands to fight me. Not a joke, not an exaggeration: a real event.

I began to rapidly go through options in my head. One of which, I will admit, was to punch him. However, I chose to try to deescalate the situation. I looked down and took a step back. Looking back up, I legitimately said, "I don't know what you are talking about."

At this point, I think his rage had peaked. He seemed to start to control his emotions. He then walked away from me like the talk never happened. If there was any doubt as to what was going to occur, that night he pulled me aside and apologized for his behavior.

The problem was that this would not be the last time he and I had conflict. I had heard rumors about his temper, but I had largely dismissed them as exaggerations. They were not exaggerations; the man was mentally ill.

I later found out about the conflict that had occurred with Shane's partner and Sgt. Mirum, and I somewhat understood the interaction. The issue was the man was very frustrated. His career was very slow-moving, and he had been overlooked for various specialized assignments and promotions. Further, he was working on his fourth failed marriage and had a terrible departmental reputation. He was just a miserable person.

Accidents Happen

Police officers drive a lot of miles. Depending on the size of your area of responsibility, you can put one hundred miles on your car in a shift. The issue is, car accidents happen. I was involved in some accidents, some my fault and some not. Police officers do crash cars; it happens.

The most interesting of these occurred a few weeks after my interaction with Sgt. Mirum. Back then, there were far fewer police officers on the streets. It was not uncommon for squads to only have five officers working a shift. This creates issues with overtime and missed breaks. Skipped lunches and working late were more of the norm back then.

During this event, Shane had stopped a gentleman about five miles from the downtown police station. I was at the station dropping off some evidence. I heard Shane call out the stop on the radio. A short time after Shane made this stop, another officer on our squad responded to help him. Then Shane came over the radio, saying he was in a fight and needed help.

Fights as a police officer are very dangerous. The officers are never aware of the suspects' intentions, that is fight to escape or fight to put down the cop and then escape. The good news is that fights in policing usually only last a few seconds. Officers usually gain control over the situation quickly. Also, in an urban environment, help is usually only minutes away.

I heard the fight on the radio, ran out to my car, and headed that way. Two officers involved in a fight should be able to end it quickly. However, I was five miles away, and as I navigated the streets to get there, the officers never got back on the radio. As the seconds went by, the officers not getting on the radio saying the fight was over worried me.

As seconds turned into minutes, I really became worried that my partners were in trouble. I got closer, and still nothing on the radio. I pulled into the parking lot and, sure enough, the fight was ongoing. Two officers were unable to control a suspect who was actively fighting them off.

I pulled closer to the three combatants and exited my car. My right foot stepped in a puddle as I got out of the car, it had rained. I closed my car door to ran and help my partners.

As I approached them, Shane began screaming, "Your car!" I looked back and realized that my vehicle was still running and moving toward us. It was still in drive.

I ran back to my car so it would not run anyone over. Stepped back into the same puddle as I opened my car door. With my door open, I grabbed the steering wheel and jumped into the car. I stomped my right foot down as hard as I could onto the brake pedal.

However, my foot was wet. My foot slipped off the brake pedal and pressed the accelerator pedal to the floor, so the car was now headed at full RPM forward. The good news was that when I had grabbed the steering wheel, I had turned the wheels.

As my vehicle lurched forward, I had no control of it for about twenty feet. I missed the three fighters by about six feet, and my vehicle then drove squarely into and through the wall of a local business. In my defense, it stopped the fight!

I backed my car out of the local business that I had just given a drive-through entrance. Shane took the guy to jail for whatever the crime was. I had to explain to Sgt. Mirum how my car ended up halfway into a local store.

I called the traffic bureau; they responded and took the accident report. I was at fault, for sure. Once the investigation was complete, the risk manager was notified, my car was towed away, and everything was finished.

Enter Sgt. Mirum, who quite literally showed up after everything was done. He parked his car, exited it, walked up to me, looked around at all the damage, and said ...

OK, before I tell you what he said, place yourself in his position. Two officers he supervises were in a fight with a suspect. He did not come to help. I'm sure he was busy. A third officer he supervised had been involved in an accident, an accident that had caused major damage to private business. The traffic bureau, criminalistics (crime scene investigator), and a tow truck had been and gone. Then he responded to the scene. What do you think delayed him? What do you think his priority should have been? I will just leave you with that.

Back to Sgt. Mirum. His statement to me was, "You need to slow down." He then turned around, got back into his car, and drove away. A man of few words, I suppose.

The thing with Sgt. Mirum was, he lost his temper so often that we all accepted it as normal. He would scream and shout like a child, then apologize to you later. I tried to just avoid contact with the man.

Bad Trainees

Being a new FTO and very junior, I normally took the bad trainees, the ones who were showing patterns of not making it through the program. I remained an FTO for five years. This is abnormal now. People are usually FTOS just long enough to get another assignment, usually one or two years. Long-term FTOS are a dying breed.

I began to try to identify patterns for those who were successful and those who were not, as well as trying to figure out what it took to get someone to make it. This was frustrating, as every trainee was different and thus struggled with different things.

The senior FTO on our squad was supervising a trainee who was almost finished with the program. She was a very pretty woman who really should have been a model, not a cop. There were rumors that she and her FTO were sleeping together, but these rumors are common and usually not true.

Women do have a difficult time in law enforcement, as it is a male-dominated profession. They are usually labeled as homosexual or weak, and it creates an entire host of issues. Some women do very well; some attempt to prove themselves too much. We all wore the same uniform and made the same money, but women were treated very differently.

Anyway, the trainee's FTO was off for a week, and I was to take her on as a trainee while he was gone. Sgt. Mirum explained that she was on track to graduate in four weeks, and he saw no issues that I should be aware of. (There were.)

Halfway through our shift, one of my partners was in pursuit of a vehicle that was heading east on a major street. This trainee was driving, and we both heard the radio traffic indicating the pursuit was headed toward us. She turned around and started driving north, away from the pursuit. Like I said, she had been reported to be doing well and on track to graduating field training.

Never jump to conclusions as a trainer or supervisor. There may be something you do not know. I gave it a few seconds, thinking maybe she had heard something on the radio that I did not. I heard the pursuing officer give another location update. I realized she either was actively avoiding the pursuit or had no clue about basic geography.

So I took over the car. I told her to turn around. She challenged me and asked why. This was not the time for democratic leadership; this was the time for autocratic leadership. I told her (possibly yelled), "Turn this fucking car around and don't ever challenge my direction."

She was shocked. Obviously, no one had ever spoken to her this way. As pretty as she was, I was happily married and not interested. She turned the car around, and with some creative direction we ended up driving west on Sahara Avenue, with the pursuit heading east right toward us on the same street.

A few seconds later, the pursuit passed Sahara Avenue and Maryland Parkway. The pursuing officer broadcast this as we were approaching the same intersection. Two police cars were pursuing the suspect, lights and sirens, low traffic conditions, unavoidable to anyone. The pursuit passed us headed east about twenty-five feet from our car, and she kept driving west.

"What the hell is wrong with you?" I yelled.

I was now convinced she was actively avoiding the pursuit. Two of the most indicative behaviors of trainees that shows they are not going to make it are either identifying criminal behavior and ignoring it or not being able to identify observed behavior as criminal behavior. Just like any job, either knowing what needs to be done and not doing it or not being able to see what needs to be done. Only in this case, either of those actions (or inactions) could cost people their life.

I again screamed for her to turn the car around. She did, and we worked our way back to the pursuit as the driver crashed into a fence.

A little suspect psychology when it comes to pursuits: they seem to end when the suspect unintentionally crashes the car and it is no longer able to be driven; police act and cause the vehicle to be inoperative, usually by ramming into it; the suspect intentionally crashes it to give up; or the suspect reaches a destination considered safe and runs from the now, abandoned vehicle.

I have never been involved in a pursuit where the suspect stopped the car and gave up. Even when I have deployed spike strips and deflated suspects' tires, they will drive on the rim(s) until they can no longer drive. There are exceptions, but for the most part, this is how most pursuits end.

We arrived at the termination point, and I was very upset at my trainee. I told the pursuing officer that we would take the case from him for training purposes. I told my newly acquired trainee that we would be taking the case, and she should prepare to take the case. I told her that I would be there to help her, and we would get through it.

Ideally, she should have taken a leadership role. She should have been assigning duties, such as someone to take care of the towing of the car, someone else to collect evidence, someone to interview the suspect, and more. She would need to obtain all the needed information to generate an arrest report.

At first, things seemed promising, as she was asking all the right questions, assigning tasks, and getting all of the needed evidence. The case involved many fraud forgery crimes, as well as the felony evading charges for the pursuit. We made our way to the jail.

A case like this has a tremendous amount of paperwork. Back then, almost no reports were on the computer. However, all the forms were very easy, fill-in-the-box forms, except one: the arrest report. This is a narrative report that tells the story of what happened. It requires the most effort, as it is what the district attorney will primarily use to prosecute the suspect.

At this late juncture in field training, trainees are expected to manage almost all the events they are on. They are expected to delegate work and get the job done. Training progression is like a mortgage that starts with a large percentage of interest and a small percentage of principle and then gradually, as time passes, switches to a large percentage of principle and small percentage of interest. Early in field training, the trainee is responsible for a small percentage of the work, and the FTO is responsible for the larger percentage. As time goes on, the trainee takes on more, and the FTO does less. At this point in the program, she should really have been performing about 99 percent of the work, and her FTO should be only interjecting if she is about to make a catastrophic mistake.

After she had released our prisoner to the jail staff, she turned to me to give her direction. I was expecting her to tell me that she was going to do most of the work and then assign me either nothing or some small tasks. Had she not assigned me anything. I would have told her that I would do some of the reports.

She said, "I will manage all of the paperwork." Great start; I was impressed.

Then she continued, "If you can just do the arrest report."

I asked her to confirm, "You want me to do the most detailed, longest report, while you do all of the fill-in-the blank forms?"

She said, "Yes."

I told her that was not going to happen, and she was now going to do all the paperwork, even if we spent the entire shift at the jail. I had previously been absolutely prepared to do all the fill-in-the-blank reports; however, this work avoidance had just become a pattern of behavior. A supervisory hint: if an employee displays an undesirable behavior, if you wait and observe, if it is a problem, it will be repeated. If it does not repeat, it may be a fluke incident and not a problem.

She was very quick to inform me that this was not how she and her other FTOS worked together. I do not know if that was true or not; however, she was now in a position where she had to prove her ability to me. We spent the next six hours at the jail. Realistically, at this point in the program, we should have been at the jail for no more than two hours. A veteran officer would have had this done in about an hour.

I reported to my old friend Sgt. Mirum that this trainee was not ready to work on her own. I explained everything that had happened. He told me that what I said sounded bad, but her previous FTO was senior to me, so his opinion was more valid than mine. That was it. I put in a transfer to swing shift. I'd had enough.

Later in her career, this trainee officer was involved in a stalking incident with another officer she was dating. She had been stalking him after he cheated on her. It was bad, and she left the agency after only about four years to avoid repercussions.

My transfer to swing shift was approved, as Sgt. Mirum's squad was a rotating door of personnel. It is very telling when you have a weekend-off, day-shift training squad that is full of brand new FTOs who transfer away to other squads with bad days off as soon as they can.

Spike Strips

One week prior to transferring, I was assigned a trainee named Richard Rounders. Rich was a veteran corrections officer who had chosen to transfer to the police side. He was later in the program and was doing well. Just before lunch, we were advised of a vehicle pursuit that was working on the other side of Las Vegas, about four stations over. The event had started with a violent attempted homicide that progressed into a carjacking.

A quasi-barricade followed. A *barricade* is a generic term for someone in a car, building, or open field who was refusing to submit to police. After a short barricade, the suspect had stolen a police car, shot and killed the canine who was in the car, and was now being chased toward downtown Las Vegas.

The best way to stop a pursuit is to get in front of it. The pursuit was headed toward us. I directed my trainee to a position on the interstate where we could safely set up spike strips to stop the pursuit. When a vehicle drives over spike strips, the rubber of the tires is pierced by hollow quills that remain in the tire. This causes a controlled deflation of the tire.

Spike strips consist of the actual spikes, which are concealed in three narrow strips shaped in a triangle. Each strip is connected end-to-end. When they are pulled end-to-end, they stretch just over the width of the traffic lane. At one end of the strips is a string, and the string is connected to a reel device that allows you to spin a handle to reel them in, like a fishing rod. The device is placed on the shoulder, or off the road. The string is then run perpendicular to the travel lanes, across the lanes.

The officer stands on the opposite shoulder or off the road on the opposite side. As non-violator vehicles drive by, they harmlessly run over the string. As the violator approaches, the officer pulls the string, pulling the device into the travel lane. After the violator runs over the spikes, you then pull the device out of the road so pursuing officers' tires are not deflated.

My trainee and I set up on the interstate about five miles from the pursuit. We placed the device in the passing lane shoulder (the far-left shoulder), ran the string across the four lanes of US-95, and stood in the far-right-lane shoulder.

This portion of the interstate is very unusual. When you drive south on US-95, going through downtown Las Vegas, there is about a two-hundred-yard stretch of road where your vehicle subtly bounces up and down. It's very strange, but your car will lift to its highest point as the shocks expand, and then your car bounces down. If you are traveling too fast, you will hear your vehicle scrape the interstate. We were right in the middle of this area. We watched as vehicles drove by, passing us at 70 to 80 miles per hour, all bouncing in the same spot.

The pursuit was close now, only about two miles away. I looked left toward the oncoming traffic, and I saw a large landscaping truck traveling in the far-right travel lane. It was driving at about 70 miles per hour. What caught my attention was that under the flatbed of the truck, there had been welded a square metal box. These boxes contained stakes, the kind of stakes that are used to set forms for concrete.

The sound caught my attention. As that truck began to bounce, the welded metal boxes were scraping the interstate. As my brain was processing the source of the scraping sound, I watched the truck pass us. As it approached us, the boxes scraped the interstate, up and down several times. As the truck passed us, the boxes hooked and caught the string, and pulled the spike strips into the far-left travel lane. Five vehicles, all traveling 70 to 80 miles per hour, ran over the spikes, creating pandemonium. Vehicles were scattered all over the interstate, and traffic backed up for miles very quickly. I had just facilitated giving five innocent people four flat tires each.

First things first, apologies. I walked up to the car closest to me, the car whose tires I had flattened last, and spoke with the driver, a very nice woman in a beige sedan who was very understanding, I looked over and saw that her passenger, a younger woman, quite literally had her head in a small plastic trash can. The driver saw my gaze and then said, "Oh, she's OK. It's my daughter. She just got out of surgery and is feeling a little sick." I felt about an inch tall.

I called LVMPD's risk manager and explained what had happened. To his credit, before offering me his solution, he made fun of me for quite a while. In the police academy, you are taught never to promise anyone money or repairs for anything you break. The reason is that there are some statutes that specifically place the liability for claims on the suspect, if their actions cause the damage, or create a circumstance where police have to cause damage.

After making fun of me, he gave me instructions. I was to call tow trucks for each car I had affected. They were to be towed to any tire store of their choosing, and then they were to select four of whichever tire they desired, and the agency would cover the cost. It was the right thing to do. The pursuit, by the way, got caught up in the traffic jam I created, and the suspect was arrested a short distance from us after crashing the stolen police car.

Plaza Desk

The next week, I was off to swings. Policing on each shift is different; there are different people out, different crimes occurring, and each shift has a different culture and pace. I preferred the pace of swings to days. It started very busy and ended very busy, and shifts went by very fast. Day shift was traditionally slow in comparison; however, I noticed that when things got crazy on days, they tend to be very severe.

The downside to working swings was a rotating position at city hall. It was called the Plaza Desk. Each day, an officer had to cover it. It was a position that allowed the public access to the police. When officers were hurt, they might get the Plaza Desk for an extended period. Barring this, it was a rotation. I pulled the job for one week about every four to six months, depending on staffing.

The Plaza Desk was easy. You sat behind a glass partition, and people came in. They asked questions or wanted to report crimes. You had an administrative staff that would take the report from the citizen after you triaged it. When someone called dispatch and dispatch was not able to answer the question, they would transfer the call to you. People would want to know the legality of having a gun in their car, or how long until they had to get Nevada license plates, or general legal information.

If someone walked in and was reporting a crime, you would investigate it and figure out if a crime occurred. If a crime occurred, you would fill out a slip with the victim's name and the crime. Your support would come over from police records, which was in the same building; take the slip from you; and take the crime report.

When you are a cop and the general public can find you, it tends to attract crazy people. I had some crazy interactions at the Plaza Desk. The most memorable was a gentleman who came in, placed a felt bag of something on the counter, and began asking me mining law questions. I knew nothing about mining; however, there was a mini law library at the Plaza Desk. I began pulling books and looking up mining laws. He was a nice guy, and the conversation went from mining to precious metals. He then began asking me about laws regarding transporting radioactive material.

Now my interest had been piqued. "What's in the bag?" I asked.

This man, whom I had been speaking with for about thirty minutes about mining, gold, and silver, told me what was in the bag. He had exposed the rocks in the bag to radiation. He had driven the rocks to Las Vegas from a mine in northern Nevada. There were rocks four feet from me, in a felt bag, that were radioactive.

Well, the academy does not train for this. We evacuated city hall, police records, and various other businesses. The hazardous materials team responded and took the stupid rocks. They turned out to be pyrite (fool's gold) and were in fact slightly radioactive.

On Patrol

While I worked through the next few years, I gained quite a bit of experience. I was also training. I found that training new officers is a very different experience from being a trainee. When you are in training, you are moving at the only speed you know. You think you're moving fast; however, you are moving at a mind-numbingly slow pace. I had some great trainees and some terrible trainees.

Working as a patrol cop in downtown Las Vegas, you really do see it all, countless suicides, homicides, sexual assaults, all the way down to a beer theft. I remember when a fifteen-year-old boy jumped off of a very tall tower in downtown Las Vegas and killed himself, and when we pulled an eighteen-month-old baby out of a bathtub dead. Things move very fast, and you experience a lot of things that a normal human being was never meant to deal with, at least not every day. Cops see it all, and it's rough, even though they may not admit it.

Late into a shift, I was stopped at a stop sign. I was in a small residential area of downtown Las Vegas. It was around midnight and there were no cars around me, but something told me not to move.

After about two minutes, I saw a young woman walking toward me. Like I explained before, you develop a very adept sense of finding bad things. Sometimes you can explain later how you knew; other times, you go your entire life and have no idea how you knew. You will see how this occurs repeatedly in my stories.

I watched her for about fifteen seconds. I then saw the only other person on the street, a man, walking very quickly toward her. My headlights were on, so he knew I was a car, just not a police car. He walked up to her and quite literally snatched her purse from her shoulder and began running toward me. After about five seconds of sheer shock, I turned on my overhead lights and got out of my car. He ran. Quick tip: If you are in a police car and the guy runs, just drive after him. Don't run unless you have to.

I chased him for about half a block, and he jumped over a fence. As I was going over the fence, he was climbing up a fire-escape ladder. I heard my friends coming to help me, so onto the roof of an apartment building I headed. When I topped the ladder, he and I were now alone on a flat roof that was about forty feet by forty feet.

I did not want to fight this guy two stories off the ground. I started telling him to lay down. As a lot of cops showed up, he was contemplating either jumping or pushing me off and then jumping. The problem with committing a crime at midnight is you have late swing shift working and early graveyard working. That is a lot of cops. As he and I were having our exchange, about ten more cops were topping the ladder. Realizing he was trapped, he did what trapped people do.

When it comes to suspect psychology and suspects fleeing police, I've noticed that when someone is running on foot or in a vehicle from the police, they develop a narrow tunnel vision. This tunnel vision only allows them to perceive a very small aspect of the world. When people are in flight, all they can process is the flight. Therefore, they have no initial remorse when they run that red light and kill a family, fleeing in a car from the police. They always say the same stupid lie when you ask why they ran, so I just stopped asking.

For those of you who don't know, their answer is, "I was scared." I really wish someone would just admit, "I thought I could get away."

When people run, they are not trained for that activity, so they almost always behave in a very predictable way. Interestingly, when in flight, suspects will feel very comfortable turning right. Studies have been done to find out why. Some people falsely believe that it is because of a person's dominant hand. I see no evidence of this. Whether in a car or on foot, left or right-handed, there will be a lot of right turns. If you force them to turn left by cutting off the right option, they tend to stop running and hide. I think it may have something to do with the fact that it is easy to turn right in a vehicle at an intersection, well, easier than turning left, that is. Perhaps this becomes ingrained into you at some subconscious level, I really don't know.

The second thing is that when people have convinced themselves that they are going to die, or that they are going to kill you to get away, they get a very strange look in their eyes. When you have someone trapped, and they decide they are going to pull out a gun, knowing they will be shot, they have a thousand-yard stare. They are looking at you, but straight through you.

If you ever see anyone with this look, be very careful. It's about to get very dangerous. They stare through you and completely ignore you. I was once told that it is a mechanism of them dehumanizing the cop in case they kill the cop. I don't know if that is true. This thousand-yard stare usually occurs when the suspect is trapped and assumes there is no way out.

Back to the roof. I was talking to the guy, and it happened. He stopped talking and began staring straight through me. Up to this point, I had never seen the look, but I had been trained to see it. Once I saw it, I immediately knew what it was. Everyone on the roof knew what was coming. He ran. I spun my body 45 degrees, and he went straight past me. Not anticipating this, he had too much speed built up, and he just about went over the roof. The only thing that stopped him was a partner of mine, Jake Carrington, who quite literally grabbed the guy by the waist and stopped him from going over. We all grabbed Jake and pulled the two back onto the roof.

Then the suspect started to fight, so much so that he was injured. We called for medical help, and we had a hell of a time getting him down from the roof. We ended up sandwiching him between two backboards and lowering him down using rappelling rope.

Drunk Driving

I learned that DUI was a serious problem. Too many people drive impaired. It is interesting that people will argue with the police about speeding tickets or a DUI arrest with incredible passion. Perhaps it is the insurance ramifications, or societal pressure. Which is puzzling because these cases are by far the easiest to prove. Drunk drivers are everywhere; just pay attention.

I found that drunk drivers would follow similar behavioral patterns. Headlights are challenging, apparently, on during the day, off at night. Inside secret: most new cops fear DUI arrests. It stems from the number of times you are taught about defense attorneys beating your case. DUI is such a simple crime, with strict statutes. However, attorneys fight you tooth and nail to win. They fight tooth and nail to establish you made some very minor error in your paperwork to illustrate your absolute incompetence. I think it's a perfect storm. Legislatures pass very strict DUI laws to attempt to dissuade you from doing it. However little thought is given to the cop who must enforce the law. A quality DUI arrest contains a lot of observational and scientific data, as well as a large amount of documentation.

Driving drunk kills people. It's a very tragic and avoidable crime. However, when the police start aggressively enforcing it and the wrong person is arrested, or a person with money is arrested. This creates an environment for defense attorneys to develop strategies to overcharge clients and find loopholes or small errors as ammunition to have the case dismissed. There are entire law firms dedicated to nothing except DUI defense, and they are good.

Vehicle Pursuit

One evening, I saw a vehicle driving with its headlights off, and it ran a stop sign. I initiated a vehicle stop. It was dark and just after seven p.m. The driver failed to stop. This was the first of dozens of vehicle pursuits I was involved in during my career. The driver led me on a chase across Las Vegas. Four minutes of a vehicle pursuit is an eternity.

For anyone reading this who is under the illusion that a vehicle pursuit is exciting and fun, well … it is. Laws and policies have changed, mostly based on the actions of suspects. As these events occurred in the early 2000s, there was a trend, and the trend was very similar to what we saw in 2020 and 2021. Police were being blamed for actions that were only partially under their control. As I have explained, policing is an evolving career. As vehicle pursuits began to be televised and shared on social media questions were being asked. The public correctly was questioning the reasons innocent members of the public were being murdered. Stolen vehicle or other offences were being pursued by police. Suspects were driving vehicles at speeds that were far beyond their capability to control. Suspects would run a stop sign or a red light killing an innocent citizen, or family.

When suspects nationwide led police officers on those high-speed, very dangerous pursuits, the news media was attracted to these events like it was a drug addiction. Media helicopters getting in the way of police helicopters was common.

The media was not following the pursuit out of a fascination with high-speed driving. The media wanted what they always want: tragedy. They craved carnage and crashed cars. When this occurred, the blame was firmly placed on the head of the police officer. As we saw in 2021 and 2022 the police were being held accountable for the deaths caused by suspects. The term they used was that the officer was "pushing" the suspect. As technology grew and more of these events were televised, it became clear that tragedy was occurring. The suspects in these events would run a red light or stop sign and crash into a car, killing innocent citizens.

Laws and policies did what they could to remove the liability of pursuit coupled with the need to stop negative media attention. To be fair culpability was shared by both parties. The suspect fleeing was the greatest threat. However, the police had failed to use the technology that was available to us to prevent the pursuit. Vehicle pursuits have now been reduced to all but only the most heinous criminals. Most agencies forbid a pursuit unless the suspect is wanted for a violent felony. Was this progress? Well, it was some progress, but I don't know if it was the correct progress. Was there a way to stop innocent people from violently dying while holding the violators accountable? I don't know.

Police agencies began to use GPS tracking technologies, CCTV and helicopters to either stop the pursuit or end it as quickly as possible. If suspect drivers were identified there was little need to pursue. Police agencies began to realize that physically pursuing a suspect in a vehicle should be limited to only those circumstances where the suspect needed to be physically stopped immediately. Other than that, other options were explored. Some examples may help the reader understand. If your car was stolen by a relative or friend, and police attempted to stop the car. There is little reason to initiate a vehicle pursuit. Assumably the vehicle is insured, and in this case it is realistic to assume that the victim is unlikely to actually prosecute a relative or friend, so why put innocent peoples lives in danger? Contrast this with a truly dangerous person. A gang member who is armed and has carjacked a vehicle. They are clearly a threat to society, perhaps they injured a victim, and further, maybe they are shooting at the police as they respond. The latter person must be stopped to prevent loss of life.

Back to my first pursuit. The driver of that pickup truck who ran a stop sign led me on a short pursuit at one point throwing the contents of his methamphetamine lab out of his window at me. As we drove, speeds increased to 70 to 80 miles per hour. We blasted through red light after red light. The problem was, I was leaving my area and entering the Southeast Station area. This is problematic, because back then, we only had analog radios. The people on my channel were all in downtown Las Vegas, as I was tearing through the southeastern portion of the city.

During vehicle pursuits, I have found that violators run, or rather drive, to one of two destinations. The first and most common is their home. Where else do you flee to when you are in danger? You go home. The second, and less common, is the absolute middle of nowhere. I have chased cars miles out of Las Vegas. Once drivers realized we were not going to simply turn around, they often would intentionally crash their car and surrender.

In this case, he drove home. The driver parked in front of his house and ran into a shed in his backyard. I took him to jail and moved on.

The next part of the story is the hardest to believe. About six years later, I was involved in another vehicle pursuit. As we drove through the streets of Las Vegas, for whatever offence I can't remember, I began to recognize the streets. We pulled up to the same house, but he did not run into the shed this time; he ran into the house. It was the son of the first man I ever chased in a vehicle, years prior. Clark County is a county of two million citizens, but that day it seemed very small.

While we are talking about vehicle pursuits, looking back, I can tell you how horrendously dangerous they are. I had many terminate miles out of Las Vegas; some terminated after a vehicle crash. One terminated because the fourteen-year-old boy who was driving the stolen car crashed into the security guard hut at the entrance to his apartment complex. Movies make these events look fun, and they are to a point, but people do die as a result.

Homicide Suspects

In 2004, it seemed like a string of homicide suspects would come to Las Vegas to hide, more specifically Fremont Street. It was very strange, and not uncommon to literally stumble across a homicide suspect who was a fugitive from somewhere. I think the allure was the plethora of anonymous hotels on Fremont Street back then that would lease daily, weekly, or monthly to anyone with cash. I personally contacted about twenty in the period of one year.

One time, I was driving to lunch and saw a guy run across the road, crossing out of the crosswalk. Heading to lunch, usually I would just ignore this. Cops don't control a lot. They don't control the calls they go on, they don't control the suspect's actions, and they don't control when they must stay late in their shift. They do control lunch, unless they are called off it.

Heading to lunch, I would rarely act on anything I saw, unless it was serious. However, I got that feeling I had to stop this guy. I stopped him and ran a records check on him. He was wanted for a homicide, attempted homicide, and some firearms violations. The crimes occurred in the Midwest. I arrested him, and he was extradited back to stand trial for his crimes.

Later that month, a triple homicide had occurred somewhere in California, and the suspect had called his mother from a Las Vegas hotel. A team was set up to surveil the hotel. I knew about the surveillance, and I was parked around the corner, in a local apartment complex. It was pouring rain, and I kept reminding myself that if something happened, my car would have limited traction. It rains very little in Las Vegas, and as a result, when it does, the roads become very slick from the various automotive fluids that have spilled on the road over the dry months.

Just like clockwork, the radio screamed, "Shots fired, officer down!" Fortunately, this was only the first time I was involved with an officer being shot; unfortunately, it would not be my last, and there were too many to count or write about.

I pulled into the parking lot where the shooting occurred. The team's sergeant had been shot in the hand, and they had shot and killed the suspect. The suspect had walked out of the hotel room, the team had identified themselves, and he had produced a pistol. He got one shot off that hit the sergeant, then he was promptly shot several times by the cops.

I arrived and helped with the scene and getting the ambulance in. The ambulance started treating the sergeant, then one of them pointed to the suspect, who was face down with a hood over his head rain pouring down and a pistol two feet from his hand, and asked, "What about him?"

It was eerie as the rain poured and mixed with the suspect's blood. I said, "He's dead." He was very dead.

The ambulance staff loaded up the ambulance with the shot sergeant, and as we do, we stopped all traffic from our location to the trauma center. I was the escort car. I pulled in front of the ambulance. Before we left I asked the ambulance driver.

"You are going *code three?*" I asked. *Code three* was cop talk for lights and siren.

He said, "He's only shot on the hand."

Understand something: It doesn't matter where you are shot. It can kill you. There is no shoot-to-wound nonsense. I have seen people die from being shot in the foot and live being shot in the head.

I responded to Mr. Ambulance Driver, "Oh, OK. Well, either you turn on that siren when we leave, or when we get to the hospital, *you* will need to go in."

The siren went on, and away we went. He wasn't a bad guy, just a little overwhelmed I think.

A short time after this, another homicide suspect was known to be hiding on Fremont Street somewhere. He had killed his mother-in-law and his wife. Fremont Street is a very long street, and it was, at the time, full of hotels. The homicide happened in another state, but we had information that the suspect was in the area.

A detective took the initiative to check every hotel, an impossible task. However, when he checked the third hotel, he found the suspect checked in. We set up a perimeter, and the suspect refused to come out. SWAT was called, and the suspect, an Asian male, began to make various demands.

I was able to set up a surveillance position on a nearby rooftop with other officers. SWAT placed an explosive breach on the front door of the room. Explosive breaching is a very good tool for removing the front door. It also has a great psychological effect. When suspects see their front door blown off, it tends to remove a sense of security and reduces the likelihood they will remain barricaded. After the smoke cleared from the door being blown off, I watched him as, sitting at the foot of his bed. He was holding a sword to his chest. I watched as he impaled himself with a sword. SWAT moved in; however, he was dead.

A short time later, I took a transfer to work back on the historic west side of Las Vegas. I needed weekdays off, more specifically Tuesday, Wednesday, and Thursdays. We worked four, ten hour shifts at the time. I wanted to continue to train, so I looked for squads that were training teams. At the time there was only one squad of FTOs with those days off, and it was on the west side. When I transferred, it was 2006. I was placed on a squad that I can say today was the best squad I ever worked on. It was a group of fearless cops who were led by a great chain of command. Today, there is only one of them left. The rest of us have retired, and two died.

The pace on the west side in 2006 was not something I was used to. It was the dawn of the hybrid gang era, and the westside was incredibly violent. The violence was so severe, you were able to track the shootings and anticipate when the next one would occur. Many times, while putting up crime scene tape on one homicide, you heard the shots of the retaliation shooting blocks away.

The hybrid gang was a Las Vegas phenomenon at first. As various politicians tried to solve the violence on the west side, they came up with an idea to demolish various government housing developments. In theory, if the complex is violent, and it was demolished, there was no more violence. In theory. In fact, the gangsters just move to new neighborhoods and set up new gangs. These new gangs were the hybrid gangs.

Gangsters who were part of one gang and were displaced to another high school would clique up with other groups and form more gangs. Feuding gang members would move and then join each other. Crime displacement is only a solution in a politician's eye. Economics played a huge part in the crime and the incredible violence I saw in 2006.

In 2005, the economy was good. Because of this, home ownership in Las Vegas was high. As a by-product, apartment complexes' occupancy rates dipped to below 50 percent in some cases. To increase profit, some turned into condo complexes, selling units individually. Others lowered rent and began accepting HUD vouchers. Further, I found that when the economy was good, there were far more drugs on the streets, which led to more violence.

I worked the area for a few months and began to get used to it again. I had worked in this area in phase two of my field training. I was acquainted with a lot of the neighborhood gang members. The violence was escalating, and it was out of control. There was so much violence the department was looking for solutions. However, other than the sheriff, political leaders were disinterested in acting.

Block Party

Memorial Day of 2006 was a terribly violent day. Early in my shift, I drove down a neighborhood street and saw that it was blocked off for a party. I walked up and spoke with some of the partiers, and they produced a permit to have their block party. The city had issued them a permit. The city had issued a permit for a block party during one of the most violent summers I ever saw, in an area known for violent gang activity. Who was having the party? A local car club. Car clubs really run the gamut from legitimate car enthusiasts to just plain thugs with cars.

I called my sergeant, Dennis Borders. He and I parked about a hundred yards from the event, just to make sure nothing happened. The crowd began to grow and grow. I looked toward the crowd and estimated it was about a thousand people, all gathered on a residential, two-lane street about one hundred and fifty yards in length.

We both had a bad feeling about the event. My sergeant called the rest of our squad, and they were on the way. While they were headed to us, Dennis and I heard the shots, about twenty in total. I grabbed my shotgun, and we both headed into the crowd.

After the shooting, the crowd began to run from the shots, and Dennis and I were running toward them. The sea of people made it almost impossible to make it to the center of the crowd. Fighting a sea of people is exhausting. Dennis took the south sidewalk, and I took the north as we ran, pushing, shoving, and yes, punching our way to the middle of the crowd. This is a small residential street, it seemed that we were never going to make it to the center of the shooting. As we made progress, I could smell recently discharged shots, and knew we were headed into a disaster. When we got to the middle of the crowd, we were greeted by three bodies on the ground.

Dennis and I tried to start rendering aid. However, the crowd, realizing the shots had stopped, began returning. They completely cut Dennis and I off from the street. The rest of our squad arrived, but they were unable to get to us because of the crowd.

On one end, a cop ran into another person who was bleeding to death from being shot in the leg, and on the other end another cop ran into a shooting suspect, who the crowd was turning on. As this occurred, ambulances began to arrive and leave with numerous victims who had made it to the exterior of the crowd.

The problem was, no one could get to us. The crowd saw ambulances coming and going and thought that we were stopping the ambulances from coming in to treat the three bodies. We were separated and cut off. Dennis and I were in the center of the crowd. We were surrounded by hundreds of angry and scared people. There were so many of them that there was no way to get to us, we were simply cut off. The crowd became violent, and the medical personnel refused to respond. Ambulances and firefighters will not enter an active scene. Jurisdictions differ, however most fire fighters and paramedics are bound by policies that forbid them from responding to active criminal scenes until the police deem it safe. This is great in theory, but as this incident shows, at times that assurance cannot be given.

As the crowd began to hurl both insults, bottles, and other items at Dennis and me, we realized we were in trouble. We tried to call for help, but the crowd was so loud that our radio traffic was not understood. The crowd began to assume the ambulances leaving was race-based, so they were further incited. You can see how the three victims did not have to bleed to death.

As the crowd became more violent, Dennis tried to start treatment on the three-shot people. This further enraged the crowd, who thought we were now intentionally keeping medical staff away. I was convinced Dennis and I were not leaving the area alive. The crowd began to attack us, some by punching, others by throwing bottles and garbage. As the mob mentality grew the crows began to feed on its won furry. Dennis and I knew that we were likely going to be injured, but we were willing to accept this, as long as we could provide some aid. We took turns in attempting to provide aid to the shooting victims, while the other fought the crowd back.

I took my shotgun, gripped it like a baseball bat (not an academy trained technique), and began swinging at people. I hit many, but they just kept coming. Dennis had returned to my side, he had realized that rendering aid was no longer and option and survival was our goal; he then said, "I don't care what you do, keep them back." I'm not sure what he thought I was doing. We were convinced the crowd was going to kill us. We were unable to maintain our perimeter around the three bodies because the crowd was uncontrollable. The three shot people were dying because of the crowd.

As I was swinging for the fences, and Dennis was preparing to start shooting people who got too close. It was our last stand, and if we were going to die, we had to get medical aid to the fallen citizens first. I looked past the crowd and saw a very strange thing, I saw a man wearing all blue who had what looked like a sword. He had jumped over a fence and was working his way toward us. The funny thing was, the crowd was moving as he approached them from their rear. As he walked up to people from behind, they appeared to just know he was there and would jump out of his way.

As this mysterious man in blue got closer, I saw who he was. He was a police officer from the North Las Vegas Police Department, and in his hand was not a sword but an AR15 that he was holding by the barrel, like a bat and swinging into people to get to us. Word had gotten out that two cops were cut off and being overrun. Law enforcement from many different agencies were headed to us to help. This North Las Vegas cop was on a mission to make it to us.

By the time the AR15-wielding officer was about ten yards from us, an older gang member walked up to me very calmly and asked why the ambulances were leaving. I told him because the crowd was too violent, and firefighters and ambulance drivers will not enter an active crime scene until they deem it safe. Once I told him this, a very strange thing happened. He pointed away, and the main instigators of the crowd turned around and left.

As about a hundred cops and a host of other law enforcement personnel, including parole and probation officers from various departments, arrived on the scene, the crowd began to disperse. Dennis and I began to try and render aid, however, the three people who were down were now long dead. The tragedy of that event is that three people died, eight were shot, and as of this writing in 2021, no one has ever been brought to justice. This is due to many factors, most importantly uncooperative witnesses.

One of the shooters was a then sixteen-year-old child, whose name we will say was Aaron Walker. Over the remaining fifteen years of my career, I was aware of several gang-related homicides that Aaron was involved in; however, he has never been to trial, and I don't think he ever will.

I learned later that the shooting occurred due to a handful of hybrid gang members being asked to leave the car club event. They climbed onto rooftops and shot into the crowd from an elevated position. They were climbing down from the roofs as Dennis and I arrived. Dennis and I received medals for the event; however, I would trade the medal on my wall for those three lost lives in a second.

Disturbance Call

Time went by, and I began to master my trade. I developed patterns and ways of getting things done. With time comes experience, and with experience comes wisdom. I developed very strong friendships with the members of that team. We had all literally saved each other's lives on so many occasions. These events don't make the news, and go largely unknown, but I promise they occur.

One of the members of the team was an officer named Dave Prichard. Dave died some time ago, but my time working with him was very memorable. He was a great cop and a good friend. He was injured in a car accident while working, and he had severely hurt his shoulder. A woman turned left right in front of him. Dave tried to swerve to not hit her car, which caused him to hit an entrance marque to a business.

After that event, Dave went on for a few years, struggling to find help for his shoulder. He fought with workman's compensation, and at the end of a yearlong battle, he died of an accidental overdose of pain medication. Cops have two threats: the streets and their own agencies. Just as any of us will have administrative battles with out employer, cops are the same. They fight the same battles over overtime, workers compensation injuries and the like. It is just that cops place themselves in high liability situations daily, and in addition to this they also have to fight their employers, it is tragic.

I was dispatched to help Dave on a disturbance call in the courtyard of a local apartment complex. He hadn't been answering the radio, which was strange for him. He was very good at his job, and this was odd. I found his car, but I could not find him.

I began calling him on the radio and walking around the complex. I turned a corner and saw Dave on his back being attacked by a single suspect. Dave was in great shape at that time, so I was confused, and I ran closer to see why he wasn't fighting. He looked like he was just shielding himself from punches. Then I saw why: the suspect had disengaged all of Dave's retentions on his holster, and the only thing holding the pistol in the holster was friction and Dave's hand.

I was about twenty yards from them, but I did not dare shoot, as I was scared. If the two moved, the bullet would hit Dave. I then turned on the jets. I was at a full sprint. I got to about two feet from the two and kicked the suspect as hard as I could in the head. Dave resecured his pistol, and we handcuffed the guy.

For those of you who just freaked out, suspects do not take cops' guns to add to their collection. They take guns to kill the cop. Remember the tunnel vision: anything to get away is permissible to them.

West Side Stories

Dave's best friend was on the team, Dave also, Dave Horne. He and I also became close. I could not write down all our stories, so I will just cover the highlights.

In one event, I was dispatched to a stabbed man. I knew that Dave was on the way. I arrived and saw the victim on the ground. I exited my car and walked up to him.

This guy, who literally had a knife sticking out of his side, got up and ran from me. I am chasing a guy whose right hand is holding a knife, but the blade was inside his body. We ran around a corner, and Dave was driving toward us.

When the guy saw Dave, he panicked. Dave brought his car to a ninety-degree skid as the guy attempted to run further, when Dave's car stopped, he was crashed into a wall and pinned the guy against a wall, between the front push bumpers of his car. There is no way he could have repeated this in a million years. It was amazing.

Before I tell you the next story, I must explain that times have changed. What we did in this event was good in 2007, but now it would be seen as reckless.

A fourteen-year-old boy had called 911. He was hiding in a closet of his parents' bedroom; he told the call-taker that gang members had taken his family hostage and had them tied up in the living room. We all arrived pretty much at the same time as the entire squad, with our trainees. The apartment was a second-floor unit, and we lined up on the ground floor to formulate a plan.

Before we could create a plan, one of the hostage-takers exited the apartment to come outside and smoke a cigarette, and he saw us. At that point, we were committed. We raced up the stairs. The first cop in the line grabbed our cigarette smoker, and I was number two in line.

I kicked in the front door, and we entered. Sure enough, there were four people duct-taped and lying face-down on the floor. I saw one suspect who had a pistol run into a bathroom; he must have misjudged how close I was. He ran into the bathroom and dropped his pistol. He then turned around just in time for me to apply a well-placed elbow to his jaw. The kidnappers were tried and convicted sometime later. We all received a medal for the event. However, today as policing has changed, forcing entry under these circumstances may be seen as reckless.

Trainees

As we all worked together, we began to be a very effective team. We were able to read each other and work off each other's movements. It is a skill that only repetition creates.

We were all about the same tenure and were training new cops. We each had a specialty. I always got the problem trainees; those who looked unlikely to graduate the program were sent to me. I gave them everything I had to get them to graduate. Sometimes I was successful, but sometimes I was unable to save them.

On a particular day, I had a day-one trainee straight out of the academy. As I drove him around, I explained which gangs controlled which streets. He confided in me that he had been raised in a very protective atmosphere. I felt his naivety as we drove around.

Before I tell you the story, his name was Lawrence Lunas, and Lawrence went on to be a great cop and was promoted to sergeant some years later.

As we drove around, I saw a known PCP-user cross the road between cars out of a crosswalk. I stopped him to give my new trainee his first stop. But as soon as I initiated the stop, the suspect ran. Knowing my day-one trainee had no idea where he was, I chased the suspect. I was giving radio traffic to get help more to my trainee than to me. My trainee had no idea where he was or what he was doing.

The suspect ran one block straight and one block east. I grabbed him as he tried to enter a fast food restaurant. We took him to jail, and I gave my trainee the best first-day story ever.

As the violence escalated, I saw a lot of people die. Some gang members, some bystanders, some adults, some children. As 2008 approached, one night I was dispatched to a shooting. I arrived and found a local drug addict was shot in the leg, with a particularly unusual caliber, unusual for gang members, anyway. He was shot by a very unusual hunting caliber that I had not only never seen at work, but I had never seen that caliber ever up to that day. He survived the shooting, and things went on as they do.

About a week later, it was late, around midnight, I had a trainee who was about halfway through the program with me. We were driving through a neighborhood run by a local gang set, about a block from the shooting I just told you about. As we drove slowly, I saw five teenage boys crossing between cars out of a crosswalk, one with a rifle over his shoulder (this is a clue).

My trainee was driving, and he stopped the group, but the kid with the rifle ran. He was on my side, so I chased him.

Imagine this: You are running through a known gang-infested area, at night. It is poorly lit. The area is littered with clotheslines at neck height. The guy you're chasing has a rifle, and your trainee is alone.

I chased this guy for about an eighth of a mile. He ran in one big circle. Every time we turned a corner, he attempted to work the rifle action to get a shot off at me, but he just could not manipulate it. I found out later he was drunk.

I finally was very tired of running, and I heard that officers had gotten to my trainee. I got to within twenty feet of the suspect and said in a very calm tone, "I'm going to shoot you." How do I know I said that? I was recorded on the radio; I had depressed the button when I said it.

He later said it was something about my tone that made him stop. He said that because I was not yelling, he thought I was crazy. Whatever helps him; he stopped, held that rifle above his head for a second, and then dropped it to the ground.

In these scenarios, you must be tactically sound. Actions are always faster than reactions, and changing speed or direction takes a lot of time. Had I taken the time to stop running and adjust my tactics, he would have been at a huge advantage, as these actions would have taken me some time. Remember he was standing over a presumably loaded hunting rifle, and had, up to this point attempted to kill me. I had no time to stop. I just kept running, pulled out my taser, and blasted the kid. As he fell, I ran right over him and kicked the rifle like a field goal. I inspected the rifle and found it to be of the unusual caliber used during the other shooting. It was a short time later that this suspect was linked to that shooting.

I had a particularly difficult trainee one time. He was assigned to me because our sergeant was worried he was not going to graduate from the program. He was very far behind, so much so that when we went to calls that were even remotely dangerous, I would leave him in the car.

Around this time, there was a series of robberies at local pharmacies. We received a call of a man at a local pharmacy who was threatening the pharmacist. We arrived at the pharmacy, and we walked in. This was a typical commercial pharmacy with aisles and the actual pharmacy counter in the back.

When I walked into the store, I heard the argument. Being concerned that my trainee would create more danger, I told him to wait at the front door in case the guy got past me. I walked back to the pharmacy counter and saw the suspect. He was indeed screaming and threatening the pharmacist.

My first goal was to get the guy's attention onto me and away from the pharmacist. This proved very easy, because as soon as he saw me, he ripped off his tank top and said, "Let's fight." He wasn't necessarily very tall, but he was obviously very strong. He was very muscular, and his skin seemed to be very thin because of his abnormally large muscles.

As I closed the distance, the fight was on. We fought, and it went to the ground. I was able to get back on my feet, and as he attempted to stand up, I tried to keep him down. However, the guy was very strong. He basically did a push-up and launched me backward into a display of over-the-counter pill bottles. The display exploded, and now we were fighting and falling over bottles and pills all over the floor.

At one point, I was able to get above him, and he started to curl his arms under his body like a turtle. I wasn't sure if he was reaching for a gun or a knife, or just preventing me from handcuffing him. I told him several times to put his hands behind his back, and he just kept hiding them.

I was able to grab his left elbow, and I started hitting him in his left shoulder with my baton. The thing is, when you're in this type of fight, your senses are dull. I did not realize what was occurring, so I will not tell you yet either.

I hit him once, pulled back, hit him twice, three times, then four. I then realized the baton was not working. He was expecting a fifth baton hit, so I put it away, partially stood up, and deployed my taser. He was not wearing a shirt, so the thing worked. I must tell you, in my experience, tasers work about 50 percent of the time.

Dennis arrived and we handcuffed the guy. As I began to calm down, I noticed all the blood. There was blood everywhere.

Blood patterns are very predictable, and you can tell a lot about what happened based on the blood pattern. You can tell the direction a bleeding person was moving, and you can tell when blood is transferred to a wall by a hand, foot, or hair. You can also establish how a person was hit with a weapon based on a blood pattern called *cast off*.

Cast off occurs when you hit or stab a bleeding person, and you swing back or up for another hit. When you stop your upward or backward movement and adjust to the forward motion to make your second strike, some of the blood that was on your fist, knife, or say, baton is cast off onto walls and ceilings.

I saw cast off blood all over the ceiling of the pharmacy. However, I wasn't injured. I then realized that each time I hit the guy with the baton, his skin split wide open and bled a lot. We spoke with the suspect, and his demeanor changed significantly when he was under control. He was actually very nice and cordial.

He told me that he was on a twelve-month steroid cycle and had gained a significant amount of muscle mass. He was concerned because he noticed his skin was becoming very thin and like paper, almost like an elderly person's skin. He was concerned that his muscle growth would inhibit his ability to fight, so he went to the pharmacy and began threatening the pharmacist in the hope someone would call the police. He knew when the police arrived, they would fight him. It was very strange.

This last story leads me to a great point: don't use the police to fight you or kill you. If your plan is to produce a gun to get shot by police, or you decide to fight because you know the police will defend the weak or themselves, you are a coward. Police officers are human beings. When you dehumanize the police and attempt to force their hands, you propagate this 2021 idea that police are the enemy or a corrupted tool of the government. Please just stop. When cops are killed, some people dismiss it as a job hazard. Using the police to facilitate suicide or a fight, does nothing but create further problems.

I went to church with a lady who was telling a story about her brother. He was in prison for killing a police officer in Northern Nevada. She went into detail on how he robbed a bank and shot at a clerk, but she breezed over the killing of a police officer, saying, "Then he killed some policeman and went to prison." When cops die, they leave behind a family. Their lives really do matter. It's not simply a job hazard. When police are killed, it is symbolic of a comp0lete disregard of our societal norms. Never dismiss these actions as necessary, when a cop is murdered it is an attack on our very freedom itself.

Kids and Guns

Over this incredibly violent period, there were several times I came very close to shooting someone to protect myself or someone else. There are just too many stories to tell. I had trainees freeze when suspects produced guns, and gang members who pointed a gun thinking we would stop chasing them. However, the absolute closest I ever got was the time I almost shot a twelve-year-old boy.

Someone called the police to report a child pointing a pistol at passing cars. I arrived about fifty yards from the kid and walked up to him from behind. It was dusk. I did not see a gun, but there was very little light.

I got about twenty yards from him; I was standing behind a block wall that separated one front yard from another. It was about four feet tall. I stopped behind the wall, using it as cover, and pulled out my pistol. I told the kid I was the police and not to turn around, and to put his hands above his head. He then turned around very slowly to his left, turning counterclockwise. His right hand was out of view.

He almost completed his turn and put an obvious pistol in his waistband. His hands were empty when he faced me. At twenty yards, there was no way I would miss shooting the kid, so I knew I would have the tactical advantage, as his pistol was now in his waistband.

He wouldn't put his hands up, no matter how many times I asked him to. He then very slightly tilted his head and began staring at me. He was looking directly through me. He was looking at me, but he did not see me. His brain was in neutral as he prepared to die.

I gave him several directions to turn away from me and place his hands up. He was not hearing me. I lowered my scream to a speaking level and asked him to put his hands up. He did. Now his hands were above his head, and I could see what looked like his pistol in his waistband. The problem was it was dusk, and the ambient light was not enough for me to see it clearly. I heard the sirens headed to me.

Then things got strange. His right hand began to slowly drop. I have spoken to many suspects over the years. I have noticed a pattern. Gang members, typically Black and Hispanic gang members, have a strange idea about possessing a pistol. When they are encountered by law enforcement, they want to separate themselves from the pistol. Even when they are told not to reach for their gun, they do. They reach for it, grab it, and usually throw it.

I asked one, after this happened for at least the dozenth time, and he told me that if he was not in possession of it, we, the police, could not shoot him. However, when I encountered White and Asian gang members, they only reached for their pistol when they planned on shooting the officer with it. It is a very strange pattern I noticed.

Once the kid's hands passed his ear, I told him to not reach for the gun and put his hands on his head, or I would shoot him. His hands lowered to his shoulder. I told him again to stop. His hands then began working their way down to his waist, and he grabbed the pistol.

I told him one last time that I was going to shoot and kill him. He wasn't listening. He started to lift the pistol from his waist. I processed what I was seeing, and I told myself that I did not want to kill this kid. I had a tactical advantage; I was behind a concrete block wall, my weapon was already pointed at him, and I knew I could get at least two rounds off in less than a second.

I then made a tactically poor choice. The correct thing to do would have been to shoot him, but I waited. I told myself that as soon as the barrel of the pistol cleared his belt, I would shoot. I removed every ounce of slack from the trigger and waited.

I was now convinced that I was going to shoot the kid. He lifted the pistol further, and I waited to shoot. As the middle portion of the barrel cleared his belt, I exhaled and prepared for the recoil of the shot I was going to fire.

Two things saved his life. First, the streetlights came on, and at the same time, some homeowner's lights reacted to dusk and turned on. When the lights turned on, my eyes adjusted, and I saw the top of the pistol slide. I immediately recognized it as a BB gun. I'd had the same toy as a child. It was black and had a spring-loaded slide. It wasn't very expensive or even very fun. It had a large dovetail at the rear of the slide. To operate the toy, you would pull back the slide and then push it forward, this would load a spring that would release with a trigger pull, shooting the BB.

I saw in this kid's waistband that same BB pistol I'd had as a kid. I jumped over the wall, causing the kid to release his grip on the toy, from surprise and I pushed him over into the grass.

I spoke with the kid's father about an hour later. His father lived a few blocks away. I told his dad the story, and I explained that I had come within a millisecond of killing his son. The father smiled and said, "Well, boys will be boys."

I had no idea how to react to that statement. Kids, teenage kids, and toy guns are a problem. When a cop sees a person with what looks like a pistol, and it is pointed or is in the process of potentially being pointed at someone, the cop must act. People often get very hung up on how quick police shoot, especially the media, but I never understood the obsession with how quick a cop shoots. If a cop arrives on a call, and exits his car, then someone points a gun at him, the cop can make two choices: die or to shoot. If cops all choose to die at these moments, there would be very few cops.

The media and law enforcement have an unusual relationship. They rely on each other quite a bit. If one news network will not air the new recruiting video, then we will go to another. Also, the media will publish their story with or without the police side of events. It is important for both the media and police to work together and not to be at odds. They both need each other; however, each still moves forward at its own pace. If police do not provide context, a reporter may interview a witness, or an alleged witness, to get a story. The police and media must work together to get their jobs done.

The media and the police are not enemies. They simply have different priorities. Further, with the advent of social media and the decline of print media, there is more pressure than ever to get a story out as soon as possible. Later in my career I would watch members of the media posting to social media during a press conference; rather then waiting for an editors approval. They are in fierce competition with each other, and with the police, for the story.

Posts like, "The officer shot the suspect only two seconds after the encounter" confuse me. Well, that means the cop is alive. Children, teenagers, and adults can shoot a gun; also, people who are shot can shoot a gun; further, people who are dying can shoot a gun. Death is terrible, and society and the media tend to place a suspect's life above the cop's, and further, they tend to even place blame on the cop.

If you don't point a gun at a cop, you likely won't be shot. If you point a gun at a cop, you will be shot, and you may die, and it's your fault. I noticed that most gang members have literally never been told how to interact with the police, and thus they react as they see in movies. If you do not tell your kids how to deal with the police, and they have police contact, you roll the dice. When parents avoid uncomfortable talks with their children, they risk their children learning life ending lessons.

One mother I met really managed this well. I was dispatched to a call of two teenage kids who were pointing guns at each other. It was in an area that was very violent, and it was known for its violent shootings. Various gangs were positioning for control of the area at that time.

My partner and I arrived, and we found the two sitting on a power box, the metal above-ground boxes that are about four feet square. We grabbed the kids and put them in handcuffs in front of my car. Neither had a gun. It was dark, so I began to look around.

Behind the power box were two replica pistols. The replicas were solid metal and had no moving parts. The kids admitted they were pointing them at each other. They both were sixteen and were cousins. It was past curfew, so I called their parents. Not the crime of the century.

When mother number one arrived, I was seated in my car. She saw both kids were still in handcuffs and asked why. I explained that I was going to release her kid to her, because it was past curfew. She asked why we stopped them, and I showed her one of the metal guns they had. She seemed fascinated by it; she looked at it and studied it very closely. Then she said, "It's heavy, not like a toy." I told her I thought that too, and that they were solid metal. She handed the toy back to me and asked if I would have it destroyed. I agreed, and the weight of the gun left her hand as it landed in mine.

Before I explain what happened next, let me mention that it is incredibly dangerous to speak with anyone while being seated in the police car. You should always get out of your car. Suspects can shoot or attack you when you are stationary in a vehicle. I should have gotten out of my car, I was lazy, it was a long night, I was tired, and I did not feel like getting out of the car again.

After handing me the toy gun, she closed my driver's door on me. I was momentarily trapped in my own car. She then launched herself forward, put her right foot on my left front tire, and jumped over the hood of my car. She tackled her handcuffed son to the ground and began literally punching him in the face.

It took me a second or two to process what I was seeing. I opened my door, jumped out of my car, and headed over to them. She was screaming at him that she was not going to lose a kid to the street, and something about his father who was either dead or in prison. This mom cared and was beating this emotion into her son. I pulled her off her crying teenage boy, took his handcuffs off, and the two left. I never saw the kid again.

Bad Things

I developed a reputation for finding bad things. I had a skill for finding guns and drugs, mostly by casting a large net. I pulled over thousands of cars. If they were normal taxpaying citizens, they went on their way. If they were felons, gang members, or general criminals, I pushed the issue. Normal people, I defined as people who were working and not committing crimes. Seems reasonable. When you arrest someone who is a serial armed robber for speeding, it is very hard for them to rob someone while sitting in the city jail. Thus, enforcing small crimes can prevent the larger ones. Even in casting large nets, sometimes things just fell on my lap, some fun, others tragic.

I was dispatched to a call of a three-year-old girl who was found face down in a septic tank. When I arrived, I found that there was a septic tank in the backyard, and the homeowner did not have a manhole cover for it, so over the manhole he had used a piece of plywood. His daughter moved the plywood, fell into it, and he froze.

The child was still face down in the tank when I got there. I laid on the ground and grabbed the child out of the open full septic tank by her shirt. Once I had her above ground, the fire department was there, and I literally handed her over to them. I began to prepare to scream at the dad for not doing anything, but then I heard the child crying. Crying means breathing, and breathing means not dead. Her crying broke my train of thought. No yelling, just a child neglect investigation.

Later that week, I was driving with a trainee. I was explaining something to him; I can't remember what it was. We pulled up to an intersection and saw absolute pandemonium. There were crashed cars, personal belongings, and various car parts scattered across the intersection.

I later found out a man was driving his wife somewhere. He became impatient as he approached a left turn. The vehicle that was in front of him was not moving fast enough for him, so he passed the car in the right lane, and made his left turn. He exited the left turn lane, entering the lane just to the right passing the car that was in front of him, then pulled back into the left turn lane and made his left turn. As he made that left turn, another car traveling at about 45 miles per hour had hit his car in the passenger door. His wife was unrestrained in the passenger seat and took the brunt of the impact.

When I got there, I saw him talking to his wife, who I found out later was long dead. I could only see one side of her face and head; she was half in and half out of the passenger door window. I felt for a pulse and could not feel anything. I then pulled her from the car. Her shirt pulled up, covering the side of her head I could not see.

I started chest compressions. I was at about compression fifteen when the fire truck showed up and the firefighters were screaming, "Stop CPR." Well, they are the paramedics, so I stopped. They were telling me to stop because they were able to see the side of her head I could not. It was gone, the entire right side of her upper head was missing, and most of her brain was also gone. It was tragic, no amount of CPR would help her; I don't know how her husband lived with that. He likely went to prison for killing his wife.

As time went on, my partners transferred out to different assignments and were replaced by new people. The team lost its chemistry. All great teams are temporary. Toward the end of my time on that squad, I was dispatched to a family disturbance in another gang-run complex, this one a Crip set. When I and some other officers arrived, we were greeted with a young woman, about twenty, who was holding a baby hostage. She had the baby by the neck, like a wrestler would, with her right arm around the baby's neck.

Another officer and I split her attention and began to fan out to either side of her. Once her attention came off the other officer and was on me, he reached out and snatched the baby; then when her attention switched to him, I swept her feet out from under her. To be fair, I could have been gentler, but I was worried about the baby.

When I kicked her feet out from under her, my foot pushed hers up to about waist level. I was expecting this and kept my balance; she did not, and she landed on her head. I thought I killed her. The sound was like someone dropping a melon on a sidewalk, a hollow thump.

I felt terrible for about three seconds. Then she opened her eyes and just said one thing: "OK, you are serious." She thought that she could hold the child hostage and we would simply leave.

Rapid Change

As 2008 ended, the violence was leveling out, and things were changing rapidly. I was the only person on the team from the 2005–2007 era, and things just weren't the same. A friend of mine transferred in, Braydon Clark, and he and I became close.

We were dispatched to an explosion at a local fast-food restaurant. A local drug addict had gone into the single-stall restroom. After closing the door, he had pulled out a can of butane and started to inhale it. After this failed to get him as high as he wanted, he pulled out his crack pipe and drew his lighter to it, igniting the lighter as well as an entire room of condensed butane fumes. The employees reported that a bomb had gone off. It wasn't quite a bomb, but it was an explosion nonetheless.

That night, I had a very bad cold, a fever, and a terrible sore throat. My wife had asked me to stop at a store on the way home to pick up a Christmas gift for our kids. Braydon and I had carpooled, and he was driving us home, so I asked if he would stop at the store after our shift. He did. It was December 7, 2008.

I purchased the toy, and we began to drive home. We were driving north on I-15 approaching a large hill. As we crested the hill, we both saw a car headed south in our lane. We were traveling at 80 miles per hour, and a vehicle was headed straight for us at about the same speed. I reached over to grab the steering wheel, fearing Braydon either had not seen the car or was not reacting. However, as I reached, I saw his hands move the wheel.

He was able to move us out of the car's path with about forty feet to spare. We were going interstate speeds, and so was the wrong-way driver. As our vehicle started to slide sideways at 70 miles per hour, I began to wonder how bad this would be. We spun around, hit a nearby desert hill, and flipped.

When the car flipped, it began to spin like a top. As it spun, my right hand was flung out right, breaking the passenger side window. Meanwhile, my left hand had been launched through the windshield by the airbag.

It was Friday, and our trunk was full of various police paraphernalia, including two rifles and uniforms, which were quickly scattered across the interstate. A passing nurse saw the incident and ran up to the car. I told her to call 911 and watch out for the rifles in the dark. She then asked me if the rifles were loaded. I was having a rough day, so I may have said, "What fucking difference does it make?" That was not a nice thing for me to say.

She saw the police equipment and told the operator we were cops, and the entire agency descended upon us.

Braydon had just regained consciousness and was not aware of what had happened. We were upside down, and I was drowning in blood that was running up my nose, which was broken, and from a head gash. I was able to release my seatbelt and roll into the back of the car. Then I could lay down with gravity and try not to die.

After I yelled at the nurse, I heard the mass of sirens headed to us. I waited and just tried to breathe. Breathing is hard with liquid in your lungs; don't try it. Nothing really hurt except my right hand. It felt like there were rocks pushed under my thumb nail. I began to focus on that pain to stay awake.

A few minutes later, an ambulance arrived. The car was upside down, and I was exhausted. A very young and cocky EMT squatted down and asked me if I could scoot toward him. I asked him, "Toward you?" He responded by asking me if I was deaf. I was having a rough night, so I let him have it. I started with insulting his patient care, and I think I ended my tirade by insulting his family.

As I was yelling at him, I watched a very large hand push the kid aside. The kid fell on his side, out of my sight. A very old, overweight, and tenured EMT squatted down and looked at me.

"Officer, forget him. Are you OK?" he asked.

"My thumb hurts?" I responded.

"OK, if you can move closer to me, I can look at it," he said.

I then rolled over to him, and before I could complete my roll, he had a backboard on me, a neck brace on me, and had me strapped to both. I looked up and said, "You lied to me." He just smiled.

I was placed in the ambulance, and I heard the siren turn on. I had been a cop long enough to know that if the ambulance is using its siren, it is either going to the call or it is coming from the call with someone in critical condition. I asked him how bad I was, and he told me I was in bad shape. I kept complaining about my thumb, but the EMT kept telling me there were no rocks under my nail. I finally asked him how he knew.

"Joe, your nails are gone," he said.

Well, that made sense.

I arrived at the trauma center and was treated by a doctor I had spoken to earlier that day, about the guy who blew himself up. He recognized me and started talking to me by name. He told me my right hand had serious friction burns, my left hand was severely lacerated, I had a broken nose and a split scalp, and he was sure I had at least one spinal fracture. I ended up having three broken vertebrae.

I spent about seventeen days in the ICU. I swear to you, it seemed like every cop in the nation came by. My squad had to post an officer in the waiting room to stop people from bothering me. My wife refused to leave the room, sleeping in those chairs they have in the hospital room for all seventeen days.

CHAPTER

15

Investigative Work

My injury had come as I was seven years in patrol. It had worsened my previous spinal injury. After a few months of learning to walk, I was temporarily placed in an investigative assignment while I recovered. I proofread search warrants and did various administrative work.

I was assigned to a sergeant who had a long history of investigating outlaw motorcycle gangs. We were assigned to a violent crime team; we would respond to violent events, relieve patrol, and take the cases to investigate them. Once I recovered, I was absorbed into the unit. My condition would steadily decline over the following years; however, I was committed to going back to work.

I ended up mostly investigating violent robberies and following a lot of bikers. I was assigned to that job for about eighteen months. I was able to develop in-depth investigative experience, and I was able to apply my patrol knowledge well. I was assigned some great cases. Some are more attractive than others. I was assigned to investigate a multimillion-dollar theft at a celebrity's home. He had died, and his entourage was looting his home. That was the case that got me noticed, as it was very high profile.

I then began to work robberies exclusively. The most complicated robbery I investigated was one that occurred in the victim's living room. He'd invited two prostitutes into his home. One of them produced a pistol, and they proceeded to rob him of some of his possessions. The problem was, he had no idea who they were, only that they were twins.

As I began to dig into it, I found a set of twins who frequented that apartment complex. They were identical, obviously the same birthday, the same last name. Their first names were identical except for one letter, and their Social Security numbers were one number apart from each other. It took me a while to find them and get them into a room.

It took me about four hours to interview them both and get enough information to place them in the victim's living room and identify who had the gun.

I was partnered with a former Marine, George Charney, who was also investigating robberies. I hated him at first, but I quickly grew to love him. He was the best investigator I ever met. I almost couldn't keep up with him; his mind was just built for long-term investigations. I will demonstrate that in a little bit. He was so dedicated that I had to really step up my game to keep up.

Myspace was relatively new then, and people were posting their exploits all over it. George was working a robbery event where some vintage shoes were stolen. He spent days scouring Myspace geographically, looking for anything. Police have various investigative databases, including credit agencies, advanced social media filters, and so much more. I thought he was wasting his time; at the time we really did not know a lot about social media. Then he found a photograph of the robbery suspect wearing the stolen shoes. George got a search warrant, and we served it.

We recovered several people's stolen property that night at a single home. At the end of the search warrant service, George and I were in the office late with another officer named Lincoln Riley. I was explaining to Lincoln, how George developed enough information to get the search warrant. Lincoln made a comment to George that if he ever "went bad," he did not want George going after him.

The irony of this is that many years later, George was assigned to an intelligence unit that investigated elected officials and bad cops. He ended up arresting Lincoln for a list of felony charges. Lincoln had been involved with a prostitute and was stealing evidence from search warrants to give her to sell. He went bad, and George arrested him.

I finished my time in this unit, and toward the end, I began to study to be promoted to sergeant. I took the test and did well. As I waited to be promoted, I was placed in an "acting" role. There was a sergeant who was assigned to day shift who was on extended leave. That team needed a supervisor, and my captain asked if I would be willing to be an interim sergeant on that squad until I was officially promoted. My captain was Kevin Mcmahill, who for the second time in my career had helped me.

I was an acting sergeant on a day-shift team who was relatively junior and still very active. I learned a lot of lessons on leadership while I was an acting supervisor; that means I made a lot of mistakes. I learned very quickly, as an acting sergeant, to not get involved in police work unless it is absolutely necessary. When you do this, you become supervisory ineffective.

I was driving past an intersection when I heard an officer who was assigned to me being dispatched to a call that was quite literally around the corner from me. The dispatcher told the officer that the person reporting was the wife of the suspect. The two were married and were involved in an argument. She had run out of the home when he produced a handgun. When she was in the front yard, she heard him shoot himself but was afraid to go back inside.

The officer was going alone, and I realized that I was the only person who could go with him. I assigned myself to the event and arrived on the call a few minutes later. The officer pulled up behind me as I exited my car. He misjudged the stopping distance and slammed into the back of my parked car. There was no time to deal with that, so we ignored it for now. We had a person possibly shot and this was no time to investigate a car accident. So much for stealth.

We approached the front door. At this point, we did not know if the husband was dead, alive, or alone. We forced entry to render aid.

I saw a body lying on the couch of the living room. My officer went to the body as I checked the rest of the home for anyone else. The back of the home was clear, but when I walked back into the living room, the officer and the body were involved in a MMA-style fight.

I ran toward the two, and by the time I was about six feet from them, my officer had the guy pinned up against a wall by his wrist. The two were facing each other, and it was obvious that the officer was holding the guy's wrists to prevent himself from being punched.

I struck the guy in the abdomen with my right knee. He bent over and fell to his hands and knees. He then started to crawl toward the kitchen. We found out later that his pistol was in the kitchen.

As we tried to stop him, he kept fighting us; he was committed to getting into the kitchen. As the fight escalated, I told the cop to disengage, he did, and I deployed my taser. This time, the taser worked, and we were able to arrest the guy. Being the only supervisor working at my station, I had to call the watch commander, who screamed at me for over involving myself in the event and forcing her to now investigate the car accident and use of force. It is what it is. Like I said, I don't mind being yelled at.

CHAPTER

16

Sergeant

I was officially promoted to sergeant in 2010. I was assigned to downtown. That first squad was the worst squad I ever supervised. Some of them were completely out of control; one was textbook insubordinate, and I was having a power struggle with another. The one I was having a power struggle with was mostly my fault. I made a lot of leadership mistakes, and the interesting thing is, he and I became very close later in our careers. I think we just got off on the wrong foot, and I had no idea how to lead.

Walking into the new squad, there were things I was not aware of. The prior sergeant was a terrible leader. His name was Dave Drucker. Dave had spent the last six months not supervising the squad because he was studying for a promotion. He spent his days at work reading and preparing for the test.

The cop I had a power struggle with, that again was pretty much all my fault, was named Shawn McMurtry. Shawn had been running the team while his sergeant was studying. If you look at the history of police misconduct, I mean huge scandals, it almost always comes down to absent supervision.

I found out later that Shawn had been working as a supervisor and was tired of it. I can't blame him. He and I had several arguments, but again, it was pretty much my failure to identify where the real problem was. If you ever are a police supervisor, be engaged all the time. Do not force your job onto line-level personnel; it's just not fair. Shawn had been forced to be a supervisor, but he never wanted to be one.

Further, if there is conflict, examine whether you are contributing to it. One mistake I made was expecting everyone to respond to situations the same way I would. You cannot have a team of mini clones of yourself. Everyone is different, and because of that, they all have different ways to manage things. Keep in mind that your way is not the only way; it is your way.

I was only assigned to that squad for a few months, as I was very junior as a sergeant, and I was quickly bumped to another station. However, I learned a lot. As a police supervisor you are more than a boss. Remember that cops get hurt and die. You are there to help them and their families through this.

Further, their personal issues will affect their work and thus affect the public. Effective police supervision requires a very large commitment and takes up a great deal of energy. You are responsible for a group of people who take people's freedoms, use force, and can kill if needed. If one of them has a gambling issue or is going through a divorce, it will affect the work. You really must get very deep into their lives, because even if you are off that day, you are still responsible for their conduct.

There was a night when I was assigned to go to emergency vehicle operation course (EVOC) training. My squad was working the street at the same time. I was standing under an overhang next to the urban driving course when I saw a police car driving toward me, its lights and sirens on. It was not a training car.

The car pulled up, driven by a senior officer from another station. He asked, "Sergeant Sobrio?"

"Yes," I said, puzzled.

"Get in," he responded.

"I'm sorry?" I said.

"Sir, please get in," he responded.

I got in, and we took off fast. He swung the computer screen over so I could read it and said, "We are headed to the trauma center."

I read the screen. It explained that one of my cops had been involved in a fight with a suspect. The two had been fighting in a construction area, where the road had been dug up and was dirt. His partner responded to help. When he pulled up in his car, he misjudged the traction he would have on the dirt and quite literally ran over his partner and the suspect.

By the time I got to the trauma center, my hurt officer was being treated. The bottom of the vehicle's shock mount had literally gone through his upper thigh. His partner was outside, devastated about the accident.

This is where leadership and supervision become two very different traits. I spoke with the two for an extended time. Accidents happen, and both the officer and the suspect were injured but not killed. It was insane.

I was a sergeant for five years. I worked at many stations, as is normal. Seniority builds, and then you are given more options as far as shift and days off. As a sergeant, you truly lead; you are the example your officers follow. You give them expectations, and then they watch to see if you enforce them. A sergeant's personality is contagious to the team. A good sergeant will have a good team, and an impatient sergeant will have an impatient team.

After about a year of supervising, I got comfortable with the responsibility. I became comfortable with major incidents, the incident command system (ICS), and the day-to-day of leading. Leading is learned. I don't think there are born leaders; some people learn faster than others, but leadership takes a lot of learning. You see officers making mistakes, and you must decide if you will step in or let them learn for themselves.

Dayla Pizzoferrato

Even as a sergeant, tragedy is a part of policing. As a sergeant, you see more. You supervise, so you must be at all the major incidents, screen calls for service, go to all the dead bodies, and establish whether it is a homicide or not. You must lead under calm times and times of terror. All the officers who work for you need you to be aware of what they are doing. I saw a lot of death, as a police officer. As a line level cop, you are really only exposed to what you are dispatched to. When you promote you end up seeing much more death. When you supervise a team, you are exposed to everything each of them responds to. As each officer responds to death and tragedy, you as a supervisor are involved in each officer's cases.

When children are thrust into death it really affects you, or it affected me quite a bit. I saw hundreds of dead bodies over my twenty plus years. When it came to dead children, my heart carries a scar from each of them. Because children are dependent on adults for day-to-day care, when they die, I always wanted to identify the instigating action. At times, children's deaths are accidental, but still heart breaking. Children are killed by adult neglect, abuse and at times sheer bad luck. A part of me always wanted to come up with a method to prevent all children from dying. The problem is that this is not possible. Even the most involved parents will be touched by this tragedy.

Random car accidents, sexually motivated predators, and again bad luck, permeate past your best safeguards. It is tragic when children are killed. It would take a few days for me to return to normal after seeing a small child either dying or dead. Many children died in my arms as I attempted to save them with first aid or CPR. The good news is many children lived because of my actions.

A young boy who was in the back seat of his mother's sedan was thrust into my life one afternoon. His mom was driving her son home, from a babysitter, after she had finished her work shift. While on the interstate, mom was driving behind a pickup truck. The pickup driver had purchased the truck a few days prior. He was unaware that the truck had a poorly installed bedliner. The bedliner was loose and came unattached from the truck it flew through the air and came to rest on the windshield of mom's car. Mom had no visibility and was traveling at highway speeds, having no specialized training, she attempted to reduce her speed by quickly applying the brakes. Her son's child safety seat was improperly installed, her brakes locked up and her vehicle hit the center median head on. Her son then was ejected from the sedan. His body flew from the back seat, through the front windshield, and came to rest on the ground of the interstate.

I was very close and arrived minutes after his ejection. I picked him up, told his mother to wait there, and drove him the short distance to the University Medical Center. I visited him several times over the next few months. Doctors made it clear to me that his internal damage was so severe that it was unlikely he would have survived even a short wait, in the field, for medical personnel. Stories like this are very motivating, cops save lives daily, it becomes a frequent part of the job. However, just as many lives are saved daily, many are lost. Even the most exhaustive efforts of police, paramedics, and hospital staff, at times simply are not enough.

I don't think I will ever forget the day Dayla Pizzoferrato entered my life, she was four years old. It was in 2011. I was working, and my squad was dispatched to her. Her grandfather and father had taken her target shooting in a desert area far south of Las Vegas. The call came out that she had fallen from the back of a tailgate on a truck. I thought it was strange, but I started to head that way.

The girl was unresponsive, and my cops had called for a flight-for-life helicopter. I arrived just as the helicopter was leaving with her. I have facilitated helicopter landings a few dozen times. It's always fun to direct a helicopter down onto a street; however, the circumstances are always tragic.

The family outing had been interrupted when she fell from the tailgate of the truck. As she was being flown to the trauma center, I looked at the scene. I wasn't sure how a kid could just fall off the tailgate of a truck. I looked at the truck and saw what I immediately recognized as brain matter all over the side quarter panel. I absolutely felt sick.

The group had been shooting in a low area that was just north of a large hill. On the south side of that hill, there were about twenty people all target shooting facing north. Some stray bullet had hit this little four-year-old child in the head. She was a twin, and I met her brother, too. He was with the group.

The homicide sergeant, Matt Sanford, and I were old friends, and I have to be honest, I kind of went rogue. I went to every shooter who was on the south side of that hill and took every gun I could. In the desert around Las Vegas, it is legal to shoot; however, I was in a rage. Understand, I am pro-gun, but this hurt me a lot. I took dozens of guns and did not care. I stand by that decision today and for the rest of my life.

The crime-scene analysts went to the hospital first, and I was coordinating for lights to be brought out because night was falling. One of the analysts I knew well showed me a photo of the bullet the doctor took from that little girl's head. It was a perfectly shaped 9mm bullet, with one side completely flat. The bullet had been fired, ricocheted off something, and stopped in her head.

I never got over this. I kept up on it. I would talk to Matt regularly and ask him if there was any progress. As of this writing, none of the guns I took matched, and we still don't know where that bullet came from.

The only thing I can think about is that Dayla Pizzoferrato was just too beautiful for this world, and God called her home early. If you are reading this, just take a moment please and pray for her. In my time in law enforcement, I have seen a lot. I have also forgotten a lot. I will never forget Dayla. I pray her family knows how much I care.

911 Call

Sometime later, I was driving around, watching where all my people were, when two officers were dispatched to a suicidal-person call. An eight-year-old boy had called 911 because his fifteen-year-old brother had grabbed a kitchen knife and was threatening to kill himself. I knew where all my people were and what they were doing, so I knew who should be making their way to that call. I started that way, and it was perfect. The three closest cops dropped what they were doing and headed to the house.

The four of us arrived, and the eight-year-old answered the door. I asked where his brother was, and he said up the stairs, dead. Remember when I said sergeants should lead and not get involved in calls? Well, there are exceptions.

I drew my pistol and ran upstairs, followed by my three cops. The stairs went up about twenty steps, then a flat landing turned left, and then about five more steps that led to a hallway. I made it to the landing, and standing at the top of the five stairs was the fifteen-year-old. He wasn't dead, but he was standing about seven feet from me holding a huge kitchen knife.

Tactically, I was in a very submissive position. He was armed and had the high ground on a staircase. I did not want to shoot this child; however, if I had, it would have been completely justified.

I then made a stupid decision. I said very calmly, "Put that fucking knife down."

He just stared through me. This was not going to happen the way he was thinking. In one motion, I holstered my pistol, jumped up to stair three, and punched the kid as hard as I could in the face. The knife flew from his hand, and he fell back.

We collected him and took him to a waiting ambulance. His mother arrived a short time later. I was expecting to hear about how I was going to lose my job, how I was a racist child abuser, and the rest of the insults that come with these scenarios. By the time she saw me, she knew I had punched her son. She walked up to me, and I prepared for the worst. Then she hugged me, started crying, and thanked me for not killing him. I made a tactically poor decision that saved a child's life. The kid's mom actually understood. It was very odd, but refreshing.

New Assignments

A short time later, I was given the chance to transfer out of patrol and work in the advanced training unit. I was responsible for all patrol training after field training. We did classroom, scenario, and defensive tactics training. It was a fun time.

I only spent nine months in that assignment. But in those nine months, I worked on the collaborative reform process. This was in 2012, when Sheriff Doug Gillespie invited the Department of Justice into our agency to evaluate it. They gave us several recommendations. I was responsible for one: to train supervisors how to manage large dynamic incidents under stress. I developed a classroom portion that led to a scenario-based system to evaluate the supervisor's response. I received an award for my work on the project. I left that assignment and returned to patrol after a short time.

When I returned to patrol, I was asked to supervise a utility team. These teams were very generalized. We did a little bit of everything. Traffic, vice, bike patrol, foot patrol, saturation policing, we were really a team to put where we were needed. We did a lot of bait property operations and prostitution operations. I don't really have any great stories from that time, but I did meet some great cops who I still talk to today and consider my friends.

My final sergeant assignment was the best by far. I was preparing to be promoted to lieutenant, and I was assigned to a very senior team. The team was so senior that, as their supervisor, I was the junior person on the team. They were completely independent and were a pleasure to work with. It was the first time I policed a nice area. We patrolled a residential area that had relatively low crime.

The team members were very good at their job, and I only ever had one problem with them. One very senior member of the squad, Chuck, called me and in a very angry tone asked me, no, *told* me to come to his call. A new officer had just been assigned to the team; he was from my academy. The two were on a call at a public park.

It was odd for anyone on this senior team to call me, so I drove to the call immediately. When I arrived, I saw that the newly assigned officer had a twelve-year-old child in handcuffs, and the child's family was there also. I spoke to Chuck and asked him what the issue was.

Chuck explained the following scenario: Two twelve-year-old kids were at the park. The two were playing and shooting each other with airsoft pistols. When one hid in the bathroom, the other pursued. The bathroom had two stalls with no doors. The child entered the bathroom and looked for his friend. He looked in one stall where he thought his friend was and was greeted by a man using the stall. The child ran away, and the man called 911, claiming a gun was pointed at him. The airsoft pistols were bright orange and clearly toys.

The newly assigned officer was planning to arrest the child for assault with a deadly weapon. There is a common misconception with this law. The law says if you place someone in responsible apprehension of battery with a weapon, having the present ability to do so covers it. It is meant for when someone points a gun at someone else. The person pointing the gun has the present ability to batter with substantial bodily harm, and the victim reasonably believes they could be battered.

The issue here is, even if the victim was convinced it was a real gun, the child first had no intent to commit any crime, and second there is no way an airsoft could cause substantial harm to anyone. There was no present ability. Therefore, cops need supervision. Mistakes happen and need to be corrected. I spent hours explaining the issues to the newly assigned officer, who finally gave up the argument and left it alone. It wasn't a power struggle; it was just a person who needed supervision. Everyone needs supervision.

Police sergeants are very influential over the officers they supervise. Proper police supervision prevents the misconduct scandals that hit the national media's radar. Lead by showing up, be available and interject yourself, lead your staff. Understand that your staff is not clones of you and will have different personalities, priorities, and problems. Give clear expectations, follow up and ensure your expectations are met. Most importantly support your staff. Be there for them in good and bad times. Support them and let there be no doubt your support them.

CHAPTER

17

Lieutenant

After five years as a sergeant, I was promoted to lieutenant. I transferred to the Las Vegas Strip. Policing a tourist area is nothing like policing a city. Each casino property has its own private security force. Security comes at many levels: there are the guards you see and talk to; there are the ones you don't see; then there are the highly trained and specialized contractors. I found that these contractors were Israeli military, Special Forces veterans, and prior law enforcement people. Each property has an army of surveillance and security forces. While 911 calls do come in, there is crime and then there are day-to-day issues.

The Las Vegas Strip comes with its own unique challenges. Each property is privately owned, but the street itself is not. Casinos can enforce their own private rules, but the sidewalks and streets are public. Therefore, you see street performers on the sidewalks and not in the properties. Crime on the Strip, except for prostitution, rarely goes unnoticed and unsolved. There are a lot of public and private security measures that I am unwilling to share with you, but just understand that if you are on the Strip, you are being watched. Almost every square foot of the Las Vegas Strip in under surveillance every minute of every day.

Casino properties are enormous, with hundreds of acres of land, scores of floors, and millions of guests. Especially on holiday weekends, the crowds are massive, and it is very hard to manage that many people. I am one of very few people who has ever closed down the Las Vegas Strip. The story is not very exciting, but it is worth telling.

I was eating lunch at a property when a call came on the radio of a man walking down the Strip pointing a gun at tourists. I started to make my way out of the property and toward the street. I was listening to my officers and sergeants as they arrived. The first officer to arrive pulled up to the guy, who was clearly mentally ill. The suspect then pointed his unloaded revolver at the officer.

Before I tell you what happened next, understand that it was a three-day weekend, with about 450,000 tourists on the Strip. That's a lot of people. The officer, who was defending himself and arguably a few hundred tourists, fired twice at the suspect, who immediately surrendered. Both bullets missed the suspect; one hit a wall, ricocheted, and struck a child. The child was not hurt, just scratched. The other bullet ricocheted and scratched a homeless man.

I closed the Strip to conduct the shooting investigation. I also shut down the fountains at the Bellagio; the noise was too loud, and we could not work. So, I shut down the Strip and the Bellagio fountains. That's cool, right?

Political Events

I was working on the Strip for the 2016 presidential election. Remember that Trump Tower is on the Strip. Anti-Clinton protests would occur at Trump Tower, and anti-Trump protesters picked the same place. I began to get very good at managing protests, rallies, and large gatherings. Managing these events got me noticed, and I began to get involved in some counterterrorist investigations. I assisted with large conventions and departmental consulting with various private companies. Over the years, I also worked on various dignitary protection details.

As a police officer, I worked posts, quick-reaction teams, and one-on-one protection. I supervised the same as a sergeant. As a lieutenant, I organized, planned, and managed the events. I worked with the Secret Service, developing routes of travel and itineraries. The cool thing was that at that level, I was able to interact with the dignitary most of the time. For obvious reasons, I will not be discussing any security protocols.

As law enforcement, you must remain politically neutral on duty. During events like these or at union strikes or walkouts, we are to remain neutral and not take a position. It is the right thing to do.

However, I noticed some significant differences in the Democratic rallies and events versus the Republican rallies and events. Just so you know, I'm not having a biased opinion; I should be clear that I saw these differences were consistent for each. I found these traits were relatively consistent in how each party was the same, and consistent in how they differed from each other.

First the Democrat events. During the primaries, and their various debates and visits, I saw all the primary candidates. We will start with preplanning. Both parties sometimes gave advanced notice and sometimes a day's notice. However, I found that the Democrat candidates' travel coordinators were very rigid and inflexible. If I suggested changes, they would be listened to but rarely followed. The candidates would arrive in their jet, have their event, and leave. Some candidates literally spent less than an hour in Las Vegas.

These candidates traveled with very large entourages—huge entourages. The candidates would arrive at the airport and usually be closely surrounded by two to four people. I will call this the inner circle. If it was two, it would be one on each side; if it was four, they would stand front, rear, and side to side. These close followers appeared to be all business. They would be reading something to the candidate or briefing the candidate on something. When they approached their vehicles, the candidates waited for their doors to be opened, usually by the followers or Secret Service. If they had those Secret Service protections, the driver would normally remain in the driver's seat.

The motorcade would work its way to the event. They would usually pull up as close to the event as possible, such as an alley. They would park and only have to walk a few feet to get into the venue. They would pull up and wait. The first one I saw was Hillary Clinton, so I assumed this may have been Secret Service protocol.

Someone would open the candidate's door. Usually, this was one of the inner circle people. The candidate would exit the car, and the group would walk toward the stage while being introduced. The audience, I noticed, was a mix of groups, gathered by shirt color. Early on this was strange, until I started to plan these events. When I planned the events, I would be contacted by labor unions who would tell me what color shirts their members were wearing. I started to pay attention, and it was true. Each labor union had a different shirt color.

These events were almost always outside, in a park or a closed-off street. I suppose you could say these events were very business-only-type affairs. The crowds were diverse, but not completely. I noticed that of the White attendees, a vast majority in their late teens to late twenties. Hispanic and Black attendees were the reverse; their representation started in the late twenties and went up from there. I also noticed some, but not many, families.

Then there was the content of the talk. Although I never spoke to them, I was close enough to hear Hillary Clinton, Jesse Jackson, and Michelle Obama talk. They all have their own speaking style and mannerisms, but there was a consistency. Their talks were all very laser-focused. I found that their content was either directed specifically at the group or at the geographical area they were in.

If the talk was given to several construction unions, for example, the content would be about union benefits; if it was in a traditionally high crime area, it could be about crime and safe neighborhoods. The talks were usually message-specific. In my opinion, I never really found the content of these talks to really say anything. It was usually very broad and commonly argued issues, with no direct solutions or programs recommended. Their exit was just as swift as their entrance—the entrance process in reverse.

The Republican, Libertarian, and Independent candidates seemed to be very similar to each other, but dissimilar to the Democrat candidates. Preplanning was very easy in comparison with the Democrats. They considered road closures, construction areas, and delays and adjusted their routes as needed. They were very flexible. Not all had jets; some drove in buses or flew on commercial airlines. They may have had an aide with them, but I noticed most of it was their family.

They almost always arrived a day prior to the event and stayed at a hotel. The other big difference was that they opened their own doors—except for those who had Secret Service protection—or their door was opened by the driver of the car. I never once saw any of these candidates wait for their door to be opened; if it was closed, they would open it.

They traditionally would arrive very early to their events. For a rally, they seemed to spend an entire day here before the event. When I spoke to them, which was frequent, they were pleasant but were certainly politicians.

Former President Trump, Senator Ted Cruz, and most others spoke to the police. They thanked the cops, and then at times would just have small talk about irrelevant things in the downtime before the event. When they were introduced, they would walk themselves to the stage. These events were almost always indoors.

The attendees for these events were so diverse, I couldn't give you any category. I never saw congregations of groups wearing matching shirts, except for campaigners, who had campaign shirts on. These crowds were wearing all colors, most themed red, white, and blue. Racial demographics were like someone had picked up the event and shook it. I noticed White, Black, and Hispanic attendees of all ages. To be fair, they were usually congregated by age. However, I also noticed far more families. I remember this because of the huge number of strollers we had to search.

Speech content was very diverse and seemed to focus on very broad issues: things like race relations, world trade, nationwide issues, and major news stories. There was usually a focus on the country as a country, not groups within the country. When their talk was over, they would traditionally remain either for a question-and-answer session or to walk through the crowd. Former President Trump spent a long time after a campaign event talking to the local cops, taking photos, and signing programs and that sort of thing.

They exited as they had come, opening their own doors, unless the Secret Service was involved. I noticed their model was more of a social meeting than business. Do not get mad at me; I am just telling you what I saw. I gained a lot of experience dealing with politicians, celebrities, CEOs of major corporations, convention facilitators, security. and counterterrorism strategies.

Homeless Outreach

I began to have severe pain from spinal injuries around this time. I'd always had pain; I had been injured significantly. However, in 2016, my pain became unmanageable. I ended up having some major reconstructive surgery in 2016. It took months for me to fully recover due to the lengthy recovery. I was able to gain a significant amount of administrative experience, and this built on the experiences I've already explained.

I was asked to transfer to the deputy chief of the patrol's office. I transferred and began managing manpower allocation for the agency. Manpower allocation involved evaluating how many officers, detectives, and sergeants should be assigned to a specific detail; managing patrol staffing based on crime trends; and managing promotions and transfers, essentially, putting the right people in the right place. It was a good job, but remember we policed two million citizens with a six-thousand-person agency, and I was the guy who made sure the right number of cops were where they should be. It was a lot of stress.

The chief I was working for had recently been to a local homeless outreach meeting. During the meeting, he felt that there was no accountability for governmental money going to the homeless. He asked me to find out if we, the police, needed to be involved. I began to manage manpower one week a month and spent the remaining three weeks each month researching homeless outreach. I researched governmental responses to homelessness across the country. I attended conferences and toured several police, medical, private, and public entities that had homeless outreach programs.

After just under a year of intensive study, I made some initial observations. Before I get into the specifics of what I discovered, I should lay some groundwork. When you hear that "police wear many hats," that term has real implications. The idea is that any good or service that is needed by a citizen that is either not easily made available or that is only available during business hours from the government becomes a police function.

Let me give you some examples. If family members need a social worker at two in the morning, they call the police, who will have to provide a service. If people need eviction or housing assistance through HUD at the same time of night, they call the police. The overarching problem is that outside of normal business hours, or depending on the agency during business hours, there is only one governmental agency that will always answer the phone, and that's 911.

Most of you don't have an appreciation of this, because you have probably not needed governmental services so urgently. If you need immigration assistance and it is business hours, but you either can't raise someone on the phone or when you do, they are not helpful, who do you call? 911. Someone in a mental crisis who is a threat to themselves or others may need mental health assistance. However, first there are no mobile therapists or social workers. Second, in the very few jurisdictions where there are mobile mental health professionals, if the patient is dangerous, they won't show up until the police make the scenario safe.

There is a push now to have financial resources diverted from police agencies and toward such mobile mental health programs. The reality is, regardless of their credentials, if these mental health professionals do arrive at these events prior to police making the scenario safe, a lot of therapists will die.

So, I developed a plan to have homeless-service professionals who were with the police. I worked with the city and was able to create a mobile police-led homeless outreach team. I called it the Multi-Agency Outreach Resource and Engagement team. The team developed into a nation-leading team for homeless services. We developed a model that brought the services to the homeless citizens to get them out of homelessness. It was a huge success and is still in effect today.

The team has since expanded into a far larger model that I created. When I promoted away from the team, above the rank of lieutenant, I left them with a well-researched long-term plan and vision. We had researched and learned a lot from the failed efforts of California and Washington State when it came to homeless outreach. The team was not an enforcement team; it was a resource team. The team was not to arrest the problem away but was to remove the person from homelessness with the resources that were provided. It was a great program, and I really think we made a difference.

Creating the team to bring resources to the homeless was not the only positive step. We were able to identify companies who were taking money from the government from homeless services and misallocating the money. We were essentially able to hold homeless resource agencies accountable for what they were obligated to do. This was unheard of prior to us implementing it.

18

Bureau Commander

After my time as a lieutenant, I was finally promoted to the bureau commander level. I became the director of human resources (OHR) for my agency. The OHR for the LVMPD is not like a typical OHR, as it handles selection, classification, compensation, hiring, testing, promotions, background investigations, polygraph investigations, and recruiting. Being the director of OHR put me in the middle of just about every portion of my agency.

Most of what I learned in the last two years of my career, I've already covered in the beginning portions of this book. However, there is more that I think may be beneficial. I became the director of OHR in 2019 and retired in 2021. Things were going very routinely for me initially. Learning the new job was a challenge, because I had never been trained in that specific area. I had to learn about test validation and really understand the executive level of my agency. I was able to make decisions and provide recommendations to the leaders of the LVMPD.

I found very quickly that I needed to have the correct information readily available. I was also focused on the political issues involved in policing. I had experienced some of this when I was a lieutenant; however, now I was in the front row. I had to speak directly with the Department of Justice on many issues, including recruiting strategies and staffing. I had to justify my agency's racial and ethnic statistics and why they did not necessarily reflect the population of Clark County.

Just as I was starting to get a good handle on the position, two things happened that changed my direction. The first was that my supervisor changed. This should not have been so significant, but I had a very difficult time communicating with my new boss. There was a person now supervising me who knew absolutely nothing about my bureau or its functions, and I myself had only just begun to understand it.

Further, my new supervisor was not very good at the whole humility thing. To this day, I want to say that this individual meant well; however, I just don't know. Various events came up that were very good opportunities for my new boss to get involved in my job, but there was no interest. There was a huge disconnect between this individual's intelligence and emotional intelligence. To be fair, I really think my new supervisor was very overwhelmed with the new position and was just attempting to keep up. I will say that I was not a fan; however, that really is not a huge factor.

The second big issue was COVID. When COVID hit us in March of 2020, we were very concerned, as everyone was, about money. The Las Vegas Strip shut down. When this happened, we put a stop to all new hiring, which was against my recommendation. The issue was that when you stop such a large machine, it takes a tremendous effort to get it moving again. My staff had weathered the economic recession of 2010 and warned me not to stop hiring, the issue being the sheer amount of time it takes to process a police applicant through the entire process, then through the academy, then through field training. On whatever future date we were told to start hiring again, we would be almost two years away from having replacement cops on the street.

Every week we did not hire put us in debt, because people were still leaving the agency and needed to be replaced. I suppose the idea was to not spend more money. However, my staff argued, correctly, that our job of hiring police officers didn't see fruit for at least eighteen months. So, unless we anticipated COVID shutting down the country for two years or the community no longer needing policing, we should have kept hiring.

I was overruled, and I spoke up, loudly. I explained that my staff had been through this before and was warning me not to stop hiring and recruiting. However, my new supervisor was not very good at communicating up, and the argument was lost. Over my objections, academies were cancelled, and all recruiting was stopped.

As the weeks went by, I began to realize that we were digging a hole. Civil-service lists were expiring, and we were going to be in a position soon where we had no lists, not just for police officers, but for all the positions in our agency. Recruiters were taken from my bureau and placed back into patrol. We had come to a hard stop.

This is a great leadership lesson. If you are in a position of leadership, where your decisions will have huge ramifications for years after you make them, you should really do your research. In a police agency, the executive level is full of people who really will not push back. They will just go along with whatever the head of the agency says or does, mostly because their positions are dependent on no conflict arising. So, trust your executive staff, but also maybe speak to the line-level people who make the operation run. It takes some humility, but it may help. Because if you decide in a vacuum, and things change, you may be shooting yourself in the foot.

No one person was at fault for this, but I can tell you that I spoke up, and I was ignored. If you fail to speak to the line-level people who do the job daily, you are trusting your executive staff for the correct advice. This is fine, unless of course their jobs are reliant on you. If your executive staff is serving at your pleasure, they will almost always not want to upset you, and when this happens, key issues are hidden. When key issues are hidden, you are forced to make a choice based on biased, one-sided information. If you are ever placed in an advanced leadership position, always select an executive staff that is not afraid to tell you the truth. Never hire people that are simply yes-men.

Then it happened: the tax revenue came in for fiscal year 2021, and it was far higher than expected. Further, right around the end of June 2020, we started to see that COVID was not going to cause the economic recession we had anticipated. I was told to immediately fill a one-hundred-person academy and to staff future academies. This was very bad. I had expiring lists, no recruiters, and applications were way down due to the Defund the Police nonsense of 2020, COVID, and the ramifications of the tragic killing of George Floyd.

Politics hit me hard, because people hearing the Defund the Police talk assumed all police agencies were defunding, so people stopped applying. Again, remember how long it takes to get a cop from application to the street: just about two years. Applications were down nationwide, and we were now trying to start our hiring machine again and competing with every other agency in the United States, as well as the military. Further, after the anti-police protests of 2020, applications were so low that hiring minority officers was even harder. It shocked me when I realized how much damage politicians had done to policing just by speaking of defunding agencies.

My staff was able to combine several almost-expired lists and at the last minute fill that large academy and start up testing again for the future academies. My recruiters returned; however, in-person recruiting events were very rare. College campuses and military bases were still closed due to COVID, and we all were experimenting with the virtual tools that made such an impact in 2020.

By the time 2021 arrived, I knew I was done. As the months went by, my spinal pain was becoming unmanageable. I could only work for a few hours, and then I was debilitated. Further, my pain was so severe that I was reduced to walking with a cane and was prone to falling. I would never be able to put on a uniform again.

My prior back injuries and the stress I was experiencing were causing havoc with my health, and my wife saw it coming before I did. I was in constant pain, and because of this, I was not mentally present at work; I was just showing up. I was not able to function in a policing capacity anymore, and my body was starting to shut down.

Because I would never put on a uniform again, I was in a place where I had to decide, as the agency was simply unable to accommodate a cop who had a cane. My policing career was over, and I was the last to realize it. I couldn't train anymore, I was unable to shoot, and I just couldn't be a cop.

Telling my supervisor was easy; we had never really worked well together, and I share some of this responsibility. However, there was no effort on either side. I had never worked for someone who was so checked out. It was strange.

Telling my staff was harder. We had developed a very good working relationship, and I truly enjoyed working with them all. I delayed it as long as I could, then gave ninety days' notice of my retirement in March of 2021.

My last ninety days were spent training my replacement, who was a very smart and energetic lieutenant I had recruited for the background section sometime prior. She was to be promoted in place and take my position. I had been asked who should replace me, and it was an easy selection. My recommendation was taken, and things worked out well.

I am leaving out quite a bit from the last two years of my career; perhaps I will write another book. I learned a tremendous amount about local government, money, and politics during my final two years with the agency. I also conducted quite a bit of research across the country on policing strategies and recruiting.

I left the agency June 26, 2021, having given it twenty years of my life. My time in law enforcement had come to an end, but I realized that I could still have an impact. I focused on writing this and other books as a means of formally and ceremoniously ending my time in law enforcement. Perhaps readers may be inspired and begin their journey in the trade I had chosen twenty years prior.

CONCLUSION

In writing this book, my goal was to show the reader how police agencies hire their staff. I wanted to dispel any mystery that this subject contains. Second, I really wanted to give the reader a real world view of what police work actually consist of. An unfiltered, albeit unrefined, look at what police work really is.

The reader should have a clear understanding on what police agencies will obligate you to go through as an applicant. As you read through this book, you have learned what steps you will undertake to be hired as a police officer. You were instructed by someone who did the job for over twenty years, and by a person who was responsible for all hiring for a large police agency.

Once you understand the hiring process you will be able to dispel any associated mystery to this process. Also, I really tried to expose you to a raw, front seat, unbiased idea of what policing is. Policing is a violent, dirty job. One that forces you to see humanity at its worst daily. However, you are also the only thing that stands in the way of evil entering normal, peace-loving people's lives. Policing exists as one of the remaining noble professions in the United States. It should be independent of political opinion, theory, and ideals. The police officers of our generation are the last remaining heroes. When you take up this responsibility, you are required to uphold the values necessary to maintain order in our country. Good luck and stay safe as you first make peace and then keep it.

Printed in the United States
by Baker & Taylor Publisher Services